# C for Electronic Engineering
with applied software engineering

# C for Electronic Engineering
## with applied software engineering

William Buchanan

Prentice Hall

London   New York   Toronto   Sydney   Tokyo   Singapore
Madrid   Mexico City   Munich

First published 1995 by
Prentice Hall International (UK) Limited
Campus 400, Maylands Avenue
Hemel Hempstead
Hertfordshire, HP2 7EZ
A division of
Simon & Schuster International Group

Printed in Singapore
Redwood Books, Trowbridge, Wiltshire

Library of Congress Cataloging-in-Publication Data

Available from the publisher

British Library Cataloguing in Publication Data

A catalogue record for this book is available
from the British Library

ISBN 0-13-342668-8

4 5    99 98 97

*This book is dedicated to the four most important people in my life: my wife Julie and my sons Billy, Jamie and David.*

# CONTENTS

# PREFACE

Software development has grown over the years from simple BASIC programs written on small hobby computers to large software systems that control factories. These systems are now very complex entities requiring a great deal of management and technical expertise. Many applications that at one time were implemented using dedicated hardware are now implemented using software and programmable hardware. This shift in emphasis has meant that, as a percentage, an increasing amount of time is spent on software and less on hardware development. Electronics-related students have a great advantage in field as they acquire skills in many applications and in both hardware and software. An understanding of the hardware allows an engineer to communicate with external devices, to fine-tune programs for the systems they are running on, to speed-up data transfer, to interrogate memory locations, to quickly determine hardware and software bugs, etc. Their skills in other areas such as data communications, control systems, radar applications, instrumentation, satellite communications, etc., help them develop software for many complex applications.

This book is primarily aimed at teaching the C programming language for undergraduates and postgraduates studying on electrical engineering, electronic engineering, computer engineering, applied computer science and applied information technology courses. Over the years I have observed that electronics-related students require not only a knowledge of the theory of a subject but also its practical implementation in a real-life situation. They tend to moan when given a specification to design a database for a stock control system but will eagerly tackle programs which design transistor amplifiers, display schematics or model digital circuits. The examples used in the text relate to digital electronics, analogue electronics and electrical principles. These applications should make the learning of the language more interesting and help to re-enforce fundamental principles learnt in other subjects (and to learn new subjects which are not covered in undergraduate classes). It gives a grounding in problem solving where, from an initial specification, a program is written which matches the requirements.

There are many C books currently available, but this book presents some of the concepts which an electrical, electronic, computer or software engineer may meet when working in a technical environment. It includes the coverage of key techniques such as bit-masking, bit operations, hexadecimal and binary conversion, accessing memory locations, bit-mapped graphics, direct video access, usage of structures, design of technical software, etc.

The book uses two practical examples to demonstrate the complete software engineering process. It shows how the requirements are developed, how a design is carried out, the implementation and the final testing. This is intended as an introduction to software engineering and should set good practices for future software development. Structure charts are used throughout the text as these are simple to understand and can be used to develop structured programs.

In summary, software development is an extremely practical subject which basically involves three main skills: problem solving, methodical planning and fault finding. All of which define a good engineer.

W. J. Buchanan

# CHAPTER 1

# Introduction

Electrical, electronic and software engineers require a great deal of flexibility in their approach to system development. They must have an understanding of all levels of abstraction of the system, whether it be hardware, software or firmware. The system itself could range from a small 4-bit central heating controller to a large industrial control system. In the development of any system the engineer must understand the system specification from its interface requirements, its timing requirements, its electrical characteristics, etc. The software that runs on the system must flexible in its structure as the developer could require to interrogate memory addresses for their contents or to model a part of the system as an algorithm. For this purpose the programming language C is excellent in that it allows a high-level of abstraction (e.g. algorithm specification) and allows low-level operations (such as operations on binary digits). It has a wide range of applications, from commerce and business to industry and research. This is a distinct advantage as many software languages have facilities that make them useful only in a particular environment. For example, business and commercial applications use COBOL extensively, whereas engineering and science use FORTRAN.

## 1.1 Hardware, software and firmware

A system consists of hardware, software and firmware, all of which interconnect. Hardware is "the bits that can be touched", i.e. the components, the screws and nuts, the case, the electrical wires, etc. Software is the programs that run on programmable hardware and change their operation depending on the inputs to the system. These inputs could be taken from a keyboard, interface hardware or from an external device. The program itself cannot exist without some form of programmable hardware such as a microprocessor or controller. Firmware is a hardware device that is programmed using software. Typical firmware devices are EEPROMs (Electrically Erasable Read Only Memories), and interface devices that are programmed using registers. In most applications, dedicated hardware is faster than hardware which is running software, although systems running software programs tend to be easier to modify and require less development time.

## 1.2 History of C

Dennis Ritchie initially developed the language at the AT&T Bell Laboratories. His objective was to use a high-level language to implement the UNIX operating system in a way that was easy to maintain yet powerful and portable. To achieve this he designed a language that had many influences, the most important was the language BCPL. The influence of this on C continued indirectly through the language B.

Originally, the main usage of C was in system programming. Compilers, operating systems and utilities have all been written in C. It excels in these areas and is now applied to many other areas on differing types of computer systems. After its adoption, the C language, unlike many other languages, tended not to splinter into different dialects. By 1983, it had matured to the point where it required standardization. For this purpose the ANSI (American National Standards Institute) committee X3J11 was set up to standardize it and has since produced the ANSI-C standard. Most C products now comply with this standard and not with the original implementation.

## 1.3 Basic computer architecture

The main elements of a basic computer system are a central processing unit (or microprocessor), memory, and input/output (I/O) interfacing circuitry. These connect by means of three main buses: the address bus; the control bus; and the data bus. Figure 1.1 shows a basic system. External devices such as a keyboard, display, disk drives, etc., can connect directly onto the data, address and control buses, or connect through I/O interfacing circuitry.

Memory normally consists of RAM (random access memory) and ROM (read only memory). ROM stores permanent binary information, whereas RAM is a non-permanent memory and will lose its contents when the power is taken away. RAM memory is used to run application programs and to store information temporarily.

The microprocessor is the main controller of the computer. It fetches binary instructions (known as machine code) from memory, decodes these into a series of simple actions and carries out the actions in a sequence of steps. These steps are synchronized by a system clock. To access a location in memory the microprocessor puts the address of the location on the address bus. The contents of this address are placed on the data bus and the microprocessor reads the data from the data bus. To store data in memory the microprocessor places the data on the data bus. The address of the location in memory is then put on the address bus and data are then read from the data bus into the required memory address location.

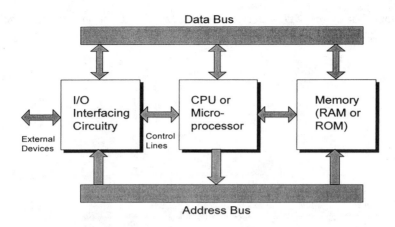

**Figure 1.1:** Block diagram of a simple computer system

## 1.4 Compiling, linking and producing an executable program

A microprocessor only understands binary information and operates on a series of binary commands known as machine code. It is extremely difficult to write large programs in machine code, so that high-level languages are used instead. A low-level language is one which is similar to machine code and normally involves the usage of keyword macros to replace machine code instructions. A high-level language has a syntax that is almost like written English and thus makes the program easy to read and to modify. In most programs the actual operation of the hardware is invisible to the programmer. A compiler then changes the high-level language into machine code. High-level languages include C, BASIC, COBOL, FORTRAN and Pascal; an example of a low-level language is 80386 Assembly Language.

Figure 1.2 shows the sequence of events that occur to generate a machine code program from a C source code program (the filenames used in this example relate to a PC-based system). An editor creates and modifies a C source code file; a compiler then converts this source code into a form which the microprocessor can understand, i.e. machine code. The file produced by the compiler is named an object code file. This file cannot be executed as it does not have all the required information to run the program. The final stage of the process is linking; this involves adding extra machine code into the program so that it can use devices such as a keyboard, a monitor, etc. A linker links the object code file with other object code files and with libraries to produce an executable program. These libraries contain other object code modules that are compiled source code.

If the compilation or linking generates errors or warnings then the source code must be modified to eliminate them. The process of compilation/linking will begin again. Warnings in the compile/ link process do not stop the compiler or linker from producing an output, but errors will. All errors in the compilation or linking stage must be eliminated, whereas it is only advisable to eliminate warnings.

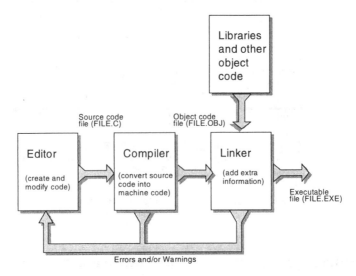

**Figure 1.2:** Edit, compile and link processes

Turbo C Version 2.0 is an integrated development package available for PC-based systems. It contains an editor, compiler, linker and debugger (used to test programs). The editor is used to create and modify the source code file and is initiated by running TC.EXE. Figure 1.3 shows a main screen with a source code file FILE1.C.

```
  File   Edit   Run   Compile   Project   Options   Debug   Break/watch
                                   Edit
      Line 1      Col 1     Insert Indent Tab Fill Unindent     C:PROG1_1.C
/*       prog1_1.c                          */
#include          <stdio.h>

/*              Simple program              */

int      main(void)
{
         puts("C for Electronic Engineering with Applied Software Engineering"
         return(0);
}








                                  Message

  F1-Help  F5-Zoom  F6-Switch  F7-Trace  F8-Step  F9-Make  F10-Menu
```

**Figure 1.3:** Turbo C Version 2.0 main screen

Figure 1.4 shows the compile menu options within this package. A source code file is compiled by selecting Compile to OBJ. If there are no errors an object code file is produced (in this case FILE1.OBJ). This is linked using Link EXE file (producing the file FILE1.EXE). A compile and link process can also be initiated using the Make EXE file option.

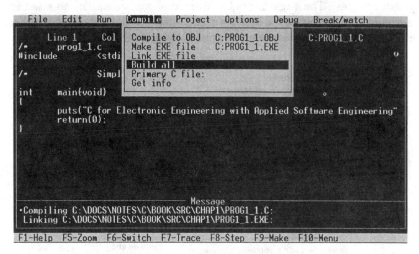

**Figure 1.4:** Turbo C Version 2.0 compile menu options

Figure 1.5 shows an integrated development package for Microsoft Windows. This package is named Borland C++ for Windows Version 3.0.

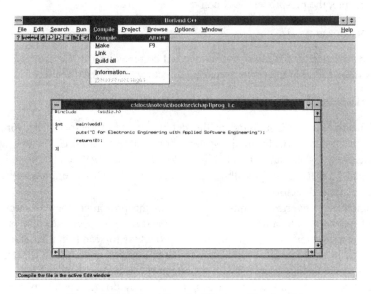

**Figure 1.5:** Borland C++ for Windows Version 3.0

## 1.5 Pre-processor

The pre-processor acts on programs before the compiler. It uses commands that have a number-sign symbol ('#') as the first non-blank character on a line. Figure 1.6 shows its main uses, these are: including special files (header files) and defining various macros (or symbolic tokens). The #include directive includes a header file and #define to define macros. By placing these directives near the top of a source code file all parts of the program can have access to the information contained in them.

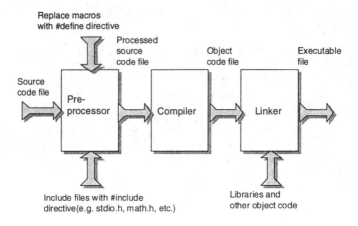

**Figure 1.6:** Operations on the program to produce an file

For example, the pre-processor directive

```
#include "main.h"
```

will include the header file *main.h*. The inverted commas inform the pre-processor that this file will be found in the current working directory, while the directive

```
#include <stdio.h>
```

will include the file *stdio.h* found in the default include directory. This directory is normally set up automatically by the system. For example, Turbo C Version 2.0 stores its header files, by default, in the directory \TC\INCLUDE and Borland C uses \BORLANDC\INCLUDE. Typically, header files on a UNIX system are stored in the /usr/include directory.

To summarize, inverted commas (" ") inform the pre-processor to search for the specified header file in the current directory (or the directory specified in the pathname). The chevron characters (<>) inform the pre-processor to search in the default include directory. It is not advisable to include any other file apart from header files. These have a '.h' file extension (although this is not obligatory). Standard header files are used in conjunction with functions contained in libraries. They do not contain program code, but have information relating to functions. A given set of functions, such as maths or

I/O, has a header file associated with it. Table 1.1 gives typical header files and their functionality.

**Table 1.1:** Typical header files

| Header file | Comment |
|---|---|
| *ctype.h* | character classification and conversion |
| *math.h* | maths functions |
| *stddef.h* | defines several common data types and macros |
| *stdio.h* | Input/Output (I/O) routines, such as input from keyboard, output to display and file handling (*stdio* is a contraction of **standard input/output**) |
| *stdlib.h* | miscellaneous routines |
| *string.h* | string manipulation functions |
| *time.h* | time functions |

A macro replaces every occurrence of a certain token with another specified token. The following examples show substitutions using the #define directive.

```
#define   PI              3.14
#define   BEGIN           {
#define   END             }
#define   _sqr(X)         ((X) * (X))
#define   SPEED_OF_LIGHT  3e8
```

Normally, as a matter of programming style, the definitions of constants, such as π, are given in uppercase characters.

## 1.6 Structure

Normally programs are split into a number of sub-tasks named functions. These are clearly distinctive pieces of code that perform particular operations. The main function (main()) is the basic routine for controlling the flow of the program and calling other sub-functions. Figure 1.7 shows a main function calling other functions.

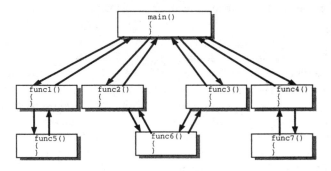

**Figure 1.7:** Modular structure

**Table 1.2:** Function names

| Function name | VALID | Notes |
|---|---|---|
| calc_impedance_RC() | ✓ | well named function as it explains what the function does |
| 3_point_rms() | ✗ | begins with an invalid character |
| get average value() | ✗ | spaces are used in the name |
| show_memory | ✗ | no parentheses at end of function name |
| $temp1() | ✗ | begins with an invalid character |
| calc1() | ✓ | valid name, but it is difficult to determine what this function does |
| calculateimpedanceofRC() | ✓ | difficult to read the name of this function; it would be better to shorten each of the words and insert underscores to delimit them |
| calc_boolean_eq() | ✓ | better than the previous example; it is easier for the user to read this as 'calculate Boolean equation' |
| CalcImpedanceRC() | ✓ | a common style is to use capital letters to signify the start of a new word |
| do() | ✗ | C keyword |

Function names are distinguishable with up to 31 characters (names with more than this will depend on the compiler implementation). All function names are followed by an opening set of parentheses and should not be one of C's reserved keywords. The first character of the name must be a letter ('a' - 'z', 'A' - 'Z' ) followed by either letters, digits, underscores ('_') or dollar signs ('$'). Other characters such as blankspaces or tabspaces are invalid. As a matter of programming style it is typical to use underscores to break up function names into readable form. Table 1.2 shows some valid and invalid function names.

Program 1.1 is a simple program which uses the puts() function to display the text "C for Electronic Engineering". The puts() function is a standard function used to output text to the display; the header file associated with this is *stdio.h*. This header file is included using the #include directive.

The statement terminator (;) is used to end a line of code (or statement) and braces ({}) show the beginning ({) and end (}) of a block of code. Comments are inserted in the program between a start comment identifier (/*) and an end identifier (*/).

All C programs have a main() function which defines the entry point into the program and, by means of calling functions, controls general program flow. It can be located anywhere in the source code program, but, is normally placed near the top of the file it is located in (making it easier to find). The int keyword preceding main() defines that the program returns a value to the operating system (or calling program). In this case, the return value is 0 (return(0)). Normally, a non-zero return value is used when the program has exited due to an error; the actual value of this gives an indication of why the program has exited. The void within the parenthesis of main() defines that there is no communication between the program and the operating system (i.e. no values are passed into the program).

**Program 1.1**

```
/* prog1_1.c                    */
#include <stdio.h>

int  main(void)
{
     puts("C for Electronic Engineering");
     return(0);
}
```

Figure 1.8 shows that the start and end of the program are defined within the main() function.

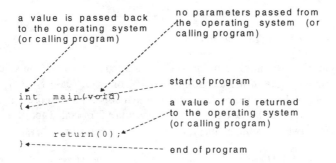

**Figure 1.8:** Start and end points of a program

## 1.7 Numbers and representations

### 1.7.1 Negative numbers

A notation, known as 2's complement, represents negative whole numbers (or integer values). In this representation the binary digits have a '1' in the most significant bit column if the number is negative, else it is a '0'. To convert a number into 2's complement notation, the magnitude of the negative number is represented in binary form. Next, all the bits are inverted and a '1' is added. The following example illustrates the 16-bit 2's complement representation of the decimal value –65.

$$
\begin{array}{ll}
+65 & 00000000\ 01000001 \\
\text{invert} & 11111111\ 10111110 \\
\text{add 1} & 11111111\ 10111111
\end{array}
$$

Thus, –65 is 11111111 1011111 in 16-bit 2's complement notation. Table 1.3 shows that with 16 bits the range of values that can be represented in 2's complement is from –32,767 to 32,768 ( i.e. 65,536 values).

**Table 1.3:** 16-bit 2's complement notation

| Decimal | 2's complement |
| --- | --- |
| -32,768 | 10000000 00000000 |
| -32,767 | 10000000 00000001 |
| :::: | :::: |
| -2 | 11111111 11111110 |
| -1 | 11111111 11111111 |
| 0 | 00000000 00000000 |
| 1 | 00000000 00000001 |
| 2 | 00000000 00000010 |
| :::: | :: |
| 32,766 | 01111111 11111110 |
| 32,767 | 01111111 11111111 |

### 1.7.2  Hexadecimal and octal numbers

It is not possible to represent bit patterns in C using a binary format. One solution is to represent the binary digits in hexadecimal (base 16) or octal (base 8) representation. This technique also helps to reduce the number of symbols used to represent the binary value by about one-quarter for hexadecimal and one-third for octal. Table 1.4 shows the basic conversion between decimal, binary, octal and hexadecimal numbers.

**Table 1.4:** Decimal, binary, octal and hexadecimal conversions

| Decimal | Binary | Octal | Hex |
| --- | --- | --- | --- |
| 0 | 0000 | 0 | 0 |
| 1 | 0001 | 1 | 1 |
| 2 | 0010 | 2 | 2 |
| 3 | 0011 | 3 | 3 |
| 4 | 0100 | 4 | 4 |
| 5 | 0101 | 5 | 5 |
| 6 | 0110 | 6 | 6 |
| 7 | 0111 | 7 | 7 |
| 8 | 1000 | 10 | 8 |
| 9 | 1001 | 11 | 9 |
| 10 | 1010 | 12 | A |
| 11 | 1011 | 13 | B |
| 12 | 1100 | 14 | C |
| 13 | 1101 | 15 | D |
| 14 | 1110 | 16 | E |
| 15 | 1111 | 17 | F |

In this text, a binary number is represented by a following b, an octal number with an o and a hexadecimal with an h. To represent a binary digit as a hexadecimal number the binary value is split into groups of four bits (starting from the least significant bit). A hexadecimal equivalent value replaces each of the binary groups. For example, to represent 0111010111000000b the bits are split into sections of four to give

| Binary | 0111 | 0101 | 1100 | 0000 |
|--------|------|------|------|------|
| Hex    | 7    | 5    | C    | 0    |

Thus, 75C0h represents the binary number 0111010111000000b. To convert from decimal to hexadecimal the decimal value is divided by 16 recursively and each remainder noted. The first remainder gives the least significant digit and the final remainder the most significant digit. For example, the following shows the hexadecimal equivalent of the decimal number 1103:

$$
16 \overline{\left| \begin{array}{l} 1103 \\ \phantom{1}68 \quad \text{r F} \;\; <<< \text{LSD (least significant digit)} \\ \phantom{11}4 \quad \text{r 4} \\ \phantom{11}0 \quad \text{r 4} \;\; <<< \text{MSD (most significant digit)} \end{array} \right.}
$$

Thus the decimal value 1103 is equivalent to 044Fh.

To convert a binary value into octal the bits are split into groups of three; each group is then represented by its equivalent octal value. For example:

| Binary | 0 | 111 | 010 | 111 | 000 | 000 |
|--------|---|-----|-----|-----|-----|-----|
| Octal  | 0 | 7   | 2   | 7   | 0   | 0   |

In C hexadecimal constants are preceded by a 0 (zero) and the character 'x' (0x), whereas an octal number is preceded only by a 0 (zero). Examples of various number formats are given next.

| Number | Base of number |
|--------|----------------|
| 0xf2c  | hexadecimal    |
| 0432   | octal          |
| 321    | decimal        |

Relatively large or small numbers can be represented in exponent format. Table 1.5 gives some examples of this format.

**Table 1.5:** Exponent format conversions

| Value (or PHYSICAL CONSTANT) | Exponent format |
|------------------------------|-----------------|
| 0.000 000 001                | 1e-9            |
| 1 234 320                    | 1.23432e6       |
| 1 000 000 000 000            | 1e12            |
| 0.023                        | 2.3e-2          |
| 0.943230                     | 9.4323e-1       |
| CHARGE OF ELECTRON           | 1.602e-19       |
| MASS OF ELECTRON             | 9.109e-31       |
| PERMITTIVITY OF FREE SPACE   | 8.854e-12       |
| SPEED OF LIGHT               | 2.998e8         |

## 1.8  Character constants

Typically, characters are stored using either ASCII or EBCDIC codes. ASCII is an acronym for American Standard Code for Information Interchange and EBCDIC for Extended Binary Coded Decimal Interchange Code. Table 1.6 gives a full listing of the ASCII character set.

**Table 1.6:** ASCII character set

| Hex | Char | Hex | Char | Hex | Char | Hex | Char | Hex | Char | Hex | Char | Hex | Char | Hex | Char |
|-----|------|-----|------|-----|------|-----|------|-----|------|-----|------|-----|------|-----|------|
| 00 | NUL | 10 | DLE | 20 | SP | 30 | 0 | 40 | @ | 50 | P | 60 | ' | 70 | p |
| 01 | SOH | 11 | DC1 | 21 | ! | 31 | 1 | 41 | A | 51 | Q | 61 | a | 71 | q |
| 02 | STX | 12 | DC2 | 22 | " | 32 | 2 | 42 | B | 52 | R | 62 | b | 72 | r |
| 03 | ETX | 13 | DC3 | 23 | # | 33 | 3 | 43 | C | 53 | S | 63 | c | 73 | s |
| 04 | EOT | 14 | DC4 | 24 | $ | 34 | 4 | 44 | D | 54 | T | 64 | d | 74 | t |
| 05 | ENQ | 15 | NAK | 25 | % | 35 | 5 | 45 | E | 55 | U | 65 | e | 75 | u |
| 06 | ACK | 16 | SYN | 26 | & | 36 | 6 | 46 | F | 56 | V | 66 | f | 76 | v |
| 07 | BEL | 17 | ETB | 27 | ' | 37 | 7 | 47 | G | 57 | W | 67 | g | 77 | w |
| 08 | BS | 18 | CAN | 28 | ( | 38 | 8 | 48 | H | 58 | X | 68 | h | 78 | x |
| 09 | HT | 19 | EM | 29 | ) | 39 | 9 | 49 | I | 59 | Y | 69 | i | 79 | y |
| 0A | NL | 1A | SUB | 2A | * | 3A | : | 4A | J | 5A | Z | 6A | j | 7A | z |
| 0B | VT | 1B | ESC | 2B | + | 3B | ; | 4B | K | 5B | [ | 6B | k | 7B | { |
| 0C | FF | 1C | FS | 2C | , | 3C | < | 4C | L | 5C | \ | 6C | l | 7C | l |
| 0D | CR | 1D | GS | 2D | - | 3D | = | 4D | M | 5D | ] | 6D | m | 7D | } |
| 0E | SO | 1E | RS | 2E | . | 3E | > | 4E | N | 5E | ^ | 6E | n | 7E | ~ |
| 0F | SI | 1F | US | 2F | / | 3F | ? | 4F | O | 5F | _ | 6F | o | 7F | DEL |

ASCII characters from decimal 0 to 32 are non-printing characters that are used either to format the output or to control the hardware. Program 1.2 displays the ASCII character for an entered decimal value. The `printf()` function is used to display the ASCII character and `scanf()` is used to get the decimal value. These functions will be discussed in more detail in Chapter 2.

📄  **Program 1.2**
```
/* prog1_2.c                                              */
/* Program to display an ASCII character for an entered   */
/* decimal value                                          */
#include <stdio.h>

int  main(void)
{
int  value;

    printf("Enter a decimal value >>");
    scanf("%d",&value);

    printf("Equivalent ASCII character is %c\n",value);

    return(0);
}
```

Test run 1.1 shows a sample run. In this case the entered decimal value is 65, which gives an ASCII equivalent of 'A'.

---

🖥 **Test run 1.1**

```
Enter a decimal value >>65

Equivalent ASCII character is A
```

---

Characters stored as ASCII codes are stored with the binary digits associated with the character. For example, the ASCII code for the character 'A' is 65 decimal (0x41); the binary storage for this character is thus 0100 0001. A string of characters "Res 1" is stored as the bit pattern given in Figure 1.9; the NULL character is used to terminate the end of a string.

| 01010010 | 01100101 | 01110011 | 0010000 | 00110001 | 00000000 |
|----------|----------|----------|---------|----------|----------|
| 'R' | 'e' | 's' | SPACE | '1' | NULL (end of string) |

**Figure 1.9:** ASCII storage for the string "Res 1"

Some examples of ASCII codes are given in Table 1.7.

**Table 1.7:** Examples of ASCII characters

| Decimal | Hex | Binary | Character |
|---------|------|-----------|-------------------|
| 32 | 0x20 | 0010 0000 | SPACE |
| 65 | 0x41 | 0100 0001 | 'A' |
| 66 | 0x42 | 0100 0010 | 'B' |
| 90 | 0x5A | 0101 1010 | 'Z' |
| 97 | 0x61 | 0110 0001 | 'a' |
| 122 | 0x7A | 0111 1010 | 'z' |
| 7 | 0x07 | 0000 0111 | Ring the bell |
| 8 | 0x08 | 0000 1000 | Perform a backspace |

Quotes enclose a single character, e.g. 'a', whereas inverted commas enclose a string of characters, e.g. "C for Electronic Engineering". Several character constants that are non-printing are defined with a backslash (\). These are given in Table 1.8.

**Table 1.8:** Character definitions used by C

| Function | ASCII macro | Character |
|---|---|---|
| audible bell | BELL | \a |
| newline | NL | \n |
| horizontal tab | HT | \t |
| backspace | BS | \b |
| form feed | FF | \f |
| backslash | \ | \\ |
| double inverted commas | " | \" |
| single quote | ' | \' |

## 1.9 Data types

Variables within a program can be stored as either numbers or characters. For example, the resistance of a copper wire would be stored as a number (a real value) and the name of a component (e.g. "R1") would be stored as characters. Table 1.9 gives the four basic data types which define the format of variables.

**Table 1.9:** Basic data types

| Type | Usage |
|---|---|
| char | single character 'a', '1' , etc. |
| int | signed integer |
| float | single-precision floating point |
| double | double-precision floating point |

There are three basic extensions for the four types; these are:

```
short
long
unsigned
```

An integer is any value without a decimal point; its range depends on the number of bytes used to store it. A floating point value is any number and can include a decimal point; this value is always in a signed format. Again, the range depends on the number of bytes used.

Integers normally take up 2 or 4 bytes in memory, depending on the compiler implementation. This gives ranges of –32,768 to 32,767 (a 2-byte int) and –2,147,483,648 to 2,147,483,647 (a 4-byte int), respectively. Table 1.10 gives some typical ranges for data types.

**Table 1.10:** Typical ranges for data types

| Type | Storage (bytes) | Range |
|------|-----------------|-------|
| char | 1 | −128 to 127 |
| unsigned char | 1 | 0 to 255 |
| int | 2<br>or<br>4 | −32,768 to 32,767<br>or<br>−2,147,483,648 to 2,147,483,647 |
| unsigned int | 2<br>or<br>4 | 0 to 65535<br>or<br>0 to 4,294,967,295 |
| short int | 2 | −32,768 to 32,767 |
| long int | 4 | −2,147,483,648 to 2,147,483,647 |
| float | 4 (typically) | $\pm 3.4 \times 10^{-38}$ to $\pm 3.4 \times 10^{38}$ |
| double | 8 (typically) | $\pm 1.7 \times 10^{-308}$ to $\pm 1.7 \times 10^{308}$ |
| long double | 10 (typically) | $\pm 3.4 \times 10^{-4932}$ to $\pm 1.1 \times 10^{4932}$ |

## 1.10  Declaration of variables

A program uses variables to store data. Before the program can use a variable, its name and its data type must first be declared. A comma groups variables of the same data type. For example, if a program requires integer variables num_steps and bit_mask, floating point variables resistor1 and resistor2, and two character variables char1 and char2, then the following declarations can be made:

```
int      num_steps,bit_mask;
float    resistor1,resistor2;
char     char1,char2;
```

Program 1.2 is a simple program that determines the equivalent parallel resistance of two resistors of 1000 and 500 $\Omega$ connected in parallel. It contains three floating point declarations for the variables resistor1, resistor2 and eq_resistance.

**Program 1.3**

```
/* prog1_3.c                                                  */
/* Program to determine the parallel equivalent              */
/* resistance of two resistors of 1000 and 500 Ohms          */


#include <stdio.h>


int     main(void)
{
float   resistor1, resistor2,equ_resistance;

    resistor1=1000.0;
    resistor2=500.0;

    equ_resistance=1.0/(1.0/resistor1+1.0/resistor2);
    printf("Equivalent resistance is %f\n",equ_resistance);

    return(0);
}
```

It is also possible to assign an initial value to a variable at the point in the program at which it is declared; this is known as variable initialization. Program 1.4 gives an example of this with the declared variables resistor1 and resistor2 initialized with 1000.0 and 500.0, respectively.

**Program 1.4**

```
/* prog1_4.c                                                  */
/* Program to determine the parallel equivalent              */
/* resistance of two resistors of 1000 and 500 Ohms          */
#include <stdio.h>


int     main(void)
{
float   resistor1=1000.0, resistor2=500.0,equ_resistance;

    equ_resistance=1.0/(1.0/resistor1+1.0/resistor2);
    printf("Equivalent resistance is %f \n",equ_resistance);

    return(0);
}
```

## 1.11  C operators

C has a rich set of operators; there are four main types:

- Arithmetic;
- Logical;
- Bitwise;
- Relational.

### 1.11.1  Arithmetic

Arithmetic operators operate on numerical values. The basic arithmetic operations are add (+), subtract (-), multiply (*), divide (/) and modulus division (%). Modulus division gives the remainder of an integer division. The following gives the basic syntax of two operands with an arithmetic operator.

---

operand *operator* operand

---

The assignment operator (=) is used when a variable 'takes on the value' of an operation. Other short-handed operators are used with it, including add equals (+=), minus equals (-=), multiplied equals (*=), divide equals (/=) and modulus equals (%=). The following examples illustrate their uses.

| Statement | Equivalent |
|-----------|------------|
| `x+=3.0;` | `x=x+3.0;` |
| `voltage/=sqrt(2);` | `voltage=voltage/sqrt(2);` |
| `bit_mask *=2;` | `bit_mask=bit_mask*2;` |
| `screen_val%=22+1;` | `screen_val=screen_val%22+1;` |

In many applications it is necessary to increment or decrement a variable by 1. For this purpose C has two special operators; ++ for increment and -- for decrement. These can either precede or follow the variable. If they precede the variable, then a pre-increment/decrement is conducted, whereas if they follow it, a post-increment/decrement is conducted. The following examples show their usage.

| Statement | Equivalent |
|-----------|------------|
| `no_values--;` | `no_values=no_values-1;` |
| `i--;` | `i=i-1;` |
| `screen_ptr++;` | `screen_ptr=screen_ptr+1;` |

When the following example code is executed the values of i, j, k, y and z will be 10, 12, 13, 10 and 10, respectively. The statement z=--i decrements i and assigns this value to z (a pre-increment), while y=i++ assigns the value of i to y and then decrements i (a post-decrement).

```
i=10;   j=11;   k=12;
y=i++; /*    assign i to y then increment i              */
z=--i; /*    decrement i then assign it to z             */
j++;   /*    increment j                                 */
++k;   /*    increment k                                 */
```

Table 1.11 summarizes the arithmetic operators.

**Table 1.11:** Arithmetic operators

| Operator | Operation | Example |
|---|---|---|
| - | subtraction or minus | 5-4→1 |
| + | addition | 4+2→6 |
| * | multiplication | 4*3→12 |
| / | division | 4/2→2 |
| % | modulus | 13%3→1 |
| += | add equals | x += 2 is equivalent to x=x+2 |
| -= | minus equals | x -= 2 is equivalent to x=x-2 |
| /= | divide equals | x /= y is equivalent to x=x/y |
| *= | multiplied equals | x *= 32 is equivalent to x=x*32 |
| = | assignment | x = 1 |
| ++ | increment | Count++ is equivalent to Count=Count+1 |
| -- | decrement | Sec-- is equivalent to Sec=Sec-1 |

## 1.11.2  Relationship

The relationship operators determine whether the result of a comparison is TRUE or FALSE. These operators are greater than (>), greater than or equal to (>=), less than (<), less than or equal to (<=), equal to (==) and not equal to (!=). Table 1.12 lists the relationship operators.

**Table 1.12:** Relationship operators

| Operator | Function | Example | TRUE Condition |
|---|---|---|---|
| > | greater than | (b>a) | when b is greater than a |
| >= | greater than or equal | (a>=4) | when a is greater than or equal to 4 |
| < | less than | (c<f) | when c is less than f |
| <= | less than or equal | (x<=4) | when x is less than or equal to 4 |
| == | equal to | (x==2) | when x is equal to 2 |
| != | not equal to | (y!=x) | when y is not equal to x |

### 1.11.3  Logical (TRUE or FALSE)

A logical operation is one in which a decision is made as to whether the operation performed is TRUE or FALSE. If required, several relationship operations can be grouped together to give the required functionality. C assumes that a numerical value of 0 (zero) is FALSE and that any other value is TRUE. Table 1.13 lists the logical operators.

**Table 1.13:** Logical operators

| Operator | Function | Example | TRUE condition |
|---|---|---|---|
| && | AND | ((x==1) && (y<2)) | when x is equal to 1 and y is less than 2 |
| \|\| | OR | ((a!=b) \|\| (a>0)) | when a is not equal to b or a is greater than 0 |
| ! | NOT | (!(a>0)) | when a is not greater than 0 |

Logical AND operation will only yield a TRUE only if all the operands are TRUE. Table 1.14 gives the result of the AND (&&) operator for the operation Operand1 && Operand2.

**Table 1.14:** AND logical truth table

| Operand1 | Operand2 | Result |
|----------|----------|--------|
| FALSE | FALSE | FALSE |
| FALSE | TRUE | FALSE |
| TRUE | FALSE | FALSE |
| TRUE | TRUE | TRUE |

The logical OR operation yields a TRUE if any one of the operands is TRUE. Table 1.15 gives the logical results of the OR (||) operator for the statement Operand1 || Operand2.

**Table 1.15:** OR logical truth table

| Operand1 | Operand2 | Result |
|----------|----------|--------|
| FALSE | FALSE | FALSE |
| FALSE | TRUE | TRUE |
| TRUE | FALSE | TRUE |
| TRUE | TRUE | TRUE |

Table 1.16 gives the logical result of the NOT (!) operator for the statement !Operand.

**Table 1.16:** NOT logical truth table

| Operand | Result |
|---------|--------|
| FALSE | TRUE |
| TRUE | FALSE |

For example, if a has the value 1 and b is also 1, then the following relationship statements would apply:

| Statement | Result |
|-----------|--------|
| (a==1) && (b==1) | TRUE |
| (a>1) && (b==1) | FALSE |
| (a==10) \|\| (b==1) | TRUE |
| !(a==12) | TRUE |

### 1.11.4  Bitwise

The bitwise operators are similar to the logical operators but they should not be confused as their operation differs. Bitwise operators operate directly on the individual bits of an operand(s), whereas logical operators determine whether a condition is TRUE or FALSE.

Numerical values are stored as bit patterns in either an unsigned integer format, signed integer (2's complement) or floating point notation (an exponent and mantissa). Characters are normally stored as ASCII characters. Figure 1.10 shows examples of the various formats.

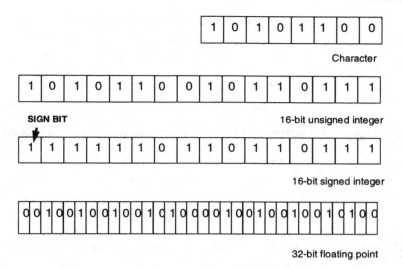

**Figure 1.10:** Example formats for differing data types

The basic bitwise operations are AND (&), OR (|), 1's complement or bitwise inversion (~), XOR (^), shift left (<<) and shift right (>>). Table 1.17 gives the results of the AND bitwise operation on two bits *Bit1* and *Bit2*.

**Table 1.17:** Bitwise AND truth table

| Bit1 | Bit2 | Result |
|------|------|--------|
| 0    | 0    | 0      |
| 0    | 1    | 0      |
| 1    | 0    | 0      |
| 1    | 1    | 1      |

Table 1.18 gives the truth table for the bit operation of the OR (|) bitwise operator with two bits *Bit1* and *Bit2*.

**Table 1.18:** Bitwise OR truth table

| Bit1 | Bit2 | Result |
|------|------|--------|
| 0    | 0    | 0      |
| 0    | 1    | 1      |
| 1    | 0    | 1      |
| 1    | 1    | 1      |

Table 1.19 gives the truth table for the EX-OR (^) bitwise function with two bits *Bit1* and *Bit2*.

**Table 1.19:** Exclusive-OR truth table

| Bit1 | Bit2 | Result |
|------|------|--------|
| 0 | 0 | 0 |
| 0 | 1 | 1 |
| 1 | 0 | 1 |
| 1 | 1 | 0 |

Table 1.20 gives the truth table for the NOT (~) bitwise operator on a single bit.

**Table 1.20:** Bitwise NOT truth table

| Bit | Result |
|-----|--------|
| 0 | 1 |
| 1 | 0 |

The bitwise operators operate on each of the individual bits of the operands, as shown in Figure 1.11.

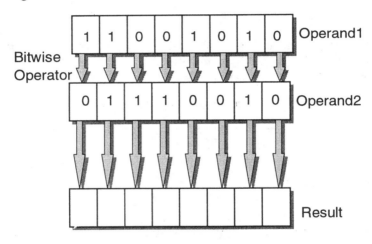

**Figure 1.11:** Bitwise operation on two operands

For example, if two decimal integers 58 and 41 (assuming eight-bit unsigned binary values) are operated on using the AND, OR and EX-OR bitwise operators, then the following will apply.

|  | AND | OR | EX-OR |
|--------|----------|----------|----------|
| 58 | 00111010 | 00111010 | 00111010 |
| 41 | 00101001 | 00101001 | 00101001 |
| Result | 00101000 | 00111011 | 00010011 |

The results of these bitwise operations are as follows:

```
58 & 41 = 40            (i.e. 00101000)
58 | 41 = 59            (i.e. 00111011)
58 ^ 41 = 19            (i.e. 00010011)
```

The 1's complement operator operates on a single operand. For example, if an operand has the value of 17 (00010001) then the 1's complement of this, in binary, will be 11101110.

To perform bit shifts, the << and >> operators are used. These shift the bits in the operand by a given number defined by a value given on the right-hand side of the operation. The left shift operator (<<) shifts the bits of the operand to the left and zeros fill the result on the right. The right shift operator (>>) shifts the bits of the operand to the right and zeros fill the result if the integer is positive; otherwise it will fill with 1's. The standard format is:

```
operand >> no_of_bit_shift_positions
operand << no_of_bit_shift_positions
```

For example, if $y = 59$ (00111011), then $y >> 3$ will equate to 7 (00000111) and $y<<2$ to 236 (11101100).

Table 1.21 gives a summary of the basic bitwise operators.

**Table 1.21:** Bitwise operators

| Operator | Function | Example |
|----------|----------|---------|
| & | AND | c = A & B |
| \| | OR | f = z \| y |
| ^ | XOR | h = 5 ^ f |
| ~ | 1's complement | x = ~y |
| >> | shift right | x = y >> 1 |
| << | shift left | y = y << 2 |

The following examples use shortened forms of the bitwise operators:

i<<=2          equivalent to i=i<<2                    *shift bits of i 2 positions to the left*

time |= 32     equivalent to time=time | 32            *OR bits of time with 32 decimal*

bitval^=22     equivalent to bitval=bitval^22          *bitval is EX-ORed with 22*

## 1.12 Precedence

There are several rules for dealing with operators, these are:

- two operators, apart from the assignment, should never be placed side by side. For example x * % 3 is invalid;
- groupings are formed with parentheses; anything within parentheses will be evaluated first. Nested parentheses can also be used to set priorities;
- a priority level or precedence exists for operators. Operators with a higher precedence are evaluated first; if two operators have the same precedence, then the operator on the left-hand side is evaluated first. The priority levels for operators are as follows:

**HIGHEST PRIORITY**

| | |
|---|---|
| ( ) [ ] . | primary |
| ! ~ ++ -- - | unary |
| * / % | multiply |
| + - | additive |
| << >> | shift |
| < > <= >= | relation |
| == != | equality |
| & | |
| ^ | bitwise |
| \| | |
| && | logical |
| \|\| | |
| = += -= | assignment |

**LOWEST PRIORITY**

The assignment operator has the lowest precedence. The following example shows how operators are prioritized in a statement (=> shows the steps in determining the result):

```
23 + 5 % 3 / 2 << 1     =>
23 + 2 / 2 << 1         =>
23 + 1 << 1             =>
23 + 2                  => 25
```

## 1.13 Data type conversion

When mixing different data types in an operation with two operands, the following rules determine the data type of the result:

1. Any character type (such as char, unsigned char, signed char and short int) converts to an integer (int).
2. Otherwise, if either operand is a long double, the other operand converts to a long double.
3. Otherwise, if either operand is a double, the other operand converts to a double.
4. Otherwise, if either operand is a float, the other operand converts to a float.
5. Otherwise, if either operand is an unsigned long, the other operand converts to an unsigned long.
6. Otherwise, if either operand is a long int, the other operand converts to a long int.
7. Otherwise, if either operand is an unsigned int, the other operand converts to unsigned int.
8. Otherwise, both operands are of type int.

A variable's data type can be changed temporarily using a technique known as casting or coercion. The cast modifier precedes the operand and the data type is defined in parentheses. Typical modifiers are (float), (int), (char) and (double). In program 1.5 two integers b and c are divided and the result is assigned to a. Since b and c are both integers, rule 8 will apply. The result will thus be 1, as an integer division is performed.

**Program 1.5**
```
/* prog1_5.c    */
#include <stdio.h>

int     main(void)
{
float   a;
int     b,c;

   b=6; c=11;
   a = c / b;
   printf("a = %f",a);
   return(0);
}
```

Program 1.6 performs a floating point division as the variable c has been recast or coerced to a float. Thus rule 4 applies.

📄 **Program 1.6**
```
/* prog1_6.c    */
#include <stdio.h>

int     main(void)
{
float   a;
int     b,c;

    b=6; c=11;
    a = (float)c /b;
    printf("a = %f",a);
    return(0);
}
```

## 1.14 Keywords

ANSI-C has very few reserved keywords (only 32); these cannot be used as program identifiers and must be in lowercase. Large programs can be built from these simple building blocks. The following gives a list of the keywords.

| | | | | |
|---|---|---|---|---|
| auto | do | for | return | switch |
| break | double | goto | short | typedef |
| case | else | if | signed | union |
| char | enum | int | sizeof | unsigned |
| const | extern | long | static | void |
| continue | float | register | struct | volatile |
| default | | | | while |

Functions are sections of code that perform a specified operation. They receive some input and produce an output in a way dictated by their functionality. These can be standardized functions which are inserted into libraries or are written by the programmer. ANSI-C defines some standard functions which provide basic input/output to/from the keyboard and display, mathematical functions, character handling, etc. They are grouped together into library files and are not an intrinsic part of the language. These libraries link into a program to produce an executable program.

## 1.15 Jargon

This section contains a glossary of some of the terms (the jargon) used in this and following chapters.

**Arguments**     Arguments are the actual values passed to a function. Commas are used to separate arguments in a function call
( *function_name(arg1,arg2,...argn)* ).

**Arrays**     An array is used to store a collection of variables of a common data type under a collective name

**Blocks**     see compound statement

| | |
|---|---|
| **Comments** | Comments are pieces of text added to a program that help to explain its operation. The compiler ignores all comments. |
| **Compiler** | A compiler converts a C program into a form the computer understands (i.e. machine code). |
| **Compound statement** | A compound statement is a number of statements enclosed by braces ( { } ). |
| **Constants** | Constants represent a fixed numeric or character constant. |
| **Declaration** | A declaration defines the type and name of a variable. |
| **Function prototype** | A function prototype defines the syntax of a function relating to how it is to be used. |
| **Definitions** | A definition introduces one or more identifier names into a program. |
| **Expression statements** | An expression followed by a semicolon is described as an expression statement. |
| **Expressions** | An expression is a sequence of operators, operands and punctuators that specifies a computation. |
| **Function** | A function performs a defined task. It has a defined interface in which arguments pass into variables known as parameters. |
| **Identifier** | Identifiers are names given such things as functions, variables, etc. |
| **Initialization** | Initialization sets the initial value of a variable, array, etc. |
| **Iteration statements** | Iteration statements allow the looping of a set of statements ( `while()`, `do..while()` and `for()` ). |
| **Keyword** | Keywords are words reserved for special purposes. |
| **Linker** | A linker adds extra information to a program to make it an executable program. |
| **Macro** | A macro replaces a token identifier with a token sequence. |
| **Operand** | Operands are operated on by operators. |
| **Operator** | Operators perform a defined action such as arithmetic, bitwise, logical and relationship. |
| **Parameters** | Parameters are the variables defined in a function header to hold the values passed. |
| **Pointers** | A pointer stores a memory address. |
| **Punctuators** | Punctuators are also known as separators. They include parentheses ( ( ) ), brackets ( [ ] ), braces ( { } ), colons ( : ), commas ( , ) and semicolons ( ; ). Parentheses can group expressions, indicate function calls and isolate conditional expressions. Brackets identify arrays. Braces indicate the start and end of a number of statements grouped as a compound statement. A colon indicates a labelled statement and a comma separates variable declarations. |
| **Selection statements** | Selection statements select from alternative courses of action by testing certain values ( `if()..else` and `switch()` ). |
| **Statement** | Statements specify the flow control of a program. |
| **Structures** | A structure is a user-defined collection of members (or components). |
| **Variables** | Variables store values and characters that the program uses. |

## 1.16  Tutorial

Q1.1   How are the start and the end of a C program defined?

Q1.2   How does the pre-processor interpret the following include directives?

```
#include <stdio.h>

#include "main.h"
```

Q1.3   Determine the octal, decimal and hexadecimal ASCII codes for the following:

- ESC (Escape)
- DEL (Delete)
- '~' (tilde)
- '_' (underscore)
- NULL (Null character)

Q1.4   What special characters does C use for the following:

- a new line
- a horizontal tab space
- an inverted comma (')
- double inverted commas (")

Q1.5   Program 1.7 allows answers in this question to be checked by replacing the 0x12 value with the required value.

📄  **Program 1.7**
```
/*    prog1_7.c                              */
#include <stdio.h>

int  main(void)
{
int  x=0x12;

    printf("Decimal %d, Hex %x, Octal %o \n",x,x,x);
    return(0);
}
```

Complete the following table, giving the equivalent decimal, hexadecimal or octal numbers.

| decimal | hexadecimal | octal |
|---------|-------------|-------|
| 15 | | |
| 201 | | |
| 14,655 | | |
| | 0x12 | |
| | 0xA1 | |
| | 0x1f0 | |
| | | 013 |
| | | 027 |
| | | 0206 |

Q1.6  Program 1.8 or 1.9 can be used to test results in this question. Replace the equations given in bold type with the required statement.

📄 **Program 1.8**
```
/* prog1_8.c                                          */

#include <stdio.h>

int main(void)
{
   printf(" The answer is %d ",5*3);

   return(0);
}
```

📄 **Program 1.9**
```
/*    prog1_9.c                                        */

#include <stdio.h>

int  main(void)
{
int  x,y;

   x=13;
   y=8;
   printf("The answer is %d ",x%y);

   return(0);
}
```

(a)  Determine the results of the following:

    i)    21 % 4 % 2 * 3 + 2
    ii)   25 + 5 % 2 * 4 - 1
    iii)  3 * 3 * 7 % 2
    iv)   (7 + 4) % 4 * 2
    v)    25 % 3

(b)  Assuming x=14 and y=8, determine the results of the following:

      i)     `x % y + 2`

     ii)    `x++`

    iii)   `--x`

    iv)   `x & y`

     v)    `x | y`

    vi)   `4 * (x + y * 2)`

    vii)  `x << 3`

  viii)  `y >> 1`

(c)   Determine the results of the following:

      i)    `0x32 + 011`

     ii)    `0x31 & 044`

    iii)   `0x4B | 013`

    iv)   `011 * 0x31`

     v)    `~32`

    vi)   `0xAA - 055`

    vii)  `0xFF + 0x10`

  viii)  `!(0xCF)`

    ix)   `~(032)`

Q1.7   Assuming x=1 and y=2, determine whether each of the following will result in a TRUE or a FALSE. Answers can be tested using the template of program 1.10.

    (a)   `( (x==1) && (y!=2) )`

    (b)   `( (x!=1) || (y==2) )`

    (c)   `( ! (x==2) )`

    (d)   `( ! ( (x==1) && (y==2) ) )`

    (e)   `( (x>0) && (y<2) )`

    (f)   `(x<=1)`

    (g)   `( (y>1) || (x==1) )`

## 🖹 Program 1.10

```c
/*    prog1_10.c                              */

#include <stdio.h>
int  main(void)
{
int  x=1,y=2;

  if (x==1)    puts("TRUE");
  else         puts("FALSE");

  return(0);
}
```

# CHAPTER 2

# Input/Output

Every program has some form of output and normally an input. Devices such as a keyboard, a file, ports (such as serial or parallel ports), mouse, etc., can provide data input to a program. Output can be sent to devices such as displays, printers, hard-disks, etc. Figure 2.1 shows some sample input and output devices. Typically, electronic engineers also communicate with devices such as ADC/DACs, LEDs, as well as with Ethernet controllers, IC programmers, etc.

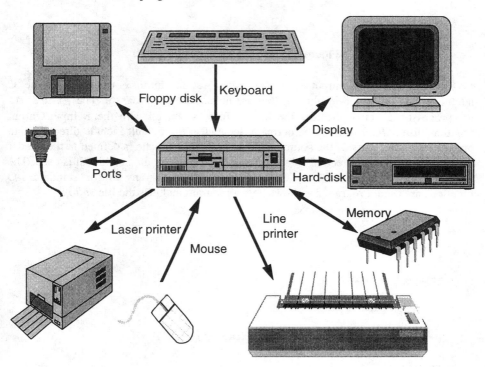

**Figure 2.1:** Input/output devices

The keyboard is normally a program's default input device and the display the default output. A redirection of this input or output is possible. For example, a text file can act as an input to a program and the printer as the output. Figure 2.2 shows an example input/output cycle where the user enters data via the keyboard; the program then processes these data and outputs the results to the display. The user can then enter new data and thus the cycle continues.

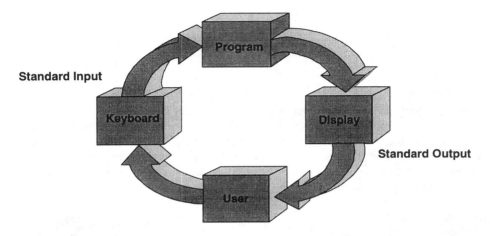

**Figure 2.2:** Program input/ output cycle

The standard input/output (I/O) functions are not intrinsic (built-in) to the C language, but are stored in libraries that are linked into the program. The #include pre-processor directive includes the header files associated with them. Input/Output functions use *stdio.h* (this file is normally located in the default include directory). In order to allow all parts of the source code access to the functions defined in the header file the pre-processor directive is located near the top of the file in which it is used. The compiler will then initiate extra error checking whenever any of the standard I/O functions are used. Program 2.1 shows how a program includes the file *stdio.h*.

**Program 2.1**

```
/*    prog2_1.c                    */

#include    <stdio.h>

int  main(void)
{
   printf("Enter a value of resistance");

   return(0);
}
```

## 2.1 Standard output (`printf()`, `puts()` and `putchar()`)

There are three basic output functions, these are:

printf(*"format",arg1,arg2...argn*)  outputs a formatted text string to the output in a form defined by *"format"* using the arguments *arg1..argn*

puts(*"string"*)  outputs a text string to the standard output and appends it with a new line

putchar(*ch*)  outputs a single character (*ch*) to the standard output

The `printf()` function sends a formatted string to the standard output (the display). This string can display formatted variables and special control characters, such as new lines ('\n'), backspaces ('\b') and tabspaces ('\t'); these are listed in Table 2.1.

The `puts()` function writes a string of text to the standard output and no formatted variables can be used. At the end of the text a new line is automatically appended.

Program 2.2 uses `puts()` to output the text *Enter a value of resistance*. A new line is automatically taken at the end of this text.

▤  **Program 2.2**
```
/*    prog2_2.c                   */
#include <stdio.h>

int main(void)
{
   puts("Enter a value of resistance");
   return(0);
}
```

▤  **Program 2.3**
```
/*    prog2_3.c                   */
#include <stdio.h>

int main(void)
{
   printf("Enter a value of resistance\n");
   return(0);
}
```

Program 2.3 shows an example of how the `printf()` statement is used with a new line character. It will write *Enter a value of resistance* to the display, then a new line is taken due to the character '\n'. The special control characters use a backslash to inform the program to escape from the way they would be normally be interpreted. For this reason, the combination of a backslash and a special character is called an escape sequence.

**Table 2.1:** Special control (or escape sequence) characters

| Characters | Function |
|---|---|
| \" | Double quotes (") |
| \' | Single quote (') |
| \\ | Backslash ( \ ) |
| \nnn | ASCII character in octal code, e.g. \041 gives '!' |
| \0xnn | ASCII character in hexadecimal code, e.g. \0x41 gives an 'A' |
| \a | Audible bell |
| \b | Backspace (move back one space) |
| \f | Form-feed |
| \n | New line (line-feed) |
| \r | Carriage return |
| \t | Horizontal tab spacing |

The parameters passed into printf() are known as arguments; these are separated commas. Program 2.3 contains a printf() statement with only one argument, i.e. a text string. This string is referred to as the message string and is always the first argument of printf(). It can contain special control characters and/or parameter conversion control characters.

### 2.1.1 Special control characters

The carriage return ('\r') is used to return the current character pointer on the display back to the start of the line (on many displays this is the leftmost side of the screen). A form-feed control character ('\f') is used to feed line printers on a single sheet and the horizontal tab ('\t') feeds the current character position forward one tab space.

Some ASCII characters are non-printing or have no special control characters assigned to them. The \nnn option allows access to these. For example, '\177' (01 111 111) defines the DEL character, '\007' (00 000 111) is BELL and '\033' (00 011 011) is ESC. Program 2.4 contains some special control characters (such as a new line and a tab space) and octal equivalents (BELL and 'H', 'E', 'L', 'L', 'O' ).

🖹  **Program 2.4**

```
/*    prog2_4.c                     */
#include  <stdio.h>

int  main(void)
{
   printf("\007");                       /* sounds the BELL    */
   printf("\tHELLO TO YOU\n");
   printf("\110\105\114\114\117\041"); /* print HELLO!    */
   return(0);
}
```

Test run 2.1 shows a sample run. When the program is executed the BELL character causes the speaker to sound (if the system has one). As this character is non-printing it will not be displayed on screen. A tab space is inserted before the "HELLO TO YOU" text and a new line taken before the "HELLO!" text. An exclamation mark is represented by \041 (00 100 001).

---

🖳 **Test run 2.1**
```
HELLO TO YOU
HELLO!
```

---

Table 2.2 lists the ASCII characters output and their octal \nnn equivalents.

**Table 2.2:** Binary and octal representations of ASCII characters

| ASCII character | Octal | Binary digits |
|---|---|---|
| BELL | 007 | 0 000 111 |
| 'H' | 110 | 1 001 000 |
| 'E' | 105 | 1 000 101 |
| 'L' | 114 | 1 001 100 |
| 'L' | 114 | 1 001 100 |
| 'O' | 117 | 1 001 111 |
| '!' | 041 | 0 100 001 |

### 2.1.2 Conversion control characters

Conversion control characters describe the format of how the message string uses the other arguments. If printf() contains more than one argument then the format of the output is defined using a percent (%) character followed by a format description character. A signed integer uses the %d conversion control characters, an unsigned integer %u. A floating point value uses the %f conversion control characters, while scientific notation uses %e. Table 2.3 lists the main conversion control characters.

**Table 2.3:** Conversion control characters

| Operator | Format | Operator | Format |
|---|---|---|---|
| %c | single character | %s | string of characters |
| %d | signed decimal integer | %o | unsigned octal integer |
| %e | scientific floating point | %% | prints % character |
| %f | floating point | %x | unsigned hexadecimal integer |
| %u | unsigned decimal integer | %g | either floating point or scientific notation |

Figure 2.3 shows an example of the printf() statement with four arguments. The first argument is the message string followed by the parameters to be printed in the message string. In this case the parameters are val1, val2 and ch; val1 is

formatted in the message string as a floating point (%f), val2 as an integer (%d) and ch as a character (%c). Finally, a new line character ('\n') is used to force a new line on the output.

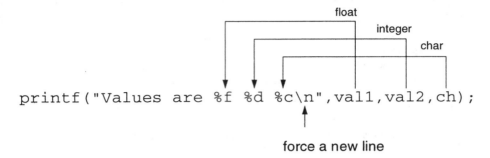

**Figure 2.3:** An example `printf()` statement

Program 2.5 gives an example of how the message string is constructed using the character control characters. Integers val1, val2 and val1+val2 use the %d control characters and float val3 uses %f.

📄 **Program 2.5**
```
/*    prog2_5.c                      */
#include <stdio.h>

int    main(void)
{
int    var1,var2;
float  var3;

    var1 = 5; var2 = 6;
    var3 = 15.0;

    printf("The sum of %d and %d is equal to %d\n",var1,var2,var1+var2);
    printf("The value of var3 is %f and var1 is %d\n",var3,var1);
    return(0);
}
```

Test run 2.2 shows the output from program 2.5.

💻 **Test run 2.2**
```
The sum of 5 and 6 is equal to 11
The value of var3 is 15.000000 and var1 is 5
```

A numerical value is output to a given specification using a precision specifier. This specifies the number of characters used to display the value and the number of places after the decimal point. The general format of a floating point value is:

%m.nX

where *m* is the width of the value (the number of digits including the decimal point), *n* is the number of digits following the decimal point, and *X* is the format type (f for float).

The general format of a string or integer is:

%mX

where *X* is the format type (c for character, s for string or d for integer) and *m* is the width of the output. Table 2.4 gives a few examples.

**Table 2.4:** Example of conversion control modifiers

| Format | Function |
|--------|----------|
| %.3f | format floating point value with 3 decimal places and a default width |
| %8.3f | format floating point with 8 reserved spaces and 3 places after the decimal point e.g.   32.453 |
| %10d | format integer for 10 reserved spaces e.g.                    23 |
| %3o | format octal integer number for 3 hexadecimal characters |
| %10.6e | format exponent format with 6 decimal places |

Program 2.6 gives an example of how different formats are output.

📄 **Program 2.6**
```
/*    prog2_6.c                      */
#include <stdio.h>

int     main(void)
{
float   x;
int     i;

  x=31.43523;
  i=143;

  printf("Value of x is <%f> <%8.2f> <%.3f>\n",x,x,x);
  printf("Value of i is <%d> <%10d>\n",i,i);
  return(0);
}
```

Test run 2.3 gives a sample run of this program. In this case, the default number of decimal places for a float is 6.

💻 **Test run 2.3**
```
Value of x is <31.435230> <   31.44> <31.435>
Value of i is <143> <       143>
```

### 2.1.3 Examples

*Capacitive reactance*

The reactance of a capacitor is dependent upon the applied frequency. At low frequencies the reactance is extremely high and at high frequencies it is low. The reactance ($X_C$) of a capacitor, of capacitance $C$ (Farads), at an applied frequency $f$ (Hertz) is be given by:

$$X_C = \frac{1}{2\pi f C} \quad \Omega$$

Figure 2.4 shows a schematic of this arrangement.

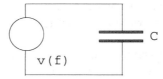

**Figure 2.4:** Capacitor connected to sinusoidal voltage source

Program 2.7 determines the capacitive reactance of a capacitor at an applied frequency. In this case, the capacitance is 1 µF (1e-6) and the frequency is 10 kHz (10e3). The #define pre-processor directive has been used to define the constant π.

**Program 2.7**
```
/*    prog2_7.c                                        */
/*    Program to calculate capactive reactance         */
/*    given frequency and capacitance                  */
#include <stdio.h>
#define PI 3.14159

int     main(void)
{
float   freq,cap,X_c;

    freq=10.0e3;               /* 1 kHz      */
    cap=1.0e-6;                /* 1 microF   */
    X_c=1/(2.0*PI*freq*cap);

    /* print freq with 3 decimal places in exponent format */
    /* print cap with 2 decimal places in exponent format  */
    /* print X_c as a floating point format with 3 decimal */
    printf("Frequency %8.2e Hz, capacitance %8.3e Farad\n",
                    freq,cap);
    printf("Capacitive reactance is %8.3f ohms\n",X_c);
    return(0);
}
```

Test run 2.4 gives a sample output of the program. Exponent format (`%8.2e`) is used to display `frequency`; this gives a width of 8 and 2 places after the decimal point; `capacitance` is also displayed in exponent format with 3 decimal places. The capacitive reactance variable (`X_c`) uses floating point format with 8 characters reserved for the answer and 3 decimal places (`%8.3f`). The number of characters reserved for the value is a minimum amount and if more are required the program will automatically use then.

---

🖳  **Test run 2.4**

```
Frequency  1.00e+04 Hz, capacitance  1.000e-06 Farad
Capacitive reactance is 15.916 ohms
```

---

### *Resistors in parallel*

Program 2.8 determines the equivalent resistance of three resistors connected in parallel. Figure 2.5 gives a schematic diagram of this set-up. The resistors connected are $R_1$, $R_2$ and $R_3$ and the equivalent input resistance is $R_{equ}$.

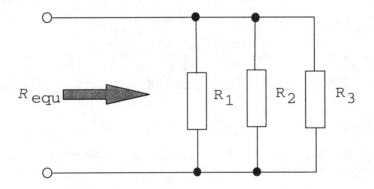

**Figure 2.5:** Three resistors connected in parallel

The formula to determine the equivalent resistance of this set-up is given by:

$$R_{equ} = \cfrac{1}{\cfrac{1}{R_1} + \cfrac{1}{R_2} + \cfrac{1}{R_3}} \ \Omega$$

Program 2.8 determines the equivalent parallel resistance of three resistors of 1 kΩ (`1e3`), 500 Ω and 250 Ω.

📄 **Program 2.8**

```
/*    prog2_8.c                                      */
/*    Program to determine equivalent resistance     */
/*    of three resistors connected in parallel        */
#include <stdio.h>

int     main(void)
{
float   R1,R2,R3,R_equ;

    R1=1.0e3;           /* 1 kohms    */
    R2=500.0;           /* 500 ohms   */
    R3=250.0;           /* 250 ohms   */

    puts("Program to determine equivalent resistance of");
    puts("three resistors connected in parallel");

    R_equ=1/(1/R1+1/R2+1/R3);

    printf("R1=%8.3f, R2=%8.3f, R3=%8.3f\n",R1,R2,R3);
    printf("Equiv. resistance is %8.3f ohms\n",R_equ);
    return(0);
}
```

Test run 2.5 shows that the equivalent resistance of this set-up is 142.857 $\Omega$.

🖥 **Test run 2.5**
```
Program to determine equivalent resistance of
three resistors connected in parallel
R1=1000.000, R2= 500.000, R3= 250.000
Equiv. resistance is  142.857 ohms
```

## Resonant frequency of a series LC circuit

When a perfect lossless inductor and a capacitor are connected in series, the input impedance is given by:

$$Z_{IN} = j\left[ 2\pi fL - \frac{1}{2\pi fC} \right] \quad \Omega$$

At low frequencies the input impedance is high due to the capacitor and at high frequencies it is also high due to the inductor. At a single frequency the reactance of the inductor and the capacitor will be equal and thus will cancel each other out. This frequency occurs when the circuit is at resonance, which results in zero input impedance. The resonant frequency is given by:

$$f_{RES} = \frac{1}{2\pi\sqrt{LC}} \quad \text{Hz}$$

Figure 2.6 gives a schematic of this setup.

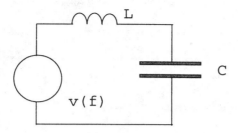

**Figure 2.6:** Series LC circuit

Program 2.9 determines the resonant frequency of a series LC circuit with an inductance of 1 mH and a capacitance of 1 μF. The values of $L$ and $C$ are assigned at the point they are declared in the program.

The program uses the square root function (sqrt()) so the *math.h* header file is included. This inclusion helps the compiler check the format of the values sent to the function as it checks the general syntax of the function call. It also informs the compiler that the value returned is a floating point (this will be discussed in greater detail in a later chapter).

**Program 2.9**

```
/*    prog2_9.c                                        */
/*    Program to determine resonant frequency of an    */
/*    LC series circuit                                */

#include <stdio.h>
#include <math.h> /* required for sqrt()              */

#define  PI 3.14159

int    main(void)
{
float  L=1e-3,C=1e-6,f_res;

   /* L is 1 mH, C is 1 uF */

   puts("Program to calculate resonant frequency of a series");
   puts("LC circuit");

   f_res=1/(2*PI*sqrt(L*C));

   printf("C=%.3e F, L=%.3e H\n" ,C,L);
   printf("Resonant frequency is %.3f Hz\n",f_res);
   return(0);
}
```

Test run 2.6 gives a sample output.

---

🖥  **Test run 2.6**

Program to calculate resonant frequency of a series

LC circuit

C=1.000e-06 F, L=1.000e-03 H

Resonant frequency is 5032.958 Hz

---

### Resonant frequency of a parallel LC circuit

In a parallel LC circuit an effect opposite to that of the series LC circuit occurs. At low frequencies the impedance is low due to the inductor short-circuiting the capacitor; at high frequencies the capacitor short-circuits the inductor causing a low impedance. At a single frequency the circuit resonates causing a very high input impedance. This is due to the current in each branch of the circuit being almost equal and opposite; thus there will be little input current. This effect is known as parallel resonance. A lossless inductor has zero resistance and there would be no input current (assuming a lossless capacitor). A perfect parallel resonator is, of course, not practical as there is some resistance in the inductor (the capacitor will also have some loss). Figure 2.7 shows a schematic of a parallel LC circuit.

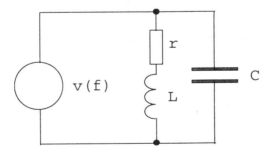

**Figure 2.7:** Parallel LC circuit

The resonant frequency can be determined using the equation:

$$f_{res} = \frac{1}{2\pi} \sqrt{\frac{1}{LC} - \frac{r^2}{4L^2}} \quad \text{Hz}$$

Program 2.10 determines the resonant frequency of a parallel LC circuit.

📄 **Program 2.10**

```c
/*    prog2_10.c                                        */
/*    Program to determine resonant frequency of a      */
/*    parallel LC circuit                               */
#include <stdio.h>
#include <math.h>          /* required for sqrt()       */

#define   PI 3.14159

int    main(void)
{
float  L=1.0e-3,C=1.0e-6,r=1.0,f_res;
   /* L is 1mH, C is 1 uF, resistance of inductor is 1 ohm */

   puts("Program to calculate resonant frequency of a parallel");
   puts("LC circuit");

   f_res=1/(2*PI)*sqrt( 1/(L*C) - (r*r)/(4*L*L));

   printf("r=%.3e ohm, C=%.3e F, L=%.3e H\n" ,r,C,L);
   printf("Resonant frequency is %.3f Hz\n",f_res);
   return(0);
}
```

Test run 2.7 shows a run with $r=1\ \Omega$, $C=1\ \mu F$ and $L=1$ mH.

---

🖥 **Test run 2.7**

```
Program to calculate resonant frequency of a parallel
LC circuit
r=1.000e+00 ohm, C=1.000e-06 F, L=1.000e-03 H
Resonant frequency is 5032.328 Hz
```

---

## 2.2 Standard input (`scanf()`, `gets()` and `getchar()`)

The keyboard is normally the standard input to a program. As with the output functions, the input functions are not part of the standard language and are contained in a standard C library. Definitions (or prototypes) of these functions are found in the header file *stdio.h*. By including this header file a degree of error checking is initiated at compilation. The compiler checks, among other things, the data types of the parameters passed into the functions. It is thus less likely that there will be any run-time errors.

There are three main input functions, these are:

| | |
|---|---|
| `scanf(`*"format",&arg1,&arg2..&argn*`)` | reads formatted values from the keyboard in a format defined by *format* and loads them into the arguments *arg1*, *arg2*, etc. |
| `gets(`*string*`)` | reads a string of text from the keyboard into *string* (up to a new line) |
| *ch=* `getchar()` | reads a single character from the keyboard into *ch* |

If a numeric or a character variable is used with the `scanf()` function an ampersand (`&`) precedes each parameter in the argument list (there are exceptions and these will be discussed in Chapters 6 and 7). This prefix causes the memory address of the variable to be used as a parameter and not the value. This allows `scanf()` to change the value of the variable (this will also be explained in more detail in Chapter 6). For now, it should be assumed that an ampersand precedes all simple numerical and character data types when using `scanf()`. The general format of the `scanf()` function is:

---

```
scanf(format,&arg1,&arg2...)
```

---

The first argument *format* is a string that defines the format of all entered values. For example, `"%f %d"` specifies that *arg1* is entered as a float and *arg2* as an integer. This string should only contain the conversion control characters such as `%d`, `%f`, `%c`, `%s`, etc., separated by spaces. Figure 2.8 shows an example of the `scanf()` function reading a float, an integer and a character into the variables `val1`, `val2` and `ch`.

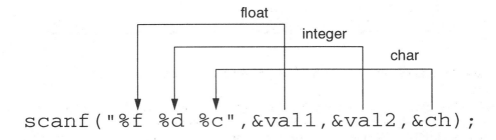

**Figure 2.8:** An example of the `scanf()` statement

Program 2.11 is an example of how variables are entered using the `scanf()` function.

📄 **Program 2.11**

```
/*    prog2_11.c                      */
#include <stdio.h>
int    main(void)
{
float  val1,val2,val3,val4;
int    i,j,k;

   printf("\nType in two float values followed by <RETURN> >>");
   scanf("%f %f",&val1,&val2);
   printf("Type in two integer values followed by <RETURN> >>");
   scanf("%d %d",&i,&j);
   printf("Type in an integer and two floats followed by <RETURN> >>");
   scanf("%d %f %f",&k,&val3,&val4);

   printf("Floats entered were %6.2f %6.2f %6.2f %6.2f\n",
                         val1,val2,val3,val4);
   printf("Integers entered were %6d %6d %6d\n",i,j,k);
   return(0);
}
```

Test run 2.8 shows a sample run.

🖥 **Test run 2.8**

```
Type in two float values followed by <RETURN> >> 1.23 23.8
Type in two integer values followed by <RETURN> >> 10 122
Type in an integer and two floats followed by <RETURN> >>
   12 12.32 0.234
Floats entered were    1.23   23.80   12.32    0.23
Integers entered were     10    122     12
```

The gets(str) function reads a number of characters into a variable (in this case str); these characters are read until the ENTER key is pressed. The getchar() function reads a single character from the input. This character is returned via the function header and not through the argument list.

A string is an array of characters which is set up using the declaration char strname[*SIZE*], where *SIZE* is the maximum number of characters in the array and strname is its name (strings and arrays are discussed in more detail in a later chapter). Program 2.12 is an example of entering strings using the gets() and the scanf() function.

📄 **Program 2.12**

```
/*    prog2_12.c                      */
#include <stdio.h>

int     main(void)
{
char    str1[100],str2[100],str3[100],text[100];
                        /* storage of text strings */
   printf("Enter a line of text >>");
   gets(text);

   printf("Entered line is %s\n",text);

   printf("Enter a line of text >>");
   scanf("%s %s %s",str1,str2,str3);

   printf("Entered line is %s %s %s\n",str1,str2,str3);
   return(0);
}
```

Test run 2.9 shows a sample run of this program. The scanf() function reads each word separated by a space. These words and spaces are interpreted as a string and the words are put into each of the string arguments. In this case only three words will be read in from the keyboard, whereas gets() reads a whole line of text until the ENTER key is pressed. The scanf() function therefore cannot read spaces in a text string.

🖥 **Test run 2.9**
```
Enter a line of text >>Some text input
Entered line is Some text input
Enter a line of text >>Some text input
Entered line is Some text input
```

### 2.2.1 Examples

*Capacitive reactance*

Program 2.13 is an improvement of program 2.7. The user enters the values of f and C using scanf(). It allows component values to be entered via the keyboard.

📄 **Program 2.13**

```
/*    prog2_13.c                                        */
/*    Program to calculate capacitive reactance  */
#include  <stdio.h>
#define    PI 3.14159

int     main(void)
{
float   freq,cap,X_c;

   puts("Enter frequency and capacitance");
   scanf("%f %f",&freq,&cap);

   X_c=1.0/(2.0*PI*freq*cap);
   printf("Capacitive Reactance is %6.3f ohms\n", X_c);
   return(0);
}
```

Test run 2.10 shows a sample run.

💻 **Test run 2.10**
```
Enter frequency and capacitance
10e3 1e-6
Capacitive Reactance is 15.916 ohms
```

### *Impedance of an RL series circuit*

The magnitude of the impedance of an RL series circuit (modulus $|Z|$) is given by the equation:

$$|Z| = \sqrt{R^2 + X_L^2} \quad \Omega$$

and the angle of the impedance (argument $\langle Z \rangle$) is given by:

$$\langle Z \rangle = \tan^{-1} \frac{X_L}{R}$$

Figure 2.9 shows a schematic of an RL series circuit.

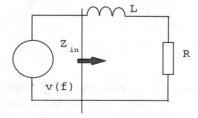

**Figure 2.9:** RL series circuit

Program 2.14 determines the magnitude and the angle of the impedance using entered values of resistance (R), inductance (L) and frequency (freq). The inverse tangent (tan⁻¹) function is defined (or prototyped) in *math.h* and is named atan(). This function returns the inverse tangent in radians; to convert it to degrees it is scaled by $\pi/180$.

📄 **Program 2.14**

```
/*    prog2_14.c                                     */
/*    Program to determine the impedance of a        */
/*    series RL circuit                              */

#include  <stdio.h>
#include  <math.h>  /*required for sqrt() and atan() */

#define   PI 3.14159

int    main(void)
{
float    R,L,freq,Xl,Zin_mag,Zin_angle;

    printf("Enter R, L and frequency >>");
    scanf("%f %f %f",&R,&L,&freq);

    Xl= 2 * PI * freq * L;

    Zin_mag = sqrt(R*R+Xl*Xl);

    Zin_angle= atan(Xl/R)*180.0/PI;
        /* atan is arc tan and returns radians    */
        /* 180/PI converts to degrees             */

    printf("Zin mag %6.2f ohm, angle %6.2f degrees\n",
                                        Zin_mag,Zin_angle);
    return(0);
}
```

Test run 2.11 is a sample output using entered values $R=100\ \Omega$, $L=100$ mH and *frequency*=1 kHz. The impedance has a magnitude of 118.10 $\Omega$ and an angle of 32.14°

🖥 **Test run 2.11**

```
Enter R, L and frequency >> 100 10e-3 1000
Zin mag 118.10 ohm, angle  32.14 degrees
```

### Resistors in parallel

Program 2.15 is an improvement of program 2.8, where values entered via the keyboard are used rather than fixed values. Three resistance values are entered using scan() with a format argument of "%f  %f  %f".

📄 **Program 2.15**

```c
/*    prog2_15.c                                    */
/*    Program to determine equivalent resistance    */
#include <stdio.h>

int     main(void)
{
float   R1,R2,R3,R_equ;

    puts("Program to determine equivalent resistance");
    puts("of three resistors connected in parallel");
    puts("Enter three values of resistance >>");

    scanf("%f %f %f",&R1,&R2,&R3);

    R_equ=1.0/(1.0/R1+1/R2+1/R3);

    printf("R1=%8.3f, R2=%8.3f and R3=%8.3f ohms\n",  R1,R2,R3);

    printf("Equivalent resistance is %8.3f ohms\n",R_equ);
    return(0);
}
```

Test run 2.12 shows a run with values of 250, 500 and 1000 $\Omega$.

💻 **Test run 2.12**

```
Program to determine equivalent resistance
of three resistors connected in parallel
Enter three values of resistance >>
1000 500 250
R1=1000.000, R2= 500.000, R3= 250.000 ohms
Equivalent resistance is 142.857 ohms
```

### Resonant frequency of a series LC circuit

Program 2.16 is an improvement of program 2.9.

**📄 Program 2.16**

```
/*    prog2_16.c                                        */
/*    Program to determine resonant frequency of a      */
/*    series LC circuit                                  */
#include  <stdio.h>
#include  <math.h>  /* required for sqrt()         */

#define   PI 3.14159

int     main(void)
{
float   L,C,f_res;

    puts("Program to resonant frequency of a series");
    puts("LC circuit");

    puts("Enter capacitance and inductance");

    scanf("%f %f",&C,&L);

    f_res=1.0/(2.0*PI*sqrt(L*C));

    printf("C=%.3e F, L=%.3e\n" ,C,L);
    printf("Resonant frequency is %.3f Hz\n",f_res);
    return(0);
}
```

Test run 2.13 is a run with input values of $C=1$ $\mu$F and $L=1$ mH.

---

**🖥 Test run 2.13**

```
Program to resonant frequency of a series
LC circuit
Enter capacitance and inductance
1e-6 1e-3
C=1.000e-06 F, L=1.000e-03
Resonant frequency is 5032.958 Hz
```

---

## Resonant frequency of a parallel LC circuit

Program 2.17 determines the resonant frequency of a parallel LC circuit for entered values of L, C and r.

### 📄 Program 2.17

```
/*    prog2_17.c                                         */
/*    Program to determine resonant frequency of a       */
/*    parallel LC circuit                                */

#include <stdio.h>
#include <math.h>

#define   PI 3.14159

int     main(void)
{
float   L,C,r,f_res;

   puts("Program to determine resonant frequency of a parallel");
   puts("LC circuit");

   puts("Enter C, L and r>>>");

   scanf("%f %f %f",&C,&L,&r);

   f_res=1.0/(2.0*PI)*sqrt( 1/(L*C) - (r*r)/(4*L*L));

   printf("r=%.3e ohm, C=%.3e F, L=%.3e\n" ,r,C,L);
   printf("Resonant frequency is %.3f Hz\n",f_res);
   return(0);
}
```

Test run 2.14 shows a run with test values of 1 μF capacitance and an inductor with inductance 1 mH and 4 Ω internal resistance.

---

### 🖥 Test run 2.14

```
Program to determine resonant frequency of a parallel
LC circuit
Enter C, L and r>>>
1e-6 1e-3 4
r=4.00e+00 ohm, C=1.00e-06 F, L=1.00e-03
Resonant frequency is 4992.531 Hz
```

---

Typically, the units of capacitance are given in μF (or even nF) and those of inductance in mH; therefore an improvement to the program is that the user is prompted to enter the values in μF and mH. Program 2.18 uses the #define directive to represent the macros MILLI and MICRO.

📄 **Program 2.18**

```
/*    prog2_18.c                                          */
/*    Program to determine resonant frequency of a        */
/*    parallel LC  circuit                                */

#include <stdio.h>
#include <math.h>
/* A few defines to help program documentation    */

#define MILLI  1e-3
#define MICRO  1e-6
#define KILO   1e3
#define PI     3.14159

int    main(void)
{
float  L,C,r,f_res;

    puts("Program to determine resonant frequency");
    puts("of a parallel LC circuit");
    puts("Enter C (in uF), L (in mH) and r (ohms)");

    scanf("%f %f %f",&C,&L,&r);

    C=C*MICRO;
    L=L*MILLI;

    f_res=1.0/(2.0*PI)*sqrt( 1/(L*C) - (r*r)/(4*L*L));

    printf("r=%.2f ohm, C=%.2f uF, L=%.2f mH\n" ,r,C/MICRO,L/MILLI);
    printf("Resonant frequency is %.3f kHz\n", f_res/KILO);
    return(0);
}
```

Test run 2.15 is a sample test run. Notice that the component values are simpler to enter than in test run 2.14. The frequency value is displayed in kHz.

🖥 **Test run 2.15**
```
Program to determine resonant frequency
of a parallel LC circuit
Enter C (in uF), L (in mH) and r (ohms)
1 10 4
r=4.00 ohm, C=1.00 uF, L=10.00 mH
Resonant frequency is 1.591 kHz
```

### Bit operations

Program 2.19 relates to digital electronics and illustrates the power of C's low-level bit operators. It uses the AND (&), OR ( | ), EX-OR (^) and NOT (~) bitwise operators to create AND, OR, EX-OR, NAND and NOR Boolean functions. The NAND and NOR functions are generated by inverting the AND and OR operations.

📄 **Program 2.19**

```
/*    prog2_19.c                                               */
/*    Program to bitwise AND, OR, NAND, NOR and EX-OR          */
/*    two hexadecimal values                                  */

#include <stdio.h>

int  main(void)
{
int  value1, value2;

        /* & - bitwise AND operator    */
        /* | - bitwise OR  operator    */
        /* ^ - bitwise EX-OR operator  */
        /* ~ - bitwise NOT operator    */

    printf("Enter two hex values >>> ");
    scanf("%x %x",&value1,&value2);

    printf("Values ANDed is %x\n",value1 & value2);
    printf("Values ORed is %x\n",value1 | value2);
    printf("Values Ex-ORed is %x\n",value1 ^ value2);
    printf("Values NANDed is %x\n",~(value1 & value2));
    printf("Values NORed is %x\n", ~(value1 | value2));
    return(0);
}
```

Test run 2.16 shows a run with test values.

---

💻 **Test run 2.16**
```
Enter two hex values >>> E215 C431
Values ANDed is c011
Values ORed is e635
Values Ex-ORed is 2624
Values NANDed is 3fee
Values NORed is 19ca
```

---

The bit patterns used in the test run are 1110  0010  0001  0101 (E215h) and 1100  0100  0011  0001 (C431h). To verify the program the hexadecimal equivalents of these values are operated on by the Boolean operators and the results checked against the test run results.

The AND operation gives the following:

| HEX | BINARY |
|-----|--------|
| E215 | 1110 0010 0001 0101 |
| C431 | 1100 0100 0011 0001 |
| C011 | 1100 0000 0001 0001 |

The OR operation gives the following:

| HEX | BINARY |
|-----|--------|
| E215 | 1110 0010 0001 0101 |
| C431 | 1100 0100 0011 0001 |
| E635 | 1110 0110 0011 0101 |

The EX-OR function gives the following:

| HEX | BINARY |
|-----|--------|
| E215 | 1110 0010 0001 0101 |
| C431 | 1100 0100 0011 0001 |
| 2624 | 0010 0110 0010 0100 |

The inverse of AND (NAND) will be 0011 1111 1110 1110 (3FEEh); the inverse of the OR (NOR) is 0001 1001 1100 1010 (19CAh). These results are identical to these in test run 2.16. Thus the test has been successful.

### Converting between decimal, hexadecimal and octal

Programs 2.20, 2.21 and 2.22 demonstrate how entered values are input/output using different number bases. Integers can be entered/output as a decimal (%d), a hexadecimal (%x) or an octal (%o). The use of hexadecimal and octal are important in bit operations and conversions. Program 2.20 displays an entered decimal number and its equivalent hexadecimal and octal representations.

**Program 2.20**

```
/*    prog2_20.c                                          */
/*    Program to display a decimal integer in hexadecimal */
/*    and octal                                           */

#include <stdio.h>

int  main(void)
{
int  value;

    puts("Enter integer value (-32768 to 32767) >> ");
    scanf("%d",&value);

    printf("Decimal = %d, Octal = %o, Hex = %x\n",value,value,value);
    return(0);
}
```

Test run 2.17 shows a sample run.

**Test run 2.17**

```
Enter integer value (-32768 to 32767)>>
36
Decimal = 36, Octal = 44, Hex = 24
```

Program 2.21 uses a hexadecimal number as the input and displays it as a decimal and as an octal.

📄 **Program 2.21**
```
/*    prog2_21.c                                            */
/*    Program to display a hexademical value as demical      */
/*    and octal                                              */

#include <stdio.h>

int  main(void)
{
int  value;

   puts("Enter a hexadecimal value ");
   scanf("%x",&value);

   printf("Decimal = %d, Octal = %o, Hex = %x\n",value,value,value);
   return(0);
}
```

Test 2.18 shows a sample test run with an entered hexadecimal value of FAh.

🖥 **Test run 2.18**
```
Enter a hexadecimal value
fa
Decimal = 250, Octal = 372, Hex = fa
```

Program 2.22 displays an ASCII decimal value as an equivalent ASCII character.

📄 **Program 2.22**
```
/*    prog2_22.c                               */
/*    Program to ASCII code to character        */

#include <stdio.h>

int  main(void)
{
int  value;
   puts("Enter ASCII code (greater than 33)>");
   scanf("%d",&value);

   printf("Code = %d, character = %c\n",value,value);
   return(0);
}
```

Test run 2.19 shows a sample run with an entered ASCII decimal value of 45; this prints the ASCII character '-'.

---

💻  **Test run 2.19**
```
Enter ASCII code (greater than 33)>
45
Code = 45, character = -
```

---

NOTE OF CAUTION: Problems can occur if getchar() is used after scanf(). This is due to the storage of carriage returns in the keyboard buffer. This can be solved using the fflush(stdin) statement before each keyboard input statement. Examples using getchar() will be given in the next chapter.

## 2.3  Tutorial

Q2.1    (i) Write a program which displays the following text using two printf() statements. Refer to program 2.3.

---

💻  **Test run 2.20**
```
The value of the resistance in the circuit
is less than the impedance of the capacitor
```

---

(ii) Modify the program in (i) so that it uses only one printf() statement.

Q2.2    Find, and correct, the three types of errors in programs 2.23, 2.24 and 2.25.

(i)

📄  **Program 2.23**
```
\*    prog2_23.c                                      *\
\*    Program to determine equivalent resistance      *\
\*    of two resistors in parallel                    *\
#include <stdio.h>

int     main(void)
{
float   R1,R2,Requ;

   puts("Enter R1 and R2");
   scanf("%d %d",&R1,&R2);


   Requ=1.0(1.0/R1+1/R2);

   printf("Parallel resistance is %f",Requ);
   return(0);
}
```

(ii)
### 📄 Program 2.24

```
/*    prog2_24.c                                    */
/*    Program to determine current flowing in       */
/*    a resistor using Ohms law                      */

#include <stdio.h>

int    main(void)
{
float    current,voltage,resistance;

   printf('Enter voltage and resistance>> ');
   scanf("%f %f",voltage,resistance);

   current=voltage/resistance;
   printf("Current is ",current," amps\n");
   return(0);
}
```

(iii)
### 📄 Program 2.25

```
/*    prog2_25.c
    */
/*    Program to bitwise OR two hexadecimal values
    */

#include <stdio.h>

int  main(void)
int  val1,val2,val3;
{
   printf("Enter two hex values>> ");
   scanf("%d %d",&val1,&val2);

   val3= val1 & val2;

   printf("%x OR %x = %x\n",val1,val2,val3);
   return(0);
}
```

Test run 2.21 shows the correct output from program 2.25.

### 🖥 Test run 2.21

```
Enter two hex values>> 12 6a
12 OR 6a = 7a
```

Q2.3    Complete Table 2.5 using a base conversion program. Refer to programs 2.20 and 2.21.

**Table 2.5:** Decimal, hexadecimal and octal equivalents

| decimal | hexadecimal | octal |
|---------|-------------|-------|
| 145     |             |       |
| -54     |             |       |
| 2222    |             |       |
|         | 0x1fff      |       |
|         | 0x81a0      |       |
|         | 0xbbb       |       |
|         |             | 093   |
|         |             | 076   |

Q2.4    (i) The parallel plate capacitor shown in Figure 2.10 consists of two parallel plates separated by an air dielectric. Write a program which determines the capacitance of this set-up. The program should prompt for the area of the plates and the separation distance. Test run 2.22 gives a sample run.

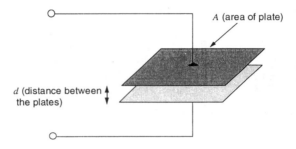

*A* (area of plate)

*d* (distance between the plates)

**Figure 2.10:** Parallel plate capacitor

$$C = \frac{\varepsilon_0 A}{d} \quad \text{F}$$

where $\varepsilon_0 = 8.854 \times 10^{-12}$ F.m$^{-1}$

---
🖳 **Test run 2.22**
Enter distance between and area of plates>> 10e-3 100e-4
Capacitance is 8.8e-12 F
---

(ii) Modify the program in (i) so the user can enter a value for the dielectric constant ($\varepsilon_r$). The capacitance of a capacitor with plates separated by a dielectric of dielectric constant $\varepsilon_r$ is given by the following.

$$C = \frac{\varepsilon_0 \varepsilon_r A}{d} \quad \text{F}$$

Table 2.6 gives typical ranges of dielectric constants.

**Table 2.6:** Typical ranges of dielectric constants for common insulating materials

| Material | Dielectric constant |
|----------|--------------------|
| Glass | 7-8 |
| Mica | 5.5-8 |
| Paper (dry) | 4.5-4.7 |
| Polyester | 2.8-3.2 |
| Polystyrene | 2.5 |

(iii) Modify the program in (ii) so that the area of the plates is entered in $mm^2$ and the distance in mm.

(iv) Modify the program in (iii) so that the capacitance is displayed in μF.

Q2.5    Figure 2.11 shows an inverting amplifier using an operational amplifier (op-amp). The magnitude of the gain of this amplifier is the ratio of $R_2$ to $R_1$. Write a program which determines the magnitude of the gain for entered resistor values.

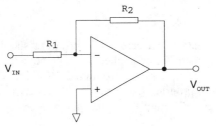

**Figure 2.11:** Inverting amplifier

Q2.6    Figure 2.12 shows an active filter using an op-amp. This circuit has high gain at low frequencies and low gain at high frequencies. It thus acts as a low-pass filter.

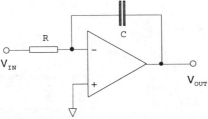

**Figure 2.12:** RC active filter

The magnitude of the gain of this circuit is given by:

$$|Gain| = \frac{1}{2\pi fRC}$$

(i) Write a program in which the user enters a frequency, resistance (for example 1 MΩ) and capacitance (for example 1 μF), and the program determines the magnitude of the gain. Refer to program 2.14.

(ii) Modify the program in (i) so that the output is displayed in decibels (dB). The log10() function determines the base-10 logarithm of a value. This is prototyped in the *math.h* header file. The gain can be found using the following:

$$Gain(dB)=20.\log_{10}(Voltage\ Gain)\ dB$$

Q2.7    Modify program 2.16 so that the program displays the reactance of the inductor at resonance ($X_L=2\pi f_{res}L$). Note that the reactance of the capacitor will be equal to this value at resonance.

Q2.8    Modify program 2.17 so that it displays the reactance of the capacitor at resonance ($X_C=1/(2\pi f_{res}C)$ ). Also, determine the magnitude of the impedance of the inductor ($Z = \sqrt{r^2 + X_L^2}$ ).

Q2.9    Program 2.26 contains an error. The program should determine the power dissipated in a resistor for an applied a.c. voltage with an entered peak voltage. Test run 2.23 is a sample run of program 2.26 and test run 2.24 is a run from a properly working program. Note that a different system and/or compiler may give a sample run different from that given in test run 2.24 (the program is unpredictable).

📄 **Program 2.26**

```
/*    prog2_26.c                                       */
/*    Program to determine power dissipated in         */
/*    a resistor with an applied a.c. waveform         */

#include <stdio.h>

int    main(void)
{
float    Vmax,Vrms,R,power;

    printf("Enter peak voltage and resistance>> ");
    scanf("%f %f",&Vmax,&R);

    Vrms=Vmax/sqrt(2);

    power=(Vrms*Vrms)/R;

    printf("Power is %6.2f\n watts",power);

    return(0);

}
```

🖳 **Test run 2.23**
```
Enter peak voltage and resistance>> 10 2
Power is   50.00 Watts
```

🖳 **Test run 2.24**
```
Enter peak voltage and resistance>> 10 2
Power is   25.00 Watts
```

Q2.10    Determine the output from program 2.27.

📄 **Program 2.27**
```
/*   prog2_27.c                           */
#include <stdio.h>

int  main(void)
{
int  y;

/*let this be a lesson to use parentheses    */

    y = -3 + 6 * 3 - 2;      printf("%d \n",y);
    y = 3 + 4 % 5 - 6;       printf("%d \n",y);
    y = -4 * 3 % - 6 / 5 ;  printf("%d \n",y);
    y = ( 7 + 6 ) % 5 / 2 ; printf("%d \n",y);
    return(0);
}
```

Q2.11    Determine the output from program 2.28.

📄 **Program 2.28**
```
/*   prog2_28.c                           */
#include <stdio.h>

int  main(void)
{
int   x=4, y ,z;

    x *= 3 + 2 ;            printf("%d\n",x);
    x *= y = z = 4 ;        printf("%d \n", x);
    x++ ;                   printf("x = %d \n",x);
    return(0);
}
```

Q2.12    Write a program in which the user enters two octal values. The program will then display the bitwise AND, OR, NAND, EX-OR and NOR octal values. Refer to program 2.19.

Q2.13    Write a program that determines the magnitude and the angle of the impedance of a series RC circuit. Refer to program 2.14.

Q2.14    Write a program which determines the magnitude of the impedance of an LC series circuit for entered values of frequency ($f$), inductance ($L$) and capacitance ($C$). The following formula can be used to determine the magnitude.

$$|Z_{in}| = \left[ 2\pi fL - \frac{1}{2\pi fC} \right] \ \Omega$$

The abs() function, which is prototyped in *math.h*, determines the magnitude of a value (or absolute value). Refer to program 2.14.

Q2.15    Modify Q2.14 so that the values are entered in mH and µF. Refer to program 2.18.

Q2.16    Figure 2.13 shows a simple base resistor biased bipolar transistor circuit.

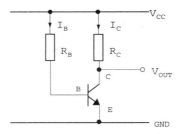

**Figure 2.13:** Simple base resistor biased bipolar transistor circuit

Typically, to produce the maximum output swing the collector voltage is biased at a point halfway between the supply rails, in this case $V_{cc}/2$. Thus, for a specific collector current ($I_c$), the collector resistance ($R_c$) can be determined (see equation 1). The base current is then determined by dividing the collector current by the DC current gain $h_{FE}$ (see equation 2). If the transistor is ON then the base-emitter junction will have a conducting silicon diode voltage across it ($V_{BE}(ON)$). Using an approximation for this voltage (~0.65 V) the base resistance can be determined (equation 3). The circuit equations are:

$$R_C = \frac{V_{cc}/2}{I_C} \qquad \Omega \quad [1]$$

$$I_B = \frac{I_C}{h_{FE}} \qquad A \quad [2]$$

$$R_B = \frac{V_{CC} - V_{BE}}{I_B} \qquad \Omega \quad [3]$$

Write a program which determines $R_B$ for given inputs of $I_c$ and $V_{cc}$. Assume that $V_{BE}(ON)$ is 0.65 V and $h_{FE}$ is 100. Entered values for $V_{cc}$ are between 5 and 30 V, and $I_c$ between 0.1 and 10 mA. Test run 2.25 gives a sample output.

---

🖳  **Test run 2.25**

```
Enter Vcc  (5->15V)>>  15
Enter Ic   (mA)      >>  1
Collector resistance is 15000  ohms
Base resistance is      1435000  ohms
```

---

Q2.17   Modify the program in Q2.16 so that it displays the collector resistance in k$\Omega$ and base resistance in M$\Omega$. Test run 2.26 gives a sample test run.

---

🖳  **Test run 2.26**

```
Enter Vcc  (5->15V)>>  15
Enter Ic   (mA)      >>  1
Collector resistance is 15 Kohms
Base resistance is      1.43 Mohms
```

# CHAPTER 3

# Selection statements

A sequential program is one in which a series of statements is executed one-by-one in a sequential manner. The path through the program will never vary. Most programs, though, make decisions on the route depending on entered or processed values. This routing is achieved with control statements. These either make a decision or are iterative. Decisive, or selection, statements allow alternative courses of action to be taken depending on the result of an operation. Two statements are used to make a decision; these are if..else and switch. An iterative process allows the looping of a set of statements. There are three forms of iteration: while, do and for. Figure 3.1 shows the flows of a sequential program and of a non-sequential program with selection and iterative statements.

Control statements operate on conditional expressions and they can route to single statement or compound statements (a block). Braces ({}) define the start and end of a blocks.

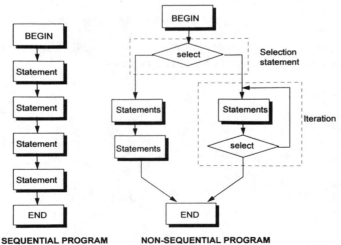

**Figure 3.1:** Sequential and non-sequential programs

## 3.1 `if..else` statements

A decision is made with the `if` statement. It logically determines whether a conditional expression is TRUE or FALSE. For a TRUE, the program executes one block of code; a FALSE causes the execution of another (if any). The keyword `else` identifies the FALSE block. Braces are used to define the start and end of the block. Note that there is no Boolean data type in C.

Relationship operators (>,<,>=,<=,==,!=) yield a TRUE or FALSE from their operation. Logical statements (&&, ||, !) can then group these together to give the required functionality. If the operation is not a relationship, such as bitwise or an arithmetic operation, then any non-zero value is TRUE and a zero is FALSE. Figure 3.2 shows how relational, bitwise and arithmetic operators group together with logical operators.

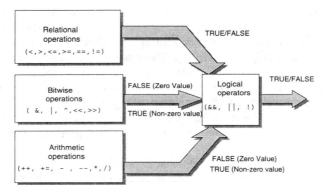

**Figure 3.2:** Outline structure of the `if` statement

The following is an example syntax of the `if` statement. **If the statement block has only one statement the braces ( { } ) can be excluded**.

```
if (expression)
{
    statement block
}
```

the following is an example format with an `else` extension.

```
if (expression)
{
    statement block1
}
else
{
    statement block2
}
```

It is possible to nest if..else statements to give a required functionality. In the next example, *statement block1* is executed if expression1 is TRUE. If it is FALSE then the program checks the next expression. If this is TRUE the program executes *statement block2*, else it checks the next expression, and so on. If all expressions are FALSE then the program executes the final else statement block, in this case, *statement block 4*:

```
if (expression1)
{
    statement block1
}
else if (expression2)
{
    statement block2
}
else if (expression3)
{
    statement block3
}
else
{
    statement block4
}
```

Figure 3.3 shows a diagrammatic represention of this example statement.

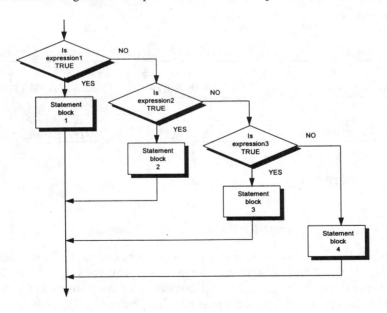

**Figure 3.3:** Structure of the compound if statement

Figure 3.4 shows three examples of the if statement. In each example the relationship operations (==,!=,>) are resolved first as these have a higher precedence than logical operations (&&, ||). After the relationship operations the program resolves the AND logical operation (&&) as this has a higher precedence than the OR logical operation (||). After the AND and OR logical operations a TRUE or FALSE is yielded from the expression. Refer to Chapter 1 for information on precedence.

In Figure 3.4 (a) the first part of the expression (x==4) yields a TRUE value as x is 4. The result of the second part (y>2) is FALSE as y is not greater than 2. The final relationship operation (i.e. ch!='x') is FALSE as the value of ch is 'x'. After these relationships have been determined the logical AND operation (&&) operates on the results of the first two relationship operations ((x==4) && (y>2)). This yields FALSE as at least one of the relationship operations is FALSE. The result of the last part of the statement (ch!='x') is also FALSE, so the overall result of the expression is FALSE.

In Figure 3.4 (b) the relationship operator for y has been changed so that the operation detemines whether the value of y is less than 2 (y<2). This yields a TRUE, making the result of the AND logical operation TRUE. This, in turn, makes the resultant expression TRUE as the OR logical operator yields a TRUE when any one of the operands is TRUE.

In Figure 3.4 (c) the (ch=='x') operation yields a TRUE which, in turn, makes the expression TRUE.

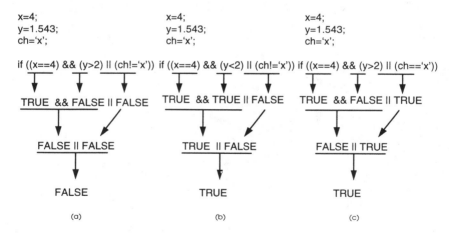

**Figure 3.4:** Examples of the if statement

Figure 3.5 illustrates how arithmetic and bitwise operators can be used within the if statement. In Figure 3.5(a) the AND logical operator regards the value of x as TRUE as its value is not 0 (zero). In Figure 3.5(b), the result of the x-- operation will be 0; thus the AND logical operator will regard this as FALSE. Similiarly, in Figure 3.5(c) the result of the bitwise operation x & 2 (00000100 & 00000010) yields a 0 value; thus the logical operator treats this as FALSE.

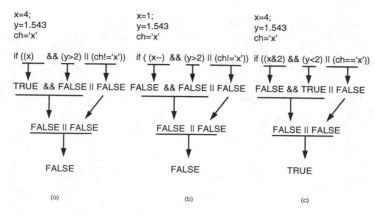

**Figure 3.5:** Examples of the `if` statement

## 3.1.1 Examples

### *Decimal to binary conversion*

The program in this section converts a decimal integer value to an 8-bit unsigned binary form. A technique known as bit-masking is used to identify individual bits by setting all other bits, other than the bit of interest, to 0. It uses the AND bitwise operator (`&`), which yields a 0 for a bit if one of the bit operands is a 0; otherwise, if one of the bit operands is a 1 it will yield the value of the other operand bit. Figure 3.6 shows an example of masking the third least significant bit ($b_2$). In this case, the bit-mask used is `0x04`; this is then bitwise AND'ed with the operand. There are only two possible results from this operation: a 0 (if $b_2$ is 0) or 4 (if $b_2$ is 1). An X indicates a don't care state in which a bit can take any binary value (i.e. 0 or 1).

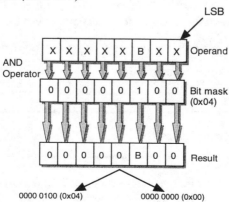

**Figure 3.6:** Bit-mask operation

Program 3.1 uses the if statement with bit-mask values 0x80 (1000 0000), 0x40 (0100 0000), etc., to determine whether each of the lower 8 bits of a decimal integer is set. The printf() statements display each of the bits on a single line as there is no new line character ('\n') at the end of each printf() format string. The most significant bit is displayed first as this will appear at the left-hand side of the screen. Note that this is not the most efficient method of implementing this problem; an iterative loop produces much less code (see program 4.2).

**Program 3.1**

```
/*    prog3_1.c                                               */
/*    Program to convert decimal to an 8-bit unsigned         */
/*    binary value                                            */
int    main(void)
{
int    i; /* only the bottom eight bits are used. An          */
          /* unsigned char data type could also be used       */

    printf("Enter decimal value (0-255)>>> ");
    scanf("%d",&i);

    printf("Binary equivalent is ");
    if (i & 0x80) printf("1"); else printf("0");
    if (i & 0x40) printf("1"); else printf("0");
    if (i & 0x20) printf("1"); else printf("0");
    if (i & 0x10) printf("1"); else printf("0");
    if (i & 0x08) printf("1"); else printf("0");
    if (i & 0x04) printf("1"); else printf("0");
    if (i & 0x02) printf("1"); else printf("0");
    if (i & 0x01) printf("1"); else printf("0");
    puts("");
    return(0);
}
```

Test runs 3.1 and 3.2 show two sample runs with entered values of 33 and 255, respectively. Both of these tests generate the correct binary values.

**Test run 3.1**
```
Enter decimal value (0-255)>>> 33
Binary equivalent is 00100001
```

**Test run 3.2**
```
Enter decimal value (0-255)>>> 255
Binary equivalent is 11111111
```

Several enhancements have been added to program 3.2, such as a trap to catch entered values which are invalid, i.e. less than 0 and greater than 255. The program will exit without printing the binary value if an invalid value is entered. Another enhancement uses the #define statement to replace the bit-mask values with tokens, e.g. the most significant bit-mask (0x80) is replaced by the token BIT7. This technique improves program readability.

📄 **Program 3.2**

```
/*    prog3_2.c                                              */
/*    Program to display an 8-bit unsigned decimal          */
/*    in a binary format                                    */
/* A few bit mask defines */
#define BIT0 0x01
#define BIT1 0x02
#define BIT2 0x04
#define BIT3 0x08
#define BIT4 0x10
#define BIT5 0x20
#define BIT6 0x40
#define BIT7 0x80

int  main(void)
{
int  i;

    printf("Enter decimal value (0-255)>>> ");
    scanf("%d",&i);

    if ( (i<0) || (i>255))
      puts("Invalid entered value");
    else
    {
      printf("Binary equivalent is ");
      if (i & BIT7) printf("1");      else printf("0");
      if (i & BIT6) printf("1");      else printf("0");
      if (i & BIT5) printf("1");      else printf("0");
      if (i & BIT4) printf("1");      else printf("0");
      if (i & BIT3) printf("1");      else printf("0");
      if (i & BIT2) printf("1");      else printf("0");
      if (i & BIT1) printf("1");      else printf("0");
      if (i & BIT0) printf("1\n");    else printf("0\n");

    }
    return(0);
}
```

Test runs 3.3 and 3.4 show sample outputs from this program. The first tests for a value within the correct range (36) and the second for an invalid entered value (430).

🖥 **Test run 3.3**
```
Enter decimal value (0-255)>>> 36
Binary equivalent is 00100100
```

🖥 **Test run 3.4**
```
Enter decimal value (0-255)>>> 430
Invalid value
```

## Bitwise operations

Program 3.3 is an enhancement of program 2.19. A simple menu option has been added
so that the user can select the Boolean function required, i.e. OR, AND, EX-OR, NOR or
NAND.

**Program 3.3**

```
/*    prog3_3.c                                        */
/*    Program which uses a simple menu to select a bitwise */
/*    operation on two entered values                  */

#include <stdio.h>
#define   OR      1
#define   AND     2
#define   EX_OR   3
#define   NOR     4
#define   NAND    5

int  main(void)
{
int  value1,value2,option;

    puts("Program to determine bitwise operation on two values");

    printf("Enter two hex values >>>");
    scanf("%x %x",&value1,&value2);

    puts("Enter function required");

    printf("1-OR \n2-AND \n3-EX-OR \n");
    printf("4-NOR \n5-NAND \nEnter >> ");
    scanf("%d",&option);

    if (option==OR)
       printf("Ans is %x (hex)\n",value1 | value2);
    else if (option==AND)
       printf("Ans is %x (hex)\n",value1 & value2);
    else if (option==EX_OR)
       printf("Ans is %x (hex)\n",value1 ^ value2);
    else if (option==NOR)
       printf("Ans is %x (hex)\n",~(value1 | value2));
    else if (option==NAND)
       printf("Ans is %x (hex)\n",~(value1 & value2));
    else puts("INVALID OPTION");

    return(0);

}
```

Test run 3.5 shows an invalid option entry, i.e. any number not equal to 1, 2, 3, 4 or 5.

---

💻 **Test run 3.5**
```
Program to determine bitwise operation on two values
Enter two hex values >>> 532e 3210
Enter function required
1-OR
2-AND
3-EX-OR
4-NOR
5-NAND
Enter Option>> 7
INVALID OPTION
```

---

Test run 3.6 is a sample test for the AND operation.

---

💻 **Test run 3.6**
```
Program to determine bitwise operation on two values
Enter two hex values >>> 532e 3210
Enter function required
1-OR
2-AND
3-EX-OR
4-NOR
5-NAND
Enter >> 2
Answer is 1200 (hex)
```

---

### Series/parallel resistances

Program 3.4 determines the equivalent resistance of two resistors connected either in series or parallel. It uses scanf() to get the two resistance values and getchar() to select the circuit configuration. Problems can occur when using getchar() after scanf() due to new-line characters being stored in the keyboard buffer. The statement fflush(stdin) has been inserted into the program in order to clear the buffer before getchar() is called (stdin represents the standard input device, i.e. the keyboard).

The program also uses tolower() to convert the entered circuit selection character to lower-case (this is protyped in the *ctype.h*).

📄 **Program 3.4**
```c
/*    prog3_4.c                                              */
/*    Program to determine the equivalent resistance of two  */
/*    resistors connected either in series or parallel       */
#include <stdio.h>
#include <ctype.h> /* required for tolower() function         */

int    main(void)
{
float  R1,R2,R_equ;
char   ch;

    printf("Enter two resistance values >>");
```

```
scanf("%f %f",&R1,&R2);

fflush(stdin); /* flush keyboard buffer                       */
printf("Do you require (s)eries or (p)arallel >>");
ch=getchar();

if (tolower(ch)=='s') /* convert character to lowercase        */
{
    R_equ=R1+R2;
    printf("Equivalent series resistance is %8.2f ohms",R_equ);
}
else if (tolower(ch)=='p')
{
    R_equ=(R1*R2)/(R1+R2);
    printf("Equivalent parallel resistance is %8.2f ohms",R_equ);
}
else puts("Invalid entry");
return(0);
}
```

### Quadratic equations

Some electrical examples require the solution of a quadratic equation. The standard form is given next:

$$ax^2 + bx + c = 0$$

The solution of $x$ in this equation is given by:

$$x_{1,2} = \frac{-b \pm \sqrt{b^2 - 4ac}}{2a}$$

This can yield three possible types of results:

1. if $b^2=4ac$, there will be a single real root $(x=-b/2a)$

2. else, if $b^2>4ac$, there will be two real roots

$$x_1 = \frac{-b + \sqrt{b^2 - 4ac}}{2a}, \qquad x_2 = \frac{-b - \sqrt{b^2 - 4ac}}{2a}$$

3. else, the roots will be complex:

$$x_1 = \frac{-b}{2a} + j\frac{\sqrt{4ac - b^2}}{2a}, \qquad x_2 = \frac{-b}{2a} - j\frac{\sqrt{4ac - b^2}}{2a}$$

Program 3.5 determines the roots of a quadratic equation. In this program the `if..else` statement is used to determine if the roots are real, complex or singular. The value passed to the square-root function (sqrt()), which is prototyped in the *math.h*, should be tested to determine if it is negative. If it is, it may cause the program to terminate as the square root of a negative number cannot be calculated (it is numerically invalid). The program may also terminate if a is zero as this causes a divide by zero error (the trap for this error is left as a tutorial question).

📄 **Program 3.5**

```
/*     prog3_5.c                                            */
/*     Program to determine roots of a quadratic equation   */

#include <stdio.h>
#include <math.h>

int     main(void)
{
float   a,b,c,real1,real2,imag;

    puts("Program to determine roots of a quadratic equation");
    printf("Enter a,b and c >>>");

    scanf("%f %f %f",&a,&b,&c);

    printf("Equation is %.2fx*x + %.2fx + %.2f\n",a,b,c);

    if  ((b*b)==(4*a*c))
    {      /*    singular root         */
       real1=(b*b)/(2*a);
       printf("Root is %.2f\n",real1);

    } else if ((b*b)>(4*a*c))
    {      /*    real roots            */
       real1=(-b+sqrt( (b*b)-4*a*c )) /(2*a);
       real2=(-b-sqrt( (b*b)-4*a*c )) /(2*a);
       printf("Roots are %.2f, %.2f\n",real1,real2);
    } else
    {      /*    complex roots         */
       real1=(b*b)/(2*a);
       imag=sqrt(4*a*c-b*b)/(2*a);
       printf("Roots are %.2f +/- j%.2f\n",real1,imag);
    }

    return(0);

}
```

Three test runs 3.7, 3.8 and 3.9 test each of the three types of roots that occur. In test run 3.7 the roots of the equation are real.

🖥 **Test run 3.7**

```
Program to determine roots of a quadratic equation
Enter a,b and c >>> 1 1 -2
Equation is 1.00x*x + 1.00x + -2.00
Roots are 1.00, -2.00
```

In test run 3.8 the roots are complex, i.e. in the form x+jy.

---

🖳  **Test run 3.8**
```
Program to determine roots of a quadratic equation
Enter a,b and c >>> 2 2 4
Equation is 2.00x*x + 2.00x + 4.00
Roots are 1.00 +/- j1.32
```
---

In test run 3.9 the result is a singular root.

---

🖳  **Test run 3.9**
```
Program to determine roots of a quadratic equation
Enter a,b and c >>> 1 2 1
Equation is 1.00x*x + 2.00x + 1.00
Root is 2.00
```
---

## Electromagnetic (EM) waves

Program 3.6 uses the if statement to determine the classification of an EM wave given its wavelength. Figure 3.7 illustrates the EM spectrum spanning different wavelengths. The classification of the wave is determined either by the frequency or the wavelength (normally radio and microwaves are defined by their frequency, whereas other types by their wavelength). For example, an EM wave with a wavelength of 10 m is classified as a radio wave, a wavelength of 500 nm as visible light and a wavelength of 50 cm is in the microwave region.

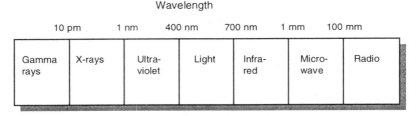

**Figure 3.7:** EM spectrum

📄  **Program 3.6**
```
/*    prog3_6.c                                               */
/*    Program to determine type of EM wave for a given wavelength */
#include <stdio.h>
int     main(void)
{
float    lambda;

    printf("Enter wavelength>>>");
    scanf("%f",&lambda);

    printf("Electromagnetic wave is ");
```

```
if          (lambda<1e-11)      puts("Gamma Ray !!!");
else if     (lambda<1e-9)       puts("X-ray");
else if     (lambda<400e-9)     puts("Ultaviolet");
else if     (lambda<700e-9)     puts("LIGHT");
else if     (lambda<1e-3)       puts("Infrared");
else if     (lambda<1e-1)       puts("Microwave");
else                            puts("Radio wave");

    return(0);
}
```

Test run 3.10 shows a sample run.

---

🖳 **Test run 3.10**
```
Enter wavelength>>> 1e-10
Electromagnetic wave is X-ray
```

---

EM waves can also be specified by their frequency. Program 3.7 allows the user to enter the frequency of the wave, and the program then determines the wavelength using the formula:

$$\lambda = \frac{c}{f}$$

where c is the speed of light and f the frequency of the wave.

📄 **Program 3.7**
```
/*    prog3_7.c                                              */
/*    Program to determine type of wave for an entered frequency */
#include  <stdio.h>
#define    SPEED_OF_LIGHT  3e8

int       main(void)
{
float     lambda,freq;

    printf("Enter frequency>>>");
    scanf("%f",&freq);

    lambda=SPEED_OF_LIGHT/freq;

    printf("Wavelength is %.2e m. EM wave is ",  lambda);
    if          (lambda<1e-11)     puts("Gamma Rays !!!");
    else if     (lambda<1e-9)      puts("X-rays");
    else if     (lambda<400e-9)    puts("Ultaviolet");
    else if     (lambda<700e-9)    puts("LIGHT");
    else if     (lambda<1e-3)      puts("Infrared");
    else if     (lambda<0.3e-1)    puts("Microwave");
    else                           puts("Radio waves");

    return(0);
}
```

Test run 3.11 shows a sample run.

---

🖳  **Test run 3.11**
```
Enter frequency>>> 10e9
Wavelength is 3.0e-02 m. EM wave is Microwave
```

---

## 3.2  `switch` statement

The `switch` statement is used when there is a multiple decision to be made. It is normally used to replace the `if` statement when there are many routes of execution the program execution can take. The syntax of `switch` is as follows.

```
switch (expression)
{
   case const1:    statement(s) : break;
   case const2:    statement(s) ; break;
   :           :
   default:        statement(s) ; break;
}
```

The `switch` statement checks the `expression` against each of the constants in sequence (the constant must be an integer or character data type). When a match is found the statement(s) associated with the constant is(are) executed. The execution carries on to all other statements until a `break` is encountered or to the end of `switch`, whichever is sooner. If the `break` is omitted, the execution continues until the end of `switch`.

If none of the constants matches the `switch` expression a set of statements associated with the default condition (`default:`) is executed.

### 3.2.1  Examples

*Resistor colour code*

Resistors are normally identified by means of a colour code system, as outlined in Table 3.1.

**Table 3.1:** Resistor colour coding system

| Digit | Colour | Multiplier | Digit | Colour | Multiplier |
|-------|--------|------------|-------|--------|------------|
|       | SILVER | 0.01       | 4     | YELLOW | 10 K       |
|       | GOLD   | 0.1        | 5     | GREEN  | 100 K      |
| 0     | BLACK  | 1          | 6     | BLUE   | 1 M        |
| 1     | BROWN  | 10         | 7     | VIOLET | 10 M       |
| 2     | RED    | 100        | 8     | GREY   |            |
| 3     | ORANGE | 1 K        | 9     | WHITE  |            |

Program 3.8 uses a `switch` statement to determine the colour of a resistor band for an entered value. The variable used (`colour`) has been declared as an `unsigned int` as the entered value will always be positive. For this purpose, `scanf()` has a `%u` format specifier.

📄 **Program 3.8**
```
/*   prog3_8.c                                         */
/*   Program to determine colour code for a single     */
/*   resistor band digit                               */
#include <stdio.h>

int  main(void)
{
unsigned int colour;
               /* char or unsigned char could also be used */
   printf("Enter value of colour band(0-9)>>");
   scanf("%u",&colour);

   printf("Resistor colour band is ");

   switch (colour)
   {
      case 0: printf("BLACK");      break;
      case 1: printf("BROWN");      break;
      case 2: printf("RED");        break;
      case 3: printf("ORANGE");     break;
      case 4: printf("YELLOW");     break;
      case 5: printf("GREEN");      break;
      case 6: printf("BLUE");       break;
      case 7: printf("VIOLET");     break;
      case 8: printf("GREY");       break;
      case 9: printf("WHITE");      break;
   }
   return(0);
}
```

Test run 3.12 shows a sample run.

💻 **Test run 3.12**
```
Enter value of colour band(0-9)>> 3
Resistor colour band is ORANGE
```

Program 3.9 uses #define directives to define each of the resistor colour bands. There may be a clash with these defines if other header files contain these definitions. If this occurs change the defines to RES_BLACK, RES_BROWN, etc.

A `default:` has been added to catch any invalid input (such as less than 0 or greater than 9).

📄 **Program 3.9**

```c
/*    prog3_9.c                                                    */
/* Program to determine colour code for resistor band digit    */
#include <stdio.h>
#define    BLACK      0
#define    BROWN      1
#define    RED        2
#define    ORANGE     3
#define    YELLOW     4
#define    GREEN      5
#define    BLUE       6
#define    VIOLET     7
#define    GREY       8
#define    WHITE      9

int  main(void)
{
unsigned int   colour;

   printf("Enter value of colour band(0-9)>>");
   scanf("%u",&colour);
   printf("Resistor colour band is ");

   switch (colour)
   {
      case BLACK: printf("BLACK");      break;
      case BROWN: printf("BROWN");      break;
      case RED:   printf("RED");        break;
      case ORANGE:printf("ORANGE");     break;
      case YELLOW:printf("YELLOW");     break;
      case GREEN: printf("GREEN");      break;
      case BLUE:  printf("BLUE");       break;
      case VIOLET:printf("VIOLET");     break;
      case GREY:  printf("GREY");       break;
      case WHITE: printf("WHITE");      break;
      default:    printf("NO COLOUR"); break;
   }
   return(0);
}
```

A modern style of defining a sequence of integer values is to use the enum data type. Program 3.10 has the same effect as the previous program; it defines BLACK as 0, BROWN as 1, etc. An enum declaration sets up a sequence of integer values. If the sequence starts at 0 then no initialization of the start value is required, else the first parameter is initialized. A sample enum declaration is given next, this initializes the start of the sequence to –2 (SILVER) and the sequence will be SILVER=–2, GOLD=–1, BLACK=0, etc. up to WHITE=9 and the variable declared is colour.

```c
enum {SILVER=-2, GOLD, BLACK, BROWN, RED, ORANGE, YELLOW, GREEN,
                  BLUE, VIOLET,  GREY, WHITE} colour;
```

One advantage of using the enum data type is that the variable can only take on the names of the declarations (e.g. colour=2 is invalid), whereas colour=RED is valid.

This improves the error checking capabilities of the program by restricting the possible uses of the variable.

📄 **Program 3.10**

```
/*    prog3_10.c                              */
#include <stdio.h>

int  main(void)
{
enum    {BLACK,BROWN,RED,ORANGE,YELLOW,
          GREEN,BLUE,VIOLET,GREY,WHITE} colours;

   printf("Enter value >>");
   scanf("%d",&colours);

   printf("Resistor colour band is ");

   switch (colours)
   {
      case BLACK: printf("BLACK");        break;
      case BROWN: printf("BROWN");        break;
      case RED:   printf("RED");          break;
      case ORANGE:printf("ORANGE");       break;
      case YELLOW:printf("YELLOW");       break;
      case GREEN: printf("GREEN");        break;
      case BLUE:  printf("BLUE");         break;
      case VIOLET:printf("VIOLET");       break;
      case GREY:  printf("GREY");         break;
      case WHITE: printf("WHITE");        break;
      default:    printf("NO COLOUR");    break;
   }
   return(0);
}
```

## TTL IC functionality

A family of integrated circuits (ICs) named the 74-series can be used to implement standard logical functions such as AND, OR, NOR, NAND, etc. For example, the 7400, 7402 and 7408 contain NAND, NOR and AND gates, respectively.

In program 3.11 the user enters the type of function required and the program determines the type of TTL IC which can implement it. It uses the `switch` statement to select from a menu for a 2-input AND, OR, NAND, NOR and NOT (inverting buffer) gates. As before, the `enum` data type is used to define the logic functions.

**Program 3.11**

```
/*    prog3_11.c                                              */
/*    Program to determine TTL ICs for a given function       */
#include <stdio.h>

int    main(void)
{
enum    {AND=1,OR,NAND,NOR,NOT} gate_type;

   puts("Enter logic gate required");
   puts("1 - 2-input AND gate");
   puts("2 - 2-input OR gate");
   puts("3 - 2-input NAND gate");
   puts("4 - 2-input NOR gate");
   puts("5 - 2-input NOT gate");
   puts("6 - exit program");
   scanf("%d",&gate_type);

   printf("TTL gate(s) available is(are) ");

   switch ( gate_type)
   {
     case AND:  puts("7408");                         break;
     case OR:   puts("7432");                         break;
     case NAND: puts("7400,7401,7403,7437,7438"); break;
     case NOR:  puts("7402,7428,7433");               break;
     case NOT:  puts("7404,7405,7505,7416");          break;
     default:   puts("Invalid option");
   }
   return(0);
}
```

Sample runs are given in test runs 3.13 and 3.14.

---

**Test run 3.13**
```
Enter logic gate required
1 - 2-input AND gate
2 - 2-input OR gate
3 - 2-input NAND gate
4 - 2-input NOR gate
5 - 2-input NOT gate
1
TTL gate(s) available is(are)  7408
```

---

**Test run 3.14**
```
Enter logic gate required
1 - 2-input AND gate
2 - 2-input OR gate
3 - 2-input NAND gate
4 - 2-input NOR gate
5 - 2-input NOT gate
3
TTL gate(s) available is(are)  7400,7401,7403,7437,7438
```

### Resistance of a conductor

The resistance of a cylindrical conductor is a function of its resistivity, cross-sectional area and length. These parameters are illustrated in Figure 3.8.

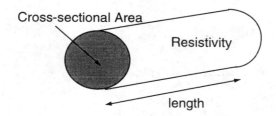

**Figure 3.8:** Cylindrical conductor

The resistance is given by:

$$R = \frac{\rho \cdot l}{A} \quad \Omega$$

where
  $\rho$  resistivity of the conductor ($\Omega$.m);
  $l$  length of the conductor (m);
  $A$  cross-sectional area of the conductor (m$^2$).

Program 3.12 determines the resistance of a cylindrical conductor made from either silver, manganese, aluminium or copper. The resistivities of these materials have been defined using #define macros.

The user enters the conductor type as a character ('c', 'a', 's' or 'm') which can either be in upper or lowercase format as the tolower() function converts the entered character to lowercase (this is protyped in *ctype.h*). When an invalid character is entered the default condition of the case statement is executed, and the text Invalid option is displayed. The program then calls the exit() function; the argument passed to this function is the termination status. A value of 0 describes a normal termination; any other value signals an abnormal program termination.

The printf() statement displays the resistance in scientific format (%e) as values are typically much less than 1 $\Omega$ (such as m$\Omega$ or $\mu\Omega$).

📄 **Program 3.12**
```
/*    prog3_12.c                              */
/*    Program to determine the resistance     */
/*    of a cylindrical conductor              */

#include <stdio.h>
#include <math.h>
#include <ctype.h>
#include <stdlib.h>

/* Define resistivities  */
```

```
#define    RHO_COPPER     17e-9
#define    RHO_AL         25.4e-9
#define    RHO_SILVER     16e-9
#define    RHO_MANGANESE 1400e-9
#define    PI             3.14

int     main(void)
{
float   radius,length,area,rho,resistance;
char    ch;

   puts("Type of conductor >>");
   puts("(c)opper");
   puts("(a)luminium");
   puts("(s)ilver");
   puts("(m)anganese");

   /* get conductor type                              */
   ch=getchar();

   printf("Enter radius and length of conductor >>");
   scanf("%f %f",&radius,&length);

   /* area of conductor                               */
   area=PI*(radius*radius);

   /* convert to lowercase and determine resistivity   */
   switch (tolower(ch))
   {
   case 'c': rho=RHO_COPPER;        break;
   case 'a': rho=RHO_AL;            break;
   case 's': rho=RHO_SILVER;        break;
   case 'm': rho=RHO_MANGANESE;     break;
   default: puts("Invalid option");    exit(0); break;
   }
   resistance= rho*length/area;
   printf("Resistance of conductor is %.3e ohm",  resistance);
   return(0);
}
```

Test run 3.15 uses an aluminium conductor with a radius of 1 mm and length 1000 m. The resistance is found to be 8.08 Ω.

---
🖳  **Test run 3.15**
```
Type of conductor >>
(c)opper
(a)luminium
(s)ilver
(m)anganese
a
Enter radius and length of conductor >> 1e-3 1000
Resistance of conductor is 8.09e+00 ohm
```
---

It is possible to have several case options in the switch statement. For example, if the tolower() function is not used in program 3.12 then the case option can be modified so that it includes the upper and lowercase options, as shown in the following code:

```
switch (ch)
{
    case 'C':case 'c': rho=RHO_COPPER;    break;
    case 'A':case 'a': rho=RHO_AL;        break;
    case 'S':case 's': rho=RHO_SILVER;    break;
    case 'M':case 'm': rho=RHO_MANGANESE; break;
    default: puts("Invalid option");      exit(0);
}
```

## 3.3 Tutorial

Q3.1    Determine the errors in programs 3.13 and 3.14.

📄 **Program 3.13**
```
/* prog3_13.c                                        */
#include <stdio.h>
int    main(void)
{
int    i;
    puts("Enter value of i");
    scanf("%d",i);
    if (i = 5) puts("i is equal to five");
    return(0);
}
```

📄 **Program 3.14**
```
/* prog3_14.c                  */
/* Simple calculator           */
#include <stdio.h>

int        main(void)
{
int        a=5,b=3;
char    ch;

    puts("Enter operator (+,-,* or /);
    ch = getchar();
    switch (ch)
      case '+': c=a+b;
      case '-': c=a-b;
      case '*': c=a*b;
      case '/': c=a/b;
    print(" %d %c %d = %d",a,ch,b,c);
    return(0);
}
```

Q3.2    Determine the output from program 3.15 if the user enters a value of 2. Modify the program so that it operates correctly.

📄 **Program 3.15**

```
/*  prog3_15.c                                    */
#include <stdio.h>

int    main(void)
{
int    a;
  puts("Enter a number);
  scanf("%d",&a);
  switch (a)
  {
     case 1:  puts("1 entered");
     case 2:  puts("2 entered");
     case 3:  puts("3 entered");
     case 4:  puts("4 entered");
     default: puts("Not 1,2,3 or 4");
  }
  return(0);
}
```

Q3.3    Modify program 3.2 so that it displays values in the range 0 to 65,535 as 16-bit unsigned binary values. The data type `unsigned int` can be used to declare a 16-bit integer with no sign bit. A sample run is given in test run 3.16.

🖥 **Test run 3.16**

```
Enter unsigned integer (0 to 65535)>> 1
Binary value is 0000000000000001
Enter unsigned integer (0 to 65535)>> 5
Binary value is 0000000000000101
Enter unsigned integer (0 to 65535)>> 43
Binary value is 0000000000101011
Enter unsigned integer (0 to 65535)>> 245
Binary value is 0000000011110101
Enter unsigned integer (0 to 65535)>> 5321
Binary value is 0001010011001001
Enter unsigned integer (0 to 65535)>> 32865
Binary value is 1000000001100001
Enter unsigned integer (0 to 65535)>> 65534
Binary value is 1111111111111110
Enter unsigned integer (0 to 65535)>>  0
Binary value is 0000000000000000
```

Q3.4    Modify the program in Q3.3 so that it displays values in the range −32,768 to 32,767 as 16-bit signed binary values. Use the data type `int` for the entered value.

Q3.5    Modify program 3.4 so that it cannot generate a divide by zero error, i.e. when a is 0 (zero). Note that if a is 0 then the root will be $-c/b$.

Q3.6    Modify program 3.7 so that the user can enter the EM wave as a frequency or a wavelength. A sample run is shown in test run 3.17.

🖥 **Test run 3.17**
```
Do you wish to enter
(f)requency or
(w)avelength  >>>
f
Enter frequency>>> 10e9
Wavelength is 3.0e-02 Electromagnetic wave is Microwave
```

Q3.7 Modify the program in Q3.6 so it uses the #define statement to define limits for the wavelength, for example:

```
#define GAMMA_RAY_LIMIT 1e-11
```

Q3.8 Write a program in which the user enters an integer and is prompted as to whether it is to be displayed as an octal number, a hexadecimal number or an ASCII character. A sample run is given in test run 3.18.

🖥 **Test run 3.18**
```
Enter decimal : 15
Do you wish (H)ex, (O)ctal or (C)har : h
Value in hexadecimal is F
```

Q3.9 Rewrite the program in Q3.8 so that the user can enter a value as either a decimal, an octal or hexadecimal number or a character.

🖥 **Test run 3.19**
```
Type of entered value (H)ex, (O)ct, (D)ecimal or (C)har: d
Enter decimal : 15
Do you wish to convert to (H)ex, (O)ctal, (C)har : h
Value in hexadecimal is F
```

Q3.10 Capacitance is normally defined as a value and a specified unit, such as pF, nF, μ F mF or F. Write a program in which a capacitance value and the unit are entered and the program displays the actual numerical value in Farads. The capacitance unit should be entered as a character. A sample test run is given in test run 3.20. Refer to program 3.12.

🖥 **Test run 3.20**
```
Enter value: 1
Enter unit p,n,u, or m : u
Capacitance value is 0.000001 Farads
```

Q3.11 Modify the program in Q3.10 so that the user enters the actual capacitance value and the program displays it in the most appropriate unit. A sample test run is given in test run 3.21. Refer to program 3.7.

---

🖥 **Test run 3.21**

```
Enter capacitance: 5e-6
Capacitance is 5 uF
```

---

Q3.12    Repeat Q3.10 for the value of the resistance. The units entered are either mΩ ('m'), Ω ('1'), kΩ ('k') or MΩ ('M'). Test run 3.22 shows a sample run.

---

🖥 **Test run 3.22**

```
Enter value: 3.21
Enter unit m,1,k, or M : k
Resistance value is 3210   Ohms
```

---

# CHAPTER 4

# Repetitive statements

An iterative, or repetitive, process allows the looping of a set of statements. There are three forms of iteration: while, do and for loops. Figure 4.1 shows the general flow of these loops. All require a test condition which determines if the loop continues or not. If this test condition is TRUE then the loop will continue; else, it will stop. The for loop has a starting condition and an operation within the loop. Loops do..while() and while() are similar, but they test the loop condition at different points.

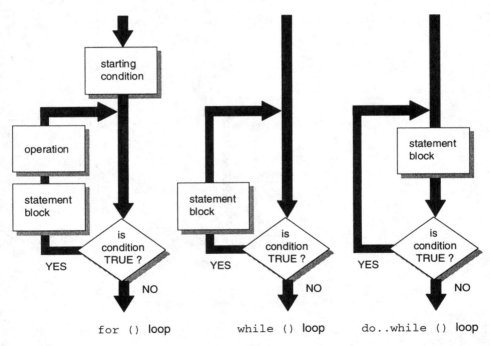

**Figure 4.1:** Flow chart representation of repetitive loops

## 4.1 `for`

Many tasks within a program are repetitive, such as prompting for data, counting values, etc. The `for` loop allows the execution of a block of code for a given control function. The following is an example format; if there is only one statement in the block then the braces can be omitted.

```
for (starting condition;test condition;operation)
{
        statement block
}
```

where

```
starting condition -   the starting value for the loop;
test condition      -   if test condition is TRUE the loop will continue
                        execution;
operation           -   the operation conducted at the end of the loop.
```

Figure 4.2 shows a flow chart representation of this statement.

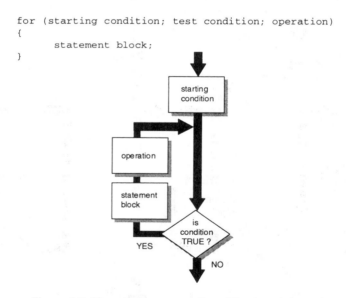

**Figure 4.2:** Flow chart representation of the `for` statement

Examples:
(a)  `for (i=1;i<10;i++)`

i will start at a value of 1, and each time round the loop it is incremented by 1 (i++). The loop will stop when it is equal to 10, i.e. the last value that i will take on within the loop will be 9.

(b) for (index=100 ; index < 500 ; index +=50)
index will start at 100; each time round the loop 50 is added to it (index += 50 is equivalent to index = index+50). Within the loop index will equal 100, 150, 200, 250.... 400, 450.

(c) for (;;)
represents an infinite loop.

(d) for (i=2;i<=128;i *= 2)
starts with i equal to 2; each time round the loop i is multiplied by 2. This continues while i is less than or equal to 128. The values of i within the loop will be 2, 4, 8, 16, 32, 64 and 128.

(e) for (k=-20.2; h>32; z--,j++)
starts with k equal to -20.2; the loop will repeat while h is greater than 32. At the end of each loop z is decremented by 1 and j incremented by 1. The comma allows more than one expression in the first and third fields of for ().

### 4.1.1 Examples

#### *ASCII characters*

Program 4.1 displays ASCII characters for entered start and end decimal values.

📄 **Program 4.1**
```
/*    prog4_1.c                              */
/*    Program to print ASCII characters      */
#include <stdio.h>
int  main(void)
{
int  i,start,end;

    printf("Enter start and end for ASCII characters >>");
    scanf("%d %d",&start,&end);

    puts("INTEGER   HEX    ASCII");

    for (i=start;i<=end;i++)
        printf("%5d   %5x   %5c\n",i,i,i);
    return(0);
}
```

Test run 4.1 displays the ASCII characters from decimal 40 (' (') to 50 ('2').

🖳 **Test run 4.1**
```
Enter start and end for ASCII characters >> 40 50
INTEGER   HEX     ASCII
   40      28        (
   41      29        )
   42      2a        *
   43      2b        +
   44      2c        ,
   45      2d        -
   46      2e        .
   47      2f        /
   48      30        0
   49      31        1
   50      32        2
```

## Integer to binary conversion

Program 4.2 is an improved version of program 3.1. It displays an entered decimal value as an unsigned 8-bit binary format. The program first masks the most significant bit (0x80 or 10000000b) and determines if the value is TRUE (i.e. the bit is set) or FALSE (i.e. the bit is set to a zero). If it is set a "1" is displayed, else a "0" is displayed. The bit-mask is then shifted down one bit position using the shift right bitwise operator (>>); a bit-masking operation is executed again. This will continue until the loop reaches to the least significant bit (i.e. 0x01 or 0000  0001b); after this the loop will end and the program will stop.

The for() loop uses the operation bit>>=1 to shift the bit-mask one place to the right; this is a shorthand equivalent of bit = bit >> 1.

📄 **Program 4.2**
```c
/*    prog4_2.c                                         */
/*    Program to determine binary equivalent of an 8-bit  */
/*    integer                                            */
int  main(void)
{
int  val, bit;

   printf("Enter value >>");
   scanf("%d",&val);

   printf("Binary value is ");
   for (bit=0x80;bit>0;bit>>=1)
   {
     if (bit & val)   printf("1");
     else             printf("0");
   }
   return(0);
}
```

Test run 4.2 gives a sample run.

🖥 **Test run 4.2**
```
Enter value >> 21
Binary value is 00010101
```

## Transient response of an RC circuit

Figure 4.3 illustrates an RC circuit with a voltage step applied at *t*=0. When a voltage step, amplitude *V* volts, is applied to this circuit an exponential current results.

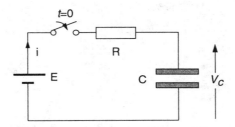

**Figure 4.3:** RC circuit with step input applied at *t*=0

The following defines the transient current in the circuit.

$$i = \frac{E}{R} e^{-\frac{t}{RC}}$$

and the voltage across the resistor will be:

$$V_R = Ee^{-\frac{t}{RC}}$$

Program 4.3 determines the voltage across the resistor at given time intervals. The user enters the end time and the number of time steps required; the program determines the voltage at each of the time steps. It uses the exponential function (exp()) which is prototyped in *math.h*.

📄 **Program 4.3**
```c
/*    prog4_3.c                               */
/*    Program to determine transient response */
/*    of an RC circuit                        */
#include <math.h> /* required for exp()       */
#include <stdio.h>

int    main(void)
{
float  R,C,tend,t,E,Vr;
int    tsteps;

    puts("Program to determine voltage across");
```

```
puts("Resistor in an RC circuit ");

printf("Enter R,C >> ");
scanf("%f %f",&R,&C);

printf("Enter number of time steps and end time>>");
scanf("%d %f",&tsteps,&tend);   /* enter integer and float*/

printf("Enter voltage step applied>>");
scanf("%f",&E);

puts("   TIME        VOLTAGE");

for (t=0;t<tend;t+=tend/tsteps)
{
   Vr=E*exp(-t/(R*C));
   printf("%8.4f %8.2f\n",t,Vr);
}
return(0);
}
```

Test run 4.3 shows that the voltage across the resistor starts at a maximum at $t=0$. This is because the voltage across the capacitor is initially zero. As the capacitor charges, the voltage across it will increase until it almost equals the applied voltage. The current in the circuit will also be at a maximum when the step is applied. It will then decay to almost zero at a rate determined by the time constant (which is a product of R and C).

---

🖥 **Test run 4.3**

```
Program to determine voltage across
Resistor in an RC circuit
Enter R,C >> 1e3 1e-6
Enter number of time steps and end time>> 20 10e-3
Enter voltage step applied>> 10
    TIME        VOLTAGE
    0.0000      10.00
    0.0005       6.07
    0.0010       3.68
    0.0015       2.23
    0.0020       1.35
    0.0025       0.82
    0.0030       0.50
    0.0035       0.30
    0.0040       0.18
    0.0045       0.11
    0.0050       0.07
    0.0055       0.04
    0.0060       0.02
    0.0065       0.02
    0.0070       0.01
    0.0075       0.01
    0.0080       0.00
    0.0085       0.00
    0.0090       0.00
    0.0095       0.00
```

Figure 4.4 shows a plot of these results (generated by a spreadsheet).

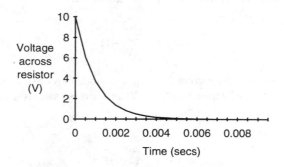

**Figure 4.4:** Transient response of an RC circuit with step input applied at *t*=0

To modify the program so that it displays the voltages across both the resistor and the capacitor, the following lines can be added to program 4.3.

```
for (t=0;t<tend;t+=tend/tsteps)
{

    vr=V*exp(-t/(R*C));
    vc=V-vr
    printf("%8.4f %8.2f %8.2f\n",t,vr,vc);

}
```

## Current flow in a diode

The current flow in a diode is dependent upon the applied voltage and the temperature. A diode circuit with an applied voltage is shown in Figure 4.5. Note that it is not advisable to connect a diode straight onto a voltage source; normally, a series resistor is inserted to protect the diode.

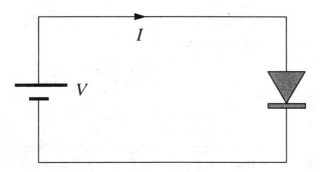

**Figure 4.5:** Diode with an applied voltage

The following equation defines the current in the diode:

$$I = I_o(e^{\frac{11600\,V}{T}} - 1)$$

Program 4.4 determines the current flowing in a diode at room temperature (27 °C or 300 K) for entered values of applied voltage ($V$) and reverse saturation current ($I_o$).

### 📄 Program 4.4

```
/*    prog4_4.c                                              */
/*    Program to determine current flowing in a diode        */
#include <math.h>
#include <stdio.h>

#define TEMPERATURE       300 /* Room temperature in Kelvin */
#define MICRO             1e-6

int     main(void)
{
float   v,Vend,Io,I;
int     tsteps;
   puts("Program to determine current flowing");
   puts("in a diode for an enter applied voltage");

   printf("Enter end voltage and number of time steps>>");
   scanf("%f %d",&Vend,&tsteps);

   printf("Enter reverse saturation current >>");
   scanf("%f",&Io);

   puts("VOLTAGE    CURRENT (uA)");

   for (v=0;v<Vend;v+=Vend/tsteps)
   {
      I=Io*exp (11600*v/TEMPERATURE-1);
      printf("%8.2f %12.2f\n",v,I/MICRO);
                              /* ^ display current in uA    */
   }
   return(0);
}
```

Test run 4.4 shows that for a large range of applied currents (between 1μA and 1 A) the diode voltage ranges from 0.4 to 0.7 volts. Typically, the voltage across the diode, when it is conducting, will range from 0.6 to 0.7 V. In the sample run notice that if 0.76 volts is applied the current will be over 2 Amps.

🖥 **Test run 4.4**

```
Program to determine current flowing
in a diode for a given applied voltage
Enter end voltage and number of time steps>> 0.8 20
Enter reverse saturation current >> 1e-12
    VOLTAGE    CURRENT (uA)
     0.00         0.00
     0.04         0.00
     0.08         0.00
     0.12         0.00
     0.16         0.00
     0.20         0.00
     0.24         0.00
     0.28         0.02
     0.32         0.09
     0.36         0.41
     0.40         1.92
     0.44         9.01
     0.48        42.29
     0.52       198.57
     0.56       932.46
     0.60      4378.63
     0.64     20561.13
     0.68     96550.87
     0.72    453383.15
     0.76   2128994.46
```

## *I-V characteristics of a MOS device*

There are two main types of MOS device. These are defined by differing diffusion types: n-channel (NMOS) and p-channel (PMOS). Figure 4.6 shows a MOS transistor with three connections: the gate, drain and source. The width and length of the gate defines the characteristics of the device.

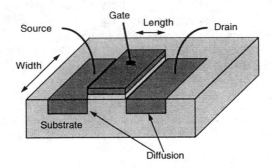

**Figure 4.6:** Structure of an MOS transistor

NMOS devices are formed in a p-type substrate of moderate doping level. The source and drain regions are formed by diffusing n-type impurity concentrations and give rise to depletion regions which extend mainly into the more lightly doped p-regions.

The MOS transistor is a transconductance device, i.e. a change in voltage between the gate and source will cause a change in the drain current. This differs from a bipolar transistor where a change in the base-emitter current causes a change in the collector-emitter current. No conduction occurs in the MOS device until a threshold voltage is reached, i.e. until the gate-source voltage is greater than a given threshold. Typically, this threshold is around 1 V for a 5 V supply. The equations for the drain-source current $I_{DS}$, can be derived to give:

$$I_{DS} = 0 \qquad\qquad\qquad V_{GS} < V_{TH}$$

$$I_{DS} = \frac{\beta}{2}\left[V_{GS} - V_{TH}\right]^2 \qquad\qquad 0 < V_{GS} - V_{TH} < V_{DS}\ (saturated)$$

$$I_{DS} = \beta\left[V_{GS} - V_{TH} - \frac{V_{DS}}{2}\right]V_{DS} \qquad V_{GS} - V_{TH} > V_{DS}\ (linear)$$

where

$$\beta = \frac{\mu\varepsilon}{T_{ox}} \cdot \frac{W}{L}$$

$\mu$   -   average mobility of the charge carrier (electron for n-channel, hole for p-channel);

$\varepsilon$   -   the permittivity of the oxide material;

$T_{ox}$   -   the thickness of the oxide (layer between gate and substrate);

$V_{GS}$   -   gate-source voltage;

$V_{DS}$   -   drain-source voltage.

A typical value of the oxide layer thickness is 700 angstroms (70 nm) and the electron mobility is typically $8 \times 10^{-2}\ m^2.V^{-1}.s^{-1}$.

Program 4.5 determines the *I-V* characteristics of a field effect transistor (FET). It uses nested loops to vary $V_{GS}$ and $V_{DS}$. $V_{GS}$ controls the outer loop and $V_{DS}$ the inner loop. Initially, $V_{GS}$ is set to $V_{TH}$, the inner loop starts with an initial condition of $V_{DS} = 0$, then is incremented by 0.5 V each time round the inner loop. After the inner loops are complete the program will return to the outer loop, which will then increment $V_{GS}$ by 1 V. This continues until $V_{GS}$ equals the supply voltage ($V_{DD}$).

▤ **Program 4.5**

```
/* prog4_5.c                                                        */
/* Program which will determine the drain current in a FET          */
/* with an entered threshold voltage, beta and Supply voltage       */

#include <stdio.h>

int     main(void)
{
float   Id,Vgs,Vth,VDD,Vds,beta;
    /* Id is the drain current,Vgs the gate-source  voltage     */
    /* Vth is the threshold voltage of the FET, VDD the supply  */
    /* voltage   and beta a constant for the FET                */
```

```
printf("Enter Supply voltage and threshold>>");
scanf("%f %f",&VDD,&Vth);
printf("Enter beta (A/V^2)>>");
scanf("%f",&beta);

for (Vgs=Vth;Vgs<=VDD;Vgs++)
        /* gate-source voltage incremented in 1V steps */
{
   printf("Vgs=%6.2f\n",Vgs);
   for (Vds=0;Vds<(Vgs-Vth);Vds+=0.5)
        /* drain-source voltage incremented in 0.5V steps */
   {
      Id=beta*Vds*(Vgs-Vth-0.5*Vds);
      printf("%6.2f %6.2f\n",Vds,Id);
   }
   for (Vds=Vgs-Vth;Vds<VDD;Vds+=0.5)
   {
      Id=0.5*beta*(Vgs-Vth)*(Vgs-Vth);
      printf("%6.2f %6.2f\n",Vds,Id);
   }
   printf("Press <RETURN> to continue");
   getchar();
}
return(0);
}
```

A test run of the program with parameters $V_{DD}$=12 V, $\beta$=1 (to create a normalized response) and $V_{TH}$=1 V, is illustrated in Figure 4.7. This shows a plot of drain-to-source current ($I_{DS}$) against drain-to-source voltage ($V_{DS}$) for different gate-to-source voltages ($V_{GS}$). The source is assumed to be connected to ground and all voltages are with respect to this point.

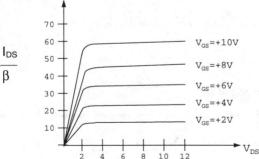

**Figure 4.7:** $I_{DS}$ - $V_{DS}$ for an n-channel MOS transistor

### Boolean logic

Program 4.6 is an example of how a Boolean logic function can be analyzed and a truth table generated. The `for` loop generates all the required binary permutations for a truth table. The Boolean function used is:

$$Z = \overline{(A.B)} + C$$

A schematic of this equation is given in Figure 4.8.

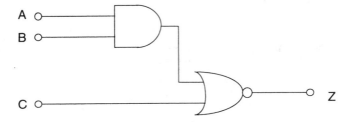

**Figure 4.8:** Digital circuit

📄 **Program 4.6**
```
/*    prog4_6.c                                                        */
/*    Program to generate truth table for boolean function            */
#include <stdio.h>

int  main(void)
{
int  A,B,C,Z;
  puts("Boolean function NOR (AND(A,B),C)");
  puts("   A    B    C    Z");
  for (A=0;A<=1;A++)
    for (B=0;B<=1;B++)
      for (C=0;C<=1;C++)
        {
          Z=!( (A && B) || C);
          printf("%4d %4d %4d %4d\n",A,B,C,Z);
        }
  return(0);
}
```

Test run 4.5 shows a sample run.

💻 **Test run 4.5**

Boolean function NOR (AND(A,B),C)

| A | B | C | Z |
|---|---|---|---|
| 0 | 0 | 0 | 1 |
| 0 | 0 | 1 | 0 |
| 0 | 1 | 0 | 1 |
| 0 | 1 | 1 | 0 |
| 1 | 0 | 0 | 1 |
| 1 | 0 | 1 | 0 |
| 1 | 1 | 0 | 0 |
| 1 | 1 | 1 | 0 |

Program 4.7 replaces the integer values 0 and 1 with FALSE and TRUE macros. This helps to make the program more readable.

📄 **Program 4.7**

```
/*    prog4_7.c                           */
/*    Program to generate truth table for a */
/*    boolean function                    */
#include <stdio.h>

#define FALSE 0
#define TRUE  1

int  main(void)
{
int  A,B,C,Z;

   puts("Boolean function NOR (AND(A,B),C)");
   puts("   A     B     C     Z");
   for (A=FALSE;A<=TRUE;A++)
      for (B=FALSE;B<=TRUE;B++)
         for (C=FALSE;C<=TRUE;C++)
         {
            Z= !( (A && B) || C) ;
            printf("%4d %4d %4d %4d\n",A,B,C,Z);
         }
   return(0);
}
```

## 4.2 `while()`

The `while` statement allows a block of code to be executed while a specified condition is TRUE. It checks the condition at the start of the block; if this is TRUE the block is executed, else it will exit the loop. The syntax is

```
while (condition)
{
   :       :
   statement block
   :       :
}
```

If the statement block contains a single statement then the braces may be omitted (although it does no harm to keep them).

Examples:

(a)  `while (i>10)` - this will repeat *statement block* while i is greater than 10.

(b)  `while ( letter != 'q')` - this will repeat *statement block* while letter is not equal to the character 'q'.

(c)  `while ((index <= 10) && (value ==3))` - this will repeat *statement block* while `index` is less than or equal to 10 and `value` is equal to 3.

## 4.3 do..while()

The `do..while()` statement is similar in its operation to `while()` except that it tests the condition at the bottom of the loop. This allows *statement block* to be excuted at least once. The syntax is

```
do
{
     statement block
} while (condition);
```

As with `for()` and `while()` loops the braces are optional. The `do..while()` loop requires a semicolon at the end of the loop, whereas the `while()` does not.

Figure 4.9 shows a flow chart representation of the `do..while()` and the `while()` loops. In both loops a TRUE condition will cause the statement block to be repeated.

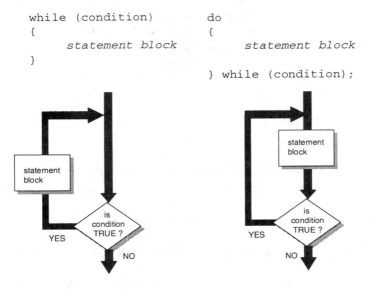

**Figure 4.9:** `do..while()` and `while()` loops

## 4.4 break

The break statement is used to exit from a repetitive loop. It can be used with the
for(), while() and do..while() loops. A few examples are given in programs
4.8, 4.9 and 4.10. The loops used in these programs are described as infinite loops
(while (1), do .. while (TRUE) and for(;;) ) and only the break
statement can cause them to terminate.

**Program 4.8**
```c
/*    prog4_8.c                                              */
/*    Program to determine resistance given                 */
/*    an applied voltage and current                        */
#include <stdio.h>
#include <ctype.h> /* required for tolower() function        */

#define    TRUE    1

int     main(void)
{
float   voltage,current,resistance;
char    ch;

   puts("Program to determine resistance given");
   puts("an applied voltage and current");

   do
   {

      printf("Enter a voltage and current >>");
      scanf("%f %f",&voltage,&current);

      resistance=voltage/current;
      printf("Resistance is %8.2f\n",resistance);

      printf("Do you wish to continue (y/n) >>");

      fflush(stdin); /* clear keyboard buffer */

      ch=tolower(getchar());

      if (ch=='n') break;
   } while (TRUE);

   puts("Program end <BYE>");
   return(0);
}
```

**Program 4.9**
```c
/*    prog4_9.c                                              */
/*    Program to determine reactance of an inductor at       */
/*    an applied frequency                                   */

#include <stdio.h>
#include <ctype.h> /* required for tolower() function        */
```

```
#define    PI     3.14159
#define    TRUE 1

int    main(void)
{
float  X_1,inductance,freq;


   puts("Program to determine reactance of an inductor");
   puts("at an applied frequency");

   while (TRUE)
   {
      puts("Enter an inductance and frequency (enter ");

      printf("a zero for any of the parameters to exit)>>");

      scanf("%f %f",&inductance,&freq);

      if ((inductance<=0) || (freq<=0)) break;

      X_1=2*PI*freq*inductance;

      printf("Reactance is %8.2f\n",X_1);
   }
   puts("Program end <BYE>");
   return(0);
}
```

Test run 4.10 shows a sample run with the exit condition.

---

🖳  **Test run 4.6**
```
Program to determine reactance of an inductor
at an applied frequency
Enter an inductance and frequency (enter
a zero for any of the parameters to exit)>> 0 0
Program end <BYE>
```

---

📄  **Program 4.10**
```
/*   prog4_10.c                              */
#include <stdio.h>
int main(void)
{
int i;
   for (;;)
   {
      puts("Enter number to be cubed");
      scanf("%d",&i);
      if (i==0) break;  /* stop infinite loop */
      printf("The cube of %d is %d\n ",i,i*i*i);
   }

   puts("Zero entered");
   return(0);
}
```

## 4.5 `continue`

The `continue` statement can be used only inside an iteration statement. It transfers control to the test condition for `while()` and `do..while()` loops and to the loop expression in a `for()` loop. The following sample code will output the values of i from 0 to 9 but will not print 5 (i.e. 0, 1, 2, 3, 4, 6, 7, 8 and 9).

```
for (i=0;i<10;i++)
{
   if (i==5) continue;
   printf("Value of i is %d",i);
}
```

## 4.6 Examples

### 4.6.1 Boolean equation

Program 4.11 uses the equation defined in program 4.6. It allows the user to enter the input states for A, B and C and the program will determine the output for these inputs. It uses the `do..while()` statement to block the entry of invalid integer values (i.e. any value which is not 0 or 1).

**Program 4.11**
```
#include <stdio.h>
/*    prog4_11.c                                           */
/*    Program which determines the output of the           */
/*    boolean equation NOR(C,AND(A,B))                     */
int  main(void)
{
int  A,B,C,Z;
   do
   {
      printf("Enter A input (0 or 1) >>");
      scanf("%d",&A);
      if ( (A!=0) && (A!=1) ) puts("Invalid input");
   } while ( (A!=0) && (A!=1)) ;
   do
   {
      printf("Enter B input (0 or 1) >>");
      scanf("%d",&B);
      if ( (B!=0) && (B!=1) ) puts("Invalid input");
   } while ( (B!=0) && (B!=1)) ;
   do
   {
      printf("Enter C input (0 or 1) >>");
      scanf("%d",&C);
      if ( (C!=0) && (C!=1) ) puts("Invalid input");
   } while ( (C!=0) && (C!=1)) ;

   Z=!((A && B) || C);
```

```
      printf("Output will be %d\n",Z);

      return(0);
}
```

Test run 4.7 shows a sample run.

---

⌨  **Test run 4.7**

```
Enter A input (0 or 1) >> 21
Invalid input
Enter A input (0 or 1) >> 0
Enter B input (0 or 1) >> -1
Invalid input
Enter B input (0 or 1) >> 1
Enter C input (0 or 1) >> 1
Output will be 0
```

---

Program 4.11 may still allow the entry of invalid values as scanf() allows the entry of other data types than the specified format. In this case the value entered should be an integer, but, scanf() will accept other data types such as floating point values, characters, etc. For example, if the user enters a floating point value into scanf() (e.g. 1.0) this may not be interpreted as a valid integer. The resulting scanned parameter would be unpredictable.

The scanf() function returns a value relating to the number of fields successfully scanned. For example, if the return is 0 then no fields were scanned. Each field is delimited by a space. The following section of code uses the return value to determine if the number of valid inputs is 1. If it is more than 1 or zero the user will be re-prompted for a valid input. The variable okay is set to FALSE if the input value is invalid. This is tested at the end of the loop, if it is FALSE then the loop will continue and the user is re-promted for a value.

```
int  okay;
     do
     {
        printf("Enter A input (0 or 1) >>");
        rtn=scanf("%d",&A);
        if ((rtn!=1) || ( (A!=0) && (A!=1)))
        {
           puts("Invalid input");
           okay=FALSE;
        }
        else okay=TRUE;
     } while ( !okay ) ;
```

Program 4.12 uses an outer do..while() loop to repeat the program. The user is prompted as to whether the program should continue or not. If the character 'y' is entered the program will repeat, else it will end. Problems can occur when getchar() is used after the scanf() as characters can be left in the keyboard buffer. For this reason the keyboard buffer is emptied using fflush(stdin).

**Program 4.12**

```
/*   prog4_12.c                                        */
/*   Program that determines the output for the        */
/*   boolean equation NOR(C,AND(A,B))                  */
#include <stdio.h>
#include <ctype.h>
#define   TRUE   1
#define   FALSE  0
int     main(void)
{
int     A,B,C,Z,okay,rtn;
char    ch;
   do
   {
      do
      {
         printf("Enter A input (0 or 1) >>");
         rtn=scanf("%d",&A);
         if ((rtn!=1) ||( (A!=0) && (A!=1)))
         {
            puts("Invalid input");
            okay=FALSE;
         }
         else okay=TRUE;
      } while ( !okay );
      do
      {
         printf("Enter B input (0 or 1) >>");
         rtn=scanf("%d",&B);
         if ((rtn!=1) ||( (B!=0) && (B!=1)))
         {
            puts("Invalid input");
            okay=FALSE;
         }
         else okay=TRUE;
      } while ( !okay );
      do
      {
         printf("Enter C input (0 or 1) >>");
         rtn=scanf("%d",&C);
         if ((rtn!=1) ||( (C!=0) && (C!=1)))
         {
            puts("Invalid input");
            okay=FALSE;
         }
         else okay=TRUE;
      } while ( !okay );
      Z=!((A && B) || C);
      printf("Output will be %d\n",Z);

      printf("Do you wish to continue (y/n) >>");
      fflush(stdin);
         /* this will flush the keyboard buffer         */
         /* as there may be characters still in it      */
      ch=getchar();
   } while (tolower(ch)=='y');
   return(0);
}
```

Test run 4.8 shows a sample run.

---

⌨ **Test run 4.8**

```
Enter A input (0 or 1) >> 0
Enter B input (0 or 1) >> 0
Enter C input (0 or 1) >> 0
Output will be 1
Do you wish to continue (y/n) >> y
Enter A input (0 or 1) >> 0
Enter B input (0 or 1) >> 0
Enter C input (0 or 1) >> 1
Output will be 0
Do you wish to continue (y/n) >> n
```

---

### 4.6.2 CR active filter

An active filter using an op-amp is given in Figure 4.10. This circuit has low gain at low frequencies and high gain at high frequencies; it therefore acts as a high-pass filter.

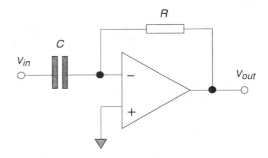

**Figure 4.10:** CR active filter

The magnitude of the gain of this circuit is given by:

$$|Gain| = 2\pi fRC$$
$$= 20\log_{10}(2\pi fRC) \quad \text{dB}$$

Program 4.13 determines the magnitude of the gain of this circuit in decibels. Valid inputs of resistance values between 1 k$\Omega$ and 1 M$\Omega$ and valid capacitance values are any value greater than or equal to 1 mF. The do..while() loop is placed around the entry of these values so that the user is re-prompted if invalid values are entered.

The function to determine the $\log_{10}$ is implemented in the standard math library, this is named log10(). To implement this function using the natural logarithm function (log()) the following conversion can be used:

$$\log_{10}(x) = \frac{\log(x)}{\log(10)}$$

**Program 4.13**

```
/*    prog4_13.c                                            */
/*    Program to determine the gain of an CR                */
/*    active filter for entered values of C and R           */
/*    and a frequency span from 1Hz up to 1 GHz in          */
/*    decade steps                                          */

#include  <stdio.h>
#include  <math.h>
#define    TRUE    1
#define    FALSE   0
#define    MILLI   1e-3
#define    KILO    1e3
#define    MEGA    1e6
#define    GIGA    1e9
#define    PI      3.14159

int     main(void)
{
float   resistance,capacitance,freq,gain,gain_dB;
int     rtn,okay;

   puts("Program to determine gain of a CR active filter");

   do
   {
      printf("Enter capacitance >>");
      rtn=scanf("%f",&capacitance);
      if ((rtn!=1) || (capacitance>MILLI))
      {
           puts("INVALID: re-enter");
           okay=FALSE;
      }
      else okay=TRUE;
   } while (!okay );

   do
   {
      printf("Enter resistance >>");
      rtn=scanf("%f",&resistance);
      if ((rtn!=1) || ((resistance>=MEGA) || (resistance<KILO)))
      {
           puts("INVALID: re-enter");
           okay=FALSE;
      }
      else okay=TRUE;
   } while (!okay);

   puts("FREQUENCY(Hz) GAIN(dB)");

   for (freq=1;freq<=GIGA;freq*=10)
   {        /* decade steps of frequency */
      gain=2*PI*freq*resistance*capacitance;
      gain_dB=20*log10(gain);
      printf("%10.1e %10.3f\n",freq,gain_dB);
   }
   return(0);
}
```

Test run 4.9 shows a sample run.

---

⌨ **Test run 4.9**
```
Program to determine gain of CR active filter
Enter capacitance >> 100
INVALID: re-enter
Enter capacitance >> 1e-6
Enter resistance  >> -43
INVALID: re-enter
Enter resistance >>  1e4
FREQUENCY(Hz)  GAIN(dB)
    1e+00    -24.036
    1e+01     -4.036
    1e+02     15.964
    1e+03     35.964
    1e+04     55.964
    1e+05     75.964
    1e+06     95.964
    1e+07    115.964
    1e+08    135.964
    1e+09    155.964
```

---

## 4.7 Tutorial

Q4.1    Determine the errors in the following programs

(i)

📄 **Program 4.14**
```
/*    prog4_14.c                                  */
/*    Prints the square of the numbers 1 to 10    */
/*    ie 1,4,9..100                               */
#include <stdio.h>

int main(void)
{
int i;
   for (i=1,i<10,i++)
      printf("The square of i is %d,i*i);
   return(0);
}
```

(ii)

📄 **Program 4.15**
```
/*    prog4_15.c                                  */
/*    Prints values from 1 to 100 in power of 3   */
/*    The step used is 0.3                         */
#include <stdio.h>

int  main(void)
{
int  i;
```

```
    while (i != 100)
    {
        printf("%d to the power of three is %d /n",      i*i*i);
        i += 0.3;
    return(0);
}
```

(iii)

### 📄 Program 4.16
```
/*    prog4_16.c                                        */
/*    Prints the square of the numbers 1 to 10          */
/*    ie 1,4,9..100                                      */
#include <stdio.h>

int  main(void)
{
int  i;
    for (i=1;i<=10;i++);
        printf("The square of i is %d,i*i);
    return(0);
}
```

(iv)

### 📄 Program 4.17
```
/*    prog4_17.c                                         */
/*    Program to determine input resistance given the    */
/*    input voltage and current                          */
#include <stdio.h>
int     main(void)
{
char    input;

    puts("Program to determine the resistance given");
    puts("input voltage and current");

    while (input == 'y')
    {
        printf("Enter voltage and current >> ");
        scanf("%f %f",voltage,current);
        printf("The resistance is %f",voltage/current);
        puts("Do you wish to continue (y/n)")
        input = getchar();
    }
    return(0);
}
```

(v)

📄 **Program 4.18**

```
/*    prog4_18.c                                        */
#include <stdio.h>

int  main(void)
{
   puts("Program to determine the resistance given");
   puts("input voltage and current");

   while (1)
   {
      printf("Enter voltage and current >> ");
      scanf("%f %f",voltage,current);
      printf("The resistance is %f",voltage/current);

      puts("Do you wish to continue(y/n)");
      ch=getchar();
      if ((ch=='n') && (ch=='N')) break;
   }
   puts("Program exited");
   return(0);
}
```

Q4.2    Determine the output from the following sections of code (beware of infinite loops).

(i)
```
for (i=0;i<10;i+=2)
   printf("%d ",i);
```

(ii)
```
for (i=1;i<120;i*=3)
   printf("%d ",i);
```

(iii)
```
for (i=19;i<12;i--)
   printf("%d ",i);
```

(iv)
```
i=6;
do
{
   i++;
   printf("%d ",i);
} while (i<10);
```

(v)
```
i=1;
while (1)
{
    i++;
    printf("%d ",i);
    if (i==4) break;
}
```

(vi)
```
i=2
for (;;)
{
    i++;
    printf("%d ",i);
    i*=2;
    if (i==256) break;
}
```

(vii)
```
i=10;
while (i<10)
{
    i--;
    printf("%d ",i);
}
```

(viii)
```
i=10;
do
{
    i--;
    printf("%d ",i);
} while (i<10);
```

(ix)
```
i=1;
while (i>0)
{
    i++;
    printf("%d ",i);
}
```

Q4.3    Determine the truth table for the following equations:

(i)

$$Z = \overline{\overline{A+B}+A\overline{B}}$$

$$Z = \overline{\overline{A+B+C}+B\overline{C}D+A}$$

$$Z = \overline{\overline{A+B+D}+(C.D)+\overline{A}}$$

Refer to program 4.7.

Q4.4    Write a program which determines the voltage across an inductor and resistor for a series RL circuit with a voltage step input applied at $t=0$. The user should enter the component values, the end time and the number of time steps. Valid ranges for the entered values are given next. Refer to program 4.3.

| Parameter | Minimum | Maximum |
|---|---|---|
| $R$ | $0 \, \Omega$ | $1 \, M\Omega$ |
| $L$ | $0 \, H$ | $100 \, mH$ |
| end time | $1 \, \mu s$ | $1 \, s$ |
| number of time steps | 10 | 100 |

Q4.5    Write a program which determines the magnitude and the angle of the impedance of an RL series circuit. The program must calculate the magnitude and the angle of the impedance and should not allow invalid input values. Valid ranges for the entered values are given next. Refer to program 2.14.

| Parameter | Minimum | Maximum |
|---|---|---|
| $R$ | $0 \, \Omega$ | $1 \, M\Omega$ |
| $L$ | $0 \, H$ | $100 \, mH$ |
| $f$ | $0 \, Hz$ | $10 \, GHz$ |

Q4.6    Modify the program in Q4.5 so that the user enters a start and an end frequency and the number of frequency points. The program will determine the magnitude and the angle of the impedance for the required frequency span. Refer to program 4.11.

Q4.7    Modify the program in Q4.6 so that it will give one page of results at a time and will then prompt the user to press the ENTER key to continue. For example, 10 values of the results table can be printed and the program pauses until the ENTER key is pressed.

Q4.8    Modify the program in Q4.6 for a series RC circuit.

Q4.9    The drain current, in milliamps, of a sample depletion-type FET is given by:

$$I_D = 6. \left[ 1 + \frac{V_{GS}}{4} \right]^2 \, mA$$

Write a program which determines the drain current (in mA) for gate-source voltages ($V_{GS}$) from $-5$ to 5 V in steps of 0.5 V. A sample run is given in test run 4.10. Refer to program 4.3.

🖥 **Test run 4.10**

| VGS(V) | IDS (mA) |
|---|---|
| -5.00 | 0.38 |
| -4.50 | 0.09 |
| -4.00 | 0.00 |
| -3.50 | 0.09 |
| -3.00 | 0.38 |
| -2.50 | 0.84 |
| -2.00 | 1.50 |
| -1.50 | 2.34 |
| -1.00 | 3.38 |
| -0.50 | 4.59 |
| 0.00 | 6.00 |
| 0.50 | 7.59 |
| 1.00 | 9.38 |
| 1.50 | 11.34 |
| 2.00 | 13.50 |
| 2.50 | 15.84 |
| 3.00 | 18.38 |
| 3.50 | 21.09 |
| 4.00 | 24.00 |
| 4.50 | 27.09 |
| 5.00 | 30.38 |

Q4.10 An active filter using an op-amp is given in Figure 4.11. This circuit has high gain at low frequencies and low gain at high frequencies; it therefore acts as a low-pass filter.

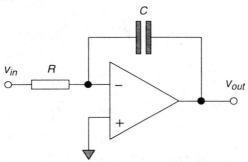

**Figure 4.11:** RC active filter

The magnitude of the gain of this circuit is given by:

$$|Gain| = \frac{1}{2\pi fRC}$$

Write a program which prints a table of frequencies and gains for frequencies from $f$=0.1 Hz to $f$=1 GHz in decade steps using

(i)    a `for()` loop;
(ii)   a `while()` loop
(iii)  a `do { } while()` loop.

Modify the programs so that the gain is displayed in decibels (dB). Refer to program 4.11.

Q4.11    A simple base resistor biased bipolar transistor circuit is shown in Figure 4.12.

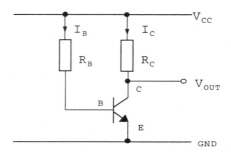

**Figure 4.12:** Simple base resistor biased transistor circuit

The following equations will apply to bias this circuit:

$$I_C = \frac{V_{CC}/2}{R_C} \qquad \text{A}$$

$$I_B = \frac{I_C}{h_{FE}} \qquad \text{A}$$

$$R_B = \frac{V_{CC} - V_{BE}(ON)}{I_B} \qquad \Omega$$

Write a program which calculates the value of $R_B$ for entered inputs of $I_C$ and $V_{CC}$. Assume that $V_{BE}(ON)$ is 0.65 V. The program should accept only valid values, such as a supply voltage ($V_{CC}$) from 5 to 30 V and the collector current $I_C$ between 0.1 and 10 mA. An error message should be displayed if the values are beyond these ranges and the program should re-prompt for valid values. A sample output is shown in test run 4.11.

| Parameter | Minimum | Maximum |
|-----------|---------|---------|
| $V_{CC}$  | 5 V     | 30 V    |
| $I_C$     | 0.1 mA  | 10 mA   |
| $h_{FE}$  | 50      | 150     |

---

💻  **Test run 4.11**

```
Enter Vcc >> 1000000
INVALID INPUT (5->15V)
Enter Vcc >> -1
INVALID INPUT (5->15V)
Enter Vcc >> 15
Enter Ic (1mA)>> 1
Enter hHE >> 100


Base resistance value is XX ohms
```

---

Q4.12   The RMS noise voltage produced by a resistor is given by:

$$v_n = \sqrt{4kTRB}$$

where

$k$  is Boltzmann's constant ($1.38 \times 10^{-23}$ J/K)
$B$  is the bandwidth of the signal (Hz);
$R$  is the equivalent resistance ($\Omega$)
$T$  is the temperature (K)

The quality of a communication systems can be measured using the signal-to-noise ratio (SNR). This is given as the ratio of the signal to the noise power, and is normally expressed in dB. This formula (in terms of RMS signal and noise voltage) is:

$$SNR(dB) = 20 \log_{10} \frac{V_s}{V_n}$$

Write a program which will display the SNR (in dB) for bandwidths from 1 Hz up to 10 GHz in decade steps. Refer to program 4.11.

Assume the following:

$T$ = 27 °C;
$R$ = 600 $\Omega$;
$V_s$ = 0.25 mV.

# CHAPTER 5

# Functions

Functions are identifiable pieces of code with a defined interface. They are called from any part of a program and allow large programs to be split into more manageable tasks, each of which can be independently tested. Functions are also useful in building libraries of routines that other programs use. Several standard libraries exist, such as a maths and input/output libraries. Programs in previous chapters have made use of some standard functions, such as `printf()`, `scanf()`, `gets()`, `getchar()`, `sqrt()`, `exp()`, and `log()`.

A function can be thought of as a 'black box' with a set of inputs and outputs. It processes the inputs in a way dictated by its function and provides some output. In most cases the actual operation of the 'black box' is invisible to the rest of the program. A modular program consists of a number of 'black box' working independently of all others, of which each uses variables declared within it (local variables) and any parameters sent to it. Figure 5.1 illustrates a function represented by an ideal 'black-box' with inputs and outputs, and Figure 5.2 shows a main function calling several sub-functions (or modules).

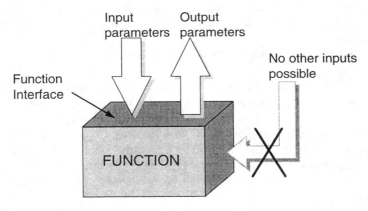

**Figure 5.1:** An ideal 'black-box' representation of a function

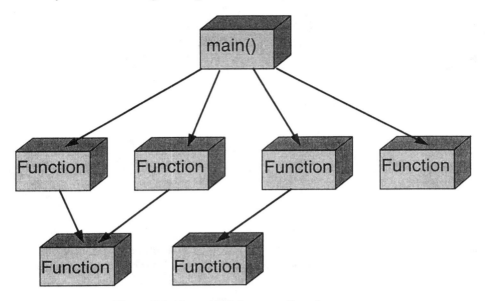

**Figure 5.2:** Hierarchical decomposition of a program

## 5.1 Parameter passing

The data types and names of parameters passed into a function are declared in the function header (its interface) and the actual values sent are referred to as arguments. They can be passed either as values (known as 'passing by value') or as pointers (known as 'passing by reference'). Passing by value involves sending a copy of it into the function. It is not possible to change the value of a variable using this method. Variables can only be modified if they are passed by reference (this will be covered in the next chapter). This chapter looks at how parameters pass into a function and how a single value is returned.

An argument and a parameter are defined as follows:

*An "argument" is the actual value passed to a function.*
*A "parameter" is the variable defined in the function header.*

Figure 5.3 shows a program with two functions, `main()` and `function1()`. Function `main()` calls `function1()` and passes three parameters to it; these are passed as values. A copy of the contents of d goes into g, e into h and f into i.

Variables declared within a function are described as local variables. Figure 5.3 shows that d, e and f are local variables within `main()`; g, h, i, j and k are local within `function1()`. These will have no links to variables of the same name declared in other functions. Local variables only exist within a function in which they are declared and do not exist once the program leaves the function. Variables declared at the top of the source file (and not within a function) are defined as global variables. These allow functions, within the source file, to access them. Care must be taken when using global variables for many reasons, one of which is that they tend to lead to programs that are unstructured and difficult to maintain.

In Figure 5.3 the function function1() makes use of the variable a as this is declared as a global variable. This function cannot be modelled as a 'black box' as it can modify a variable which is not passed to it. In a relatively small program this may not create a problem but as the size of the program increases the control of variables can become difficult.

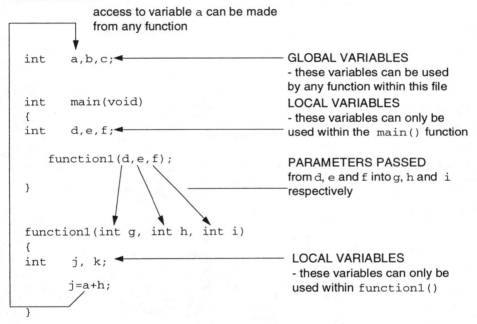

**Figure 5.3:** Local and global variables

Figure 5.4 shows an example of how thing can go wrong with global variables. In this example, a global variable i is used by two functions. Initially, the value of i within the loop in main() will be 0. The function1() function is called within this loop, which uses the variable i within another loop. Each time it is incremented the global variable takes on the incremented value. When the program leaves this function the value of i will have changed (i.e. it will be 10). This causes the for() loop in main() to end. If the variable i had been declared locally within both main() and function1() this problem would not have occurred. As a rule, called modules should be self-contained and use only the parameters sent to them.

```
int      i;

int      main(void)
{
int      d,e,f;

    for (i=0;i<5;i++)
    {
        function1(d,e,f);
        : : : : : : : : : : : : : : : : :
    }
}
function1(int x,  int y,  int z)
{
int      j,  k;

    for (i=0;i<10;i++)
    {
        : : : : : : : : : : : :
    }

}
```

Both functions make
use of global variable
i

**Figure 5.4**: An example of the use of global variables

Program 5.1 contains a function named `print_values()`. This is called from `main()` and variables a and b are passed into the parameters c and d, respectively; c and d are local parameters and only exist within `print_values()`. The values of c and d can be changed with no effect on the values of a and b.

**Program 5.1**
```
/*    prog5_1.c                                          */
/*    Simple program that shows parameter passing  */
#include <stdio.h>

void    print_values(int a,  int b);
               /* ^ function prototype, to be discussed */

int  main(void)
{
int  a=5,b=6;

   print_values(a,b);
   return(0);
}

void    print_values(int c,int d)
{
   printf("The values passed are %d %d \n",c,d);
}
```

Figure 5.5 illustrates how this program can be represented diagrammatically by a structure chart. This diagram is a high level representation of the program and displays the flow of the data between functions. In this case, it shows that `main()` is the top level function (or module) and calls function `print_values()`.

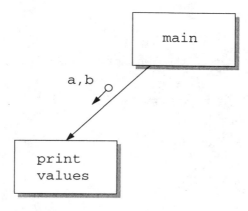

**Figure 5.5:** Structure chart for the program 5.1

## 5.2 Return value

The `return` statement returns a single value from a function to the calling routine, as illustrated in Figure 5.5.

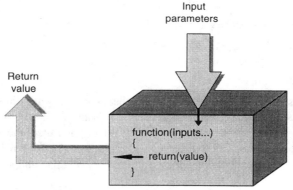

**Figure 5.6:** Black-box representation of a function with a return value

Programs in previous chapters have used functions that return values. These include the mathematical functions `sqrt()` (program 2.10), `atan()` (program 2.14), `exp()` (program 4.3), and `log10()` (program 4.13). The *math.h* header file contains declarations of these functions.

If there are no `return` statements in a function the execution returns automatically to the calling routine upon execution of the closing brace (i.e. after the final statement within the function). Program 5.2 contains functions which will add and multiply two numbers. The function `addition()` uses `return` to send back the addition of the two values to the `main()`.

📄 **Program 5.2**

```
/*    prog5_2.c                                        */
#include <stdio.h>
/* Function prototypes, these are discussed in the next section*/
int    addition(int c,int d);
int    multiply(int c,int d);
void   print_values(int c, int d, int sum,int mult);

int  main(void)
{
int  a=5,b=6,summation,multi;

   summation=addition(a,b);
   multi = multiply(a,b);
   print_values(a,b,summation,multi);
   return(0);
}

int    addition(int c,int d)
{
   return(c+d);
}

int    multiply(int c,int d)
{
   return(c*d);
}

void   print_values(int c, int d, int sum,int mult)
{
   printf("%d plus %d is %d \n",c,d,sum);
   printf("%d multiplied %d is %d \n",c,d,mult);
}
```

Figure 5.7 shows a simple structure chart of this program. The function addition() is called first; the variables sent are a and b and the return value is put into the variable summation. Next, the multiply() is called; the variables sent are also a and b and the value returned goes into multi. Finally, the function print_values() is called; the values sent are a, b, multi and summation.

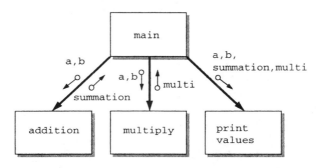

**Figure 5.7:** Basic structure chart for program 5.2

A function can have several return points, although it is normally better to have only one return point. This is normally achieved by restructuring the code. An example of a function with two `return`'s is shown next. In this example a decision is made as to whether the value passed into the function is positive or negative. If it is greater than or equal to zero it returns the same value, else it returns a negative value (`return(-value)`).

```
int  magnitude(int value)
{
   if (value >= 0)
      return (value);
   else
      return ( -value);
}
```

## 5.3 Function type

Program 5.2 contains functions that return integer data types. It is possible to return any other of C's data types, including `float`, `double` and `char`, by inserting the data type before the function name. If no data type is given then the default return type is `int`. The following gives the general syntax of a function.

```
type_def function_name(parameter list)
{
}
```

C is a flexible language in its structure. It allows the arrangement of functions in any order and even within different files. If the compiler finds a function that has not been defined (or prototyped) then it assumes the return type will be `int`. It also assumes that at the linking stage the linker will be able to find the required function either in the current compiled program, the libraries or other object codes. It is thus important that the function return data type is defined when the compiler is compiling the function; otherwise it will assume that the return type is `int`.

Function declarations (or prototypes) are normally inserted either at the top of each file, locally within a function, or in a header file (the *.h* files). These declarations allow the compiler to determine the return type and the data types of all parameters passed to the function. It thus allows the compiler to test for illegal data types passed to a function in error. For example the following are invalid uses of the function `printf()`, `sqrt()` and `scanf()`. The `printf()` has an incorrect syntax as the first argument should be a format statement (i.e. a string), the `sqrt()` function should be passed a floating point value and the `scanf()` function requires a format string as the first argument.

```
printf(23,"Value is %d\n");
b=sqrt("1233");
scanf(&val1,&val2);
```

If the *stdio.h* header is not included the compiler does not generate any errors for the incorrect usage of `printf()` and `scanf()`. The same applies to the *math.h* header file and the function `sqrt()`.

When a function prototype is inserted at the top of the file it is a global declaration of that function within the source code file. Otherwise, the declaration can be inserted into the variable declaration lists within a function; this will make the definition local only to the function in which it is defined.

If a function does not return a value then the data type definition for the return value should be `void`. Also, if no parameters are sent to the function then the argument list contains a `void`. The compiler would thus flag an error or warning if any parameters are passed to a function with a `void` argument list or if a returned value is used from a `void` return data type.

Figure 5.8 shows the operation of a function prototype. At the top of the file the prototype declares the parameter types of the arguments passed (in this case, two `float`'s) and the return data type (in this case `float`). The compiler checks all arguments sent to this function to see if they match up with these types. A warning or error is generated if there is a mismatch. The return type is also checked.

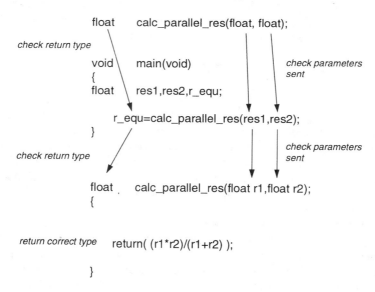

**Figure 5.8:** Checking conducted by the compiler on function prototypes

Program 5.3 contains a function `power()` which is prototyped at the top of the program. The return value is `double`; the first argument is `double` and the second is `int`. This function uses logarithms to determine the value of x raised to the power of n. The formula used is derived next; the `log()` function is the natural logarithm and the `exp()` the exponential function. Both of these require the parameter sent as `double` and the return type is also `double`.

$$y = x^n$$
$$\log(y) = \log(x^n)$$
$$\log(y) = n.\log(x)$$
$$y = \exp(n.\log(x))$$

📄 **Program 5.3**

```
/*   prog5_3.c                                    */
#include <math.h>
#include <stdio.h>

double power(double x,int n); /* declare function prototype */

int     main(void)
{
double x,val;
int     n;

   puts("Program to determine the result of a value");
   puts("raised to the power of an integer");

   printf("Enter x to the power of n >>");
   scanf("%f %d",&x,&n);

   val=power(x,n);
   printf("%f to power of %d is %f\n",x,n,val);
   return(0);
}

double power(double x,int n)
{
   return(exp(n*log(x)) );
}
```

Some compilers give a warning if the return value data type is different from the data type of the variable to which it is assigned. For example, if the data type of the variable x in program 5.3 is changed to a float then it is good practice to recast the return value to a float, as shown next.

```
int     main(void)
{
float   x,val;
int     n;

   : : : : : :
   val=(float) power(x,n);
   : : : : : : :
```

## 5.4  Using the pre-processor to define function macros

The pre-processor operates on a source code file before the compiler is called. One of its functions is to search for the required header files and insert them into the file. It also finds all the #define macros and replaces them with the required definitions. It is this facility that allows in-line function definitions by way of macros.

Program 5.4 uses the pre-processor to define the value of $\pi$ and also to declare a macro named _sqr().

**Program 5.4**

```
/*    prog5_4.c                                          */
/* FILE before the pre-processor */
#include  <stdio.h>
#include  <math.h>
#define    PI            3.14159
#define    _sqr(_X)      ((_X)*(_X))

int      main(void)
{
float    r,f,l,Z,Xl;
   printf("Enter resistance, inductance and frequency>>");
   scanf("%f %f %f",&r,&l,&f);

   Xl=2*PI*f*l;
   Z=sqrt(_sqr(r)+_sqr(Xl));

   printf("Magnitude of impedance is %f\n",Z);
   return(0);

}
```

Program 5.5 shows how the pre-processor modifies program 5.4. Note that the contents of the *stdio.h* and *math.h* file have been truncated.

### 📄 Program 5.5

```
/*   prog5_5.c                                    */
/* FILE after the pre-processor has operated */
:::::::::::::::::: contents of stdio.h:::::::::
                       ::::
:::::::::::::::::: rest of the contents of stdio.h:::::::::

:::::::::::::::::: contents of math.h:::::::::
int     abs     (int x);
double acos    (double x);
double asin    (double x);
double atan    (double x);
double tan2    (double y, double x);
double atof    (const char *s);
:::::::::::::::::: rest of the contents of math.h:::::::::

int     main(void)
{
float   r,f,l,Z,Xl;

    printf("Enter resistance, inductance and frequency>>");
    scanf("%f %f %f",&r,&l,&f);

    Xl=2*3.14159*f*l;
    Z=sqrt(((r)*(r))+((Xl)*(Xl)));

    printf("Magnitude of impedance is %f\n",Z);
    return(0);
}
```

As can be seen from program 5.5 it is possible to use the #define to generate simple macros. For example, to generate a square function the following can be used.

```
#define _sqr(_A) ((_A) * (_A))
```

In this case the pre-processor replaces every occurrence of the macro definition _sqr(ARG) with ((ARG)*(ARG)). For example,

```
Z=sqrt(_sqr(x)+_sqr(y));
```

is replaced by:

```
Z=sqrt( ((x)*(x)) + ((y)*(y)) );
```

Parameters used when declaring in-line functions, using the #define, are normally, as a matter of style, preceded by an underscore. It is also typical for function names to be preceded by an underscore (e.g. _tolower() and _toupper()). Care must be taken when using the pre-processor to replace functions as their operation is almost invisible to the programmer. Parentheses should be used to ensure that they operate correctly when inserted into the code.

An example of what can go wrong is given in the next example. In this case, it is an incorrect definition of _sqr(). With the following definition the parentheses around _X*_X have been omitted.

```
#define sqr(_X) _X*_X
```

Thus the following code

```
Z=sqr(a)/sqr(b);
```

would be replaced by

```
Z=a*a/b*b;
```

This is incorrect as the / operator has precedence over the second * operator. It will be interpreted as a multiplied by  a divided by b then multiplied by b, whereas it should have been the result of a multiplied by a divided by the result of b multiplied by b.

```
Z=(a*a)/(b*b);
```

Program 5.6 contains a practical example of how the #define can cause mistakes.

**Program 5.6**
```
/*    prog5_6.c                                        */
#include      <math.h>
#include      <stdio.h>

#define PI        3.14159
#define _sqr(_X)    (_X*_X)

/* FILE before the pre-processor */
int      main(void)
{
float    r1,r2,f,l,Z,X1;

   printf("Enter R1 and R2, inductance and frequency>>");
   scanf("%f %f %f",&r1,&r2,&l,&f);

   X1=2*PI*f*l;
   Z=sqrt(_sqr(r1+r2)+_sqr(X1));

   printf("Magnitude of impedance is %f\n",Z);
   return(0);
}
```

The pre-processor replaces _sqr(r1+r2) with r1+r2*r1+r2. This is incorrect as the multiplication operator has precedence over addition. Program 5.7 shows the processed file.

📄 **Program 5.7**

```
/*    prog5_7.c                                    */
::::::: Contents of math.h and stdio.h::::::::::::::::::::::::::::::::::
/* FILE after the pre-processor */
int    main(void)
{
float   r1,r2,f,l,Z,X1;

   printf("Enter R1 and R2, inductance and frequency>>");
   scanf("%f %f %f %f",&r1,&r2,&l,&f);

   X1=2*3.14159*f*l;
   Z=sqrt((r1+r2*r1+r2)+(X1*X1));

   printf("Magnitude of impedance is %f\n",Z);
   return(0);
}
```

Several macros, using #define statements, are shown next. The first _toupper() converts a lowercase character to uppercase; the second converts an uppercase character to lowercase. These macros are found in the header file *ctype.h*. The last example converts a value (of any data type) into its magnitude.

```
#define _toupper(c)      ((c) + 'A' - 'a')
#define _tolower(c)      ((c) + 'a' - 'A')
#define _mag(_A)         (_A<0) ? (_A) : -(_A)
```

The last statement uses a shorthand way of representing the if statement. The operators ? and : can be interpreted as 'then' and 'else', respectively.

## 5.5 Examples

### 5.5.1 Combinational logic

In this example, the following Boolean equation is processed to determine its truth table.

$$Z = \overline{(A + B + (A.C)).C}$$

Figure 5.9 gives a schematic representation of this Boolean function.

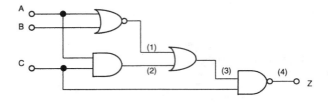

**Figure 5.9:** Schematic representation of the function $Z = \overline{(\overline{A+B}+(A.C))}.C$

The four nodes numbered on this schematic are:

(1)   $\overline{A+B}$

(2)   $A.C$

(3)   $\overline{A+B}+(A.C)$

(4)   $\overline{(\overline{A+B}+(A.C)).C}$

Table 5.1 gives a truth table showing the logical level at each point in the schematic. This table is necessary to check the program results against expected results.

**Table 5.1:** Truth table

| A | B | C | $\overline{A+B}$ (1) | $A.C$ (2) | $\overline{A+B}+(A.C)$ (3) | $(\overline{A+B}+(A.C)).C$ | $\overline{(\overline{A+B}+(A.C)).C}$ (4) |
|---|---|---|---|---|---|---|---|
| 0 | 0 | 0 | 1 | 0 | 1 | 0 | 1 |
| 0 | 0 | 1 | 1 | 0 | 1 | 1 | 0 |
| 0 | 1 | 0 | 0 | 0 | 0 | 0 | 1 |
| 0 | 1 | 1 | 0 | 0 | 0 | 0 | 1 |
| 1 | 0 | 0 | 0 | 0 | 0 | 0 | 1 |
| 1 | 0 | 1 | 0 | 1 | 1 | 1 | 0 |
| 1 | 1 | 0 | 0 | 0 | 0 | 0 | 1 |
| 1 | 1 | 1 | 0 | 1 | 1 | 1 | 0 |

Table 5.2 gives the resulting truth table.

**Table 5.2:** Truth table

| A | B | C | Z |
|---|---|---|---|
| 0 | 0 | 0 | 1 |
| 0 | 0 | 1 | 0 |
| 0 | 1 | 0 | 1 |
| 0 | 1 | 1 | 1 |
| 1 | 0 | 0 | 1 |
| 1 | 0 | 1 | 0 |
| 1 | 1 | 0 | 1 |
| 1 | 1 | 1 | 0 |

The permutations of the truth table input variables (i.e. 000, 001, 010, 011, ..., 111) are generated using 3 nested for loops. The inner loop toggles C from a 0 to a 1, the next loop toggles B and the outer loop toggles A. The Boolean functions use the logical operators && and ||. Recall that these operators treat a value of 0 (zero) as FALSE and any other value as TRUE.

📄 **Program 5.8**

```
/*    prog5_8.c                                        */
/*    Example showing use of functions in returning    */
/*    values, in this case binary values               */

#include <stdio.h>
#define    FALSE   0
#define    TRUE    1

   /* ANSI C function prototypes */
int     AND(int x,int y);
int     NAND(int x,int y);
int     NOR(int x,int y);
int     OR (int x,int y);
int     NOT(int x);

int     main(void)
{
int     a,b,c,z;

/* Go through all permutations of truth table */
   puts("     A      B      C       Result");
   puts("     ***************************");

   for (a=FALSE;a<=TRUE;a++)
      for (b=FALSE;b<=TRUE;b++)
         for (c=FALSE;c<=TRUE;c++)
         {
            z=NAND(OR(NOR(a,b),AND(a,c)),c);
            printf("%6d %6d %6d %6d\n",a,b,c,z);
         }
   return(0);
}

int     AND(int x,int y)
{
   if ( x && y ) return(TRUE);
   else return(FALSE);
}

int     NAND(int x,int y)
{
   if ( x && y ) return(FALSE);
   else return(TRUE);
}

int     OR(int x,int y)
{
   if ( x || y ) return(TRUE);
   else return(FALSE);
}

int     NOR(int x,int y)
{
```

```
if ( x || y ) return(FALSE);
else return(TRUE);
}


int     NOT(int x)
{
  if (x) return(FALSE);
  else return(TRUE);
}
```

Test run 5.1 shows a sample run of the program. Notice that the results are identical to the truth table generated by analyzing the schematic.

---

🖥 **Test run 5.1**

| A | B | C | Result |
|---|---|---|--------|
| ********************************** | | | |
| 0 | 0 | 0 | 1 |
| 0 | 0 | 1 | 0 |
| 0 | 1 | 0 | 1 |
| 0 | 1 | 1 | 1 |
| 1 | 0 | 0 | 1 |
| 1 | 0 | 1 | 0 |
| 1 | 1 | 0 | 1 |
| 1 | 1 | 1 | 0 |

---

It is possible to use in-line function definitions for the Boolean functions. The statement

```
#define _AND(_x,_y) ( (_x && _y) ? TRUE : FALSE
```

is a shorthand way of representing the if statement. If this statement is TRUE, it will yield a logical TRUE; else a FALSE. The operators ? and : can be interpreted as 'then' and 'else', respectively.

Program 5.9 is the equivalent of program 5.8 but uses #define directives for the basic Boolean functions. Care must be taken when using the #define statements instead of functions as much of the operation of the code conversion is invisible and can thus cause errors which are difficult to trace. It is important that a #define substitution is tested independently and then within a program before it can be proved to be functioning correctly.

📄 **Program 5.9**
```
/*    prog5_9.c                                          */
/*    Example showing use of macros in yielding          */
/*    values, in this case logical values               */
#include <stdio.h>

#define   FALSE   0
#define   TRUE    1

#define   _AND(_x,_y)      ((_x && _y) ? TRUE    : FALSE)
#define   _OR(_x,_y)       ((_x || _y) ? TRUE    : FALSE)
#define   _NAND(_x,_y)     ((_x && _y) ? FALSE   : TRUE)
#define   _NOR(_x,_y)      ((_x || _y) ? FALSE   : TRUE)
#define   _NOT(_x,_y)      ((_x )      ? FALSE   : TRUE)

int  main(void)
{
int  a,b,c,z;
/* Go through all permutations of truth table */
   puts("     A        B        C        Result");
   puts("     ***************************");

   for (a=FALSE;a<=TRUE;a++)
      for (b=FALSE;b<=TRUE;b++)
         for (c=FALSE;c<=TRUE;c++)
         {
            z=_NAND(_OR(_NOR(a,b),_AND(a,c)),c);
            printf("%6d %6d %6d %6d\n",a,b,c,z);
         }
   return(0);
}
```

After the in-line function macros have been fully tested, they can be placed in a user-defined header file. This file should not be placed in the directory which contains the standard header files, but should be inserted into a special user header file directory or placed in the same directory as the source code. In this case, the macros will be put into a header file *boolean.h*. The technique of using header files allows other source code files to access the pre-processor in-line functions, function prototypes or constant definitions.

Where speed of code is important, in-line function definitions are likely to operate faster than the equivalent function as they do not involve parameter passing. Program 5.10 shows the modified code with the included header file. The contents of the file *boolean.h* is shown next; this includes the definition of the Boolean function using macros and also the function declarations.

```
/* Contents of boolean.h  */

#define FALSE 0
#define TRUE  1

/*   Definition using macros                      */
#define _AND(_x,_y)   ((_x && _y) ? TRUE    : FALSE)
#define _OR(_x,_y)    ((_x || _y) ? TRUE    : FALSE)
#define _NAND(_x,_y)  ((_x && _y) ? FALSE   : TRUE)
#define _NOR(_x,_y)   ((_x || _y) ? FALSE   : TRUE)
#define _NOT(_x,_y)   ((_x )      ? FALSE   : TRUE)

/* ANSI C Boolean function prototypes */
int    AND(int x,int y);
int    NAND(int x,int y);
int    NOR(int x,int y);
int    OR (int x,int y);
int    NOT(int x);
```

A user-defined header file is inserted into the program using the `#include " "` pre-processor directive.

🗎 **Program 5.10**
```
/*   prog5_10.c                                   */
/*   Example showing use of macros in yielding    */
/*   values, in this case logical values          */

#include <stdio.h>
#include "boolean.h"

int  main(void)
{
int  a,b,c,z;

/* Go through all permutations of truth table */

    puts("    A       B       C       Result");
    puts("   ***************************");

    for (a=FALSE;a<=TRUE;a++)
      for (b=FALSE;b<=TRUE;b++)
        for (c=FALSE;c<=TRUE;c++)
        {
          z=_NAND(_OR(_NOR(a,b),_AND(a,c)),c);
          printf("%6d %6d %6d %6d\n",a,b,c,z);
        }
    return(0);
}
```

Program 5.11 uses bitwise operators to implement the Boolean functions. The single ampersand (&) operation is the bitwise AND function and should not be confused with the logical AND statement (&&). Similiarly, the verical bar (|) operation is a bitwise OR function, which should not be confused with the logical OR function (||).

📄 **Program 5.11**

```
/*    prog5_11.c                                        */
/*    Example showing use of macros in yielding        */
/*    values, in this case logical values              */

#include <stdio.h>
#include "boolean.h"

int     main(void)
{
int     a,b,c,z;

/* Go through all permutations of truth table */
   puts("     A     B     C       Result");
   puts("     ***************************");

   for (a=FALSE;a<=TRUE;a++)
     for (b=FALSE;b<=TRUE;b++)
       for (c=FALSE;c<=TRUE;c++)
       {
          z=NAND(OR(NOR(a,b),AND(a,c)),c);
          printf("%6d %6d %6d %6d\n",a,b,c,z);
       }
   return(0);
}

int     AND(int x,int y)
{
   return(x&y);
}

int     NAND(int x,int y)
{
   return( !(x&y) );
}

int     OR(int x,int y)
{
   return( x|y );
}

int     NOR(int x,int y)
{
   return ( !(x|y) );
}

int     NOT(int x)
{
   return(!(x));
}
```

## 5.5.2  Impedance of a series RL circuit

The magnitude of the impedance of an RL circuit is given by the equation:

$$|Z| = \sqrt{R^2 + X_L^2} \quad \Omega$$

and the phase angle of this impedance is given by:

$$\langle Z \rangle = \tan^{-1} \frac{X_L}{R}$$

Figure 5.10 gives a schematic of an RL series circuit.

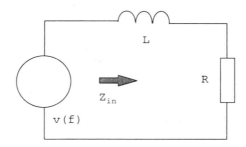

**Figure 5.10:** RL series circuit

Figure 5.11 gives a structure chart which outlines a basic design for this problem. Inputs are resistance (R), inductance (L) and frequency (f). The program determines the magnitude and phase angle of the impedance. In order to determine these values the reactance of the inductor must be determined using $X_L = 2\pi fL$.

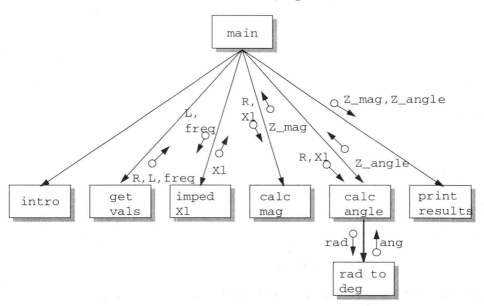

**Figure 5.11:** Structure chart for a series RL circuit program

## 🖹 Program 5.12

```
/* prog5_12.c                                     */
/* Program to determine impedance of an           */
/* RL series circuit                              */

#include <stdio.h>
#include <math.h>

#define PI       3.14159

float   calc_mag(float x, float y);
float   calc_angle(float x, float y);
float   impedance_Xl(float L,float f);
float   rad_to_deg(float rad);
void    intro(void);
void    print_results(float mag,float angle);

int     main(void)
{
float   r,l,Xl,Z_mag,Z_angle,freq;

  intro();

  printf("Enter R,L and frequency >>>");

  scanf("%f %f %f",&r,&l,&freq);

  Xl=impedance_Xl(l,freq);

  Z_mag=calc_mag(r,Xl);
  Z_angle=calc_angle(r,Xl);

  print_results(Z_mag,Z_angle);
  return(0);
}

void    intro(void)
{
  puts("Prog to determine impedance of series RL circuit");

}

void    print_results(float mag,float angle)
{
  printf("Impedance is %.2f ohms phase angle %.2f degrees\n",
      mag,angle);
}

float   calc_mag(float x, float y)
{
float   z;

  /* determine magnitude for rectangular              */
  /* co-ordinates x+jy                                */
  z=(float) sqrt( x*x + y*y ); /* sqrt() returns a double   */

  return(z);
}
```

```
float   calc_angle(float x, float y)
{
float   ang;

   /* determine angle in degrees for rectangular */
   /* co-ordinates x+jy                           */

   ang=(float) atan(y/x); /* atan() returns a double */
   ang=rad_to_deg(ang);
   return(ang);
}

float   impedance_Xl(float L,float f)
{
   /* determine impedance of inductor */
   return(2*PI*f*L);
}

float   rad_to_deg(float rad)
{
   /* convert from radians to degrees */
   return(rad*180/PI);
}
```

Test run 5.2 gives a sample run of this program. The input parameters used are resistance 1 kΩ, inductance 1 mH and applied frequency 1 MHz.

---

🖳 **Test run 5.2**

```
Program to determine impedance of series RL circuit
Enter R,L and frequency >>> 1000 1e-3 1e6
Impedance is 6362.27 ohms phase angle 80.96 degrees
```

---

Program 5.13 shows an implementation of program 5.12 using in-line function definitions to replace functions. The circuit functions defined in program 5.13 could be inserted into a file named *ac.h*. This can be included in any program that uses A.C. circuit calculations.

### 📄 Program 5.13

```c
/*    prog5_13.c                                  */
/*    Program to determine impedance of an        */
/*    series RL circuit                           */
#include <stdio.h>
#include <math.h>

/*Define functions used, these functions could    */
/*go into a header file, e.g. circuit.h            */
#define   _sqr(_X)              ((_X)*(_X))
#define   _rad_to_deg(_X)       ((_X)*180/PI)
#define   _impedance_Xl(_L,_f)  (2*PI*_f*_L)
#define   _calc_mag(_X,_Y)      (sqrt((_sqr(_X)+_sqr(_Y))))
#define   _calc_angle(_X,_Y)    (_rad_to_deg(atan(_Y/_X)))
#define   PI                    3.14159

void    intro(void);
void    print_results(float mag,float angle);

int     main(void)
{
float   r,l,Xl,Z_mag,Z_angle,freq;

    intro();

    printf("Enter R,L and frequency >>>");
    scanf("%f %f %f",&r,&l,&freq);

    Xl=_impedance_Xl(l,freq);

    Z_mag=_calc_mag(r,Xl);
    Z_angle=_calc_angle(r,Xl);

    print_results(Z_mag,Z_angle);
    return(0);
}

void    intro(void)
{
    puts("Program to determine impedance of series RL circuit");
}

void    print_results(float mag,float angle)
{
    printf("Impedance is %.2f ohms phase angle %.2f degrees\n",
            mag,angle);
}
```

Test run 5.3 is a sample run of this program.

### 🖥 Test run 5.3

```
Program to determine imdepance of series RL circuit
Enter R,L and frequency >>> 1000 1e-3 1e6
Imdepance is 6362.27 ohms phase angle 80.96 degrees
```

### 5.5.3  AC response of a series RC circuit

In the RC circuit, shown in Figure 5.12, the ratio of the output to input voltage can be used to determine the response of the circuit. Typically, this ratio is given in decibels (dB).

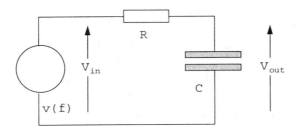

**Figure 5.12:** RC series circuit showing input and output voltages

The output voltage of this circuit can be found using:

$$V_o = V_i \cdot \frac{-jX_C}{R - jX_C}$$

where

$$X_C = \frac{1}{2\pi f C} \; \Omega$$

The magnitude of the voltage ratio is thus:

$$\left| \frac{V_o}{V_i} \right| = \frac{X_C}{\sqrt{R^2 + X_C^2}}$$

Program 5.14 determines the magnitude of this voltage ratio for entered value of R, C and $f$. One problem that can occur in this program is that there will be a divide-by-zero error when the denominator of the capacitive reactance formula is 0 (when $f$ or C is 0). To overcome this the impedance_Xc() function determines if the denominator is 0 and returns an infinity flag (INFINITYFLAG) to the calling routine if it is. The RC_response() function then detects this and returns a value of 1 of the voltage ratio. A value of $-1$ has been chosen for this flag as this value cannot occur under normal calculations.

📄 **Program 5.14**

```c
/*   prog5_14.c                                          */
/*   Program to determine the voltage ratio of an       */
/*   RC series circuit with the capacitor on the        */
/*   output                                              */
#include <stdio.h>
#include <math.h>

#define INFINITYFLAG -1
#define PI           3.14159
/* function prototypes          */

float   RC_response(float r,float C,float f);
float   impedance_Xc(float C, float F);
float   dBs(float Gain);
float   calc_mag(float x, float y);

int  main(void)
{
float   f_start,f_end,f_step,f,r,C, gain;

   printf("Enter start, end and step freq >> ");
   scanf("%f %f %f",&f_start,&f_end,&f_step);

   printf("Enter resistance and capacitance >> ");
   scanf("%f %f",&r,&C);

   puts("Frequency      Voltage gain  ");
   puts(" (Hz)          ratio     dBs");
   puts("****************************");

   for (f=f_start;f<=f_end;f+=f_step)
   {
      gain=RC_response(r,C,f);
      printf("%8.2f %8.3f %8.3f\n",f,gain,dBs(gain));
   }
   return(0);
}

float   RC_response(float r,float C,float f)
{
float   Xc,response;
   /* Determine gain of RC circuit  */

   Xc=impedance_Xc(C,f);
   if (Xc==INFINITYFLAG) response=1.0;
   else response=Xc/(calc_mag(r,Xc));

   return(response);
}

float   impedance_Xc(float C, float F)
{
   /* Calculate impedance of a capacitor */
   /* Beware when dividing by zero          */
   if ((F==0) || (C==0)) return(INFINITYFLAG);
   else return(1/(2*PI*F*C));
}
```

```
float    calc_mag(float x, float y)
{
    /* Calculate magnitude of complex value x+jy */
    return(sqrt(x*x+y*y));
}

float    dBs(float gain)
{
    /* Convert voltage ratio to dBs */
    return(20*log10(gain));
}
```

Test run 5.4 shows a sample run of the program with the values $R=1$ k$\Omega$ and $C=1$ $\mu$ F. The frequency sweeps from 0 Hz to 1 kHz in steps of 50 Hz. Notice that at 0 Hz the output voltage is a maximum and as the frequency increases the output voltage decreases. This circuit displays the characteristics of a low-pass filter (LPF).

---

⌨ **Test run 5.4**

```
Enter start, end and step freq >>  0 100 50
Enter resistance and capacitance >> 1000 1e-6
Frequency      Voltage gain
  (Hz)         ratio      dBs
**************************************
     0.00     1.000     0.000
    50.00     0.954    -0.409
   100.00     0.847    -1.445
   150.00     0.728    -2.761
   200.00     0.623    -4.115
   250.00     0.537    -5.400
   300.00     0.469    -6.583
   350.00     0.414    -7.661
   400.00     0.370    -8.643
   450.00     0.333    -9.540
   500.00     0.303   -10.362
   550.00     0.278   -11.120
   600.00     0.256   -11.822
   650.00     0.238   -12.475
   700.00     0.222   -13.084
   750.00     0.208   -13.656
   800.00     0.195   -14.194
   850.00     0.184   -14.702
   900.00     0.174   -15.182
   950.00     0.165   -15.638
  1000.00     0.157   -16.072
```

---

### 5.5.4 Harmonics of a repetitive pulse waveform

Continuously varying signals have a frequency spectrum which is also continuous, whereas a repetitive signal is made up of a series of discrete frequencies called harmonics. If a repetitive signal has a period of $T$ then the fundamental frequency is $1/T$ Hz. All other frequency components which make up the signal are multiples of this fundamental frequency, i.e. at 2, 3, 4.. times. For example, a repetitive signal with a period of 10 ms has a frequency content of 100 Hz, 200 Hz, 300 Hz, etc. If a waveform is a square wave then its frequency content will only have odd harmonics (e.g. 100 Hz, 300 Hz, etc.).

A rectangular pulse waveform is shown in Figure 5.13. The duty cycle of the waveform is the ratio of the active time of the pulse ($t$) to the period of the waveform ($T$). The duty cycle is given by:

$$\text{Duty Cycle} = \frac{t}{T}$$

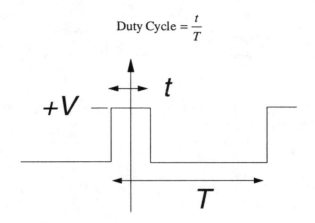

**Figure 5.13:** Duty cycle

The amplitudes of the frequency components which make up this signal are given by:

$$v_n(t) = \frac{Vt}{T} + \sum_{n=1}^{n=\infty} V_n \cos(n2\pi ft)$$

where

$$V_n = \frac{2Vt}{T} \frac{\sin Nx}{Nx}$$

and

$$x = \frac{\pi t}{T}$$

$V_1$ is the amplitude of the fundamental, $V_2$ is amplitude of the second harmonic, etc. The frequencies contained in the signal will be:

$$f_1 = \frac{1}{T} \text{ Hz}, \quad f_2 = \frac{2}{T} \text{ Hz}, \quad f_3 = \frac{3}{T} \text{ Hz, } etc.$$

The basic design of a program to determine the harmonics is given in Figure 5.14.

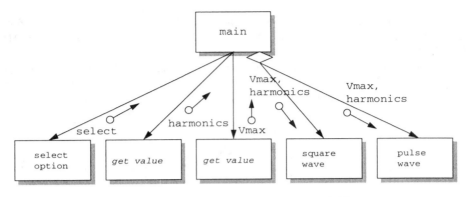

**Figure 5.14:** Structure chart for program 5.15

Program 5.15 determines the amplitude of the harmonics for a square wave or a rectangular pulse waveform.

📄 **Program 5.15**

```
/*    prog5_15.c                               */
/*    Program to determine the harmonics of    */
/*    repetitive rectangular or square pulses  */

#define    PI      3.14159
#define    TRUE    1

#include <math.h>
#include <stdio.h>

void    Square_wave(int harm,float Vmax);
void    Pulse_wave(int harm,float Vmax);
int     SelectOption(void);

int     main(void)
{
int     select,harmonics;
float   Vmax;

/* infinite loop until break */

   while (TRUE)
   {
      select=SelectOption();
      if (select==3) break;

      puts("Enter number of harmonics required");
      scanf("%d",&harmonics);

      puts("Enter max voltage ");
      scanf("%f",&Vmax);

      switch (select)
      {
         case 1: Square_wave(harmonics,Vmax);  break;
```

```
            case 2: Pulse_wave(harmonics,Vmax);    break;
        }
    }
    return(0);
}

void    Square_wave(int harm,float Vmax)
{
float   v;
int     i;

    for (i=1;i<=harm;i+=2)
    {
        v=(4*Vmax/i/PI);
        printf("Harmonic %d Amplitude %.3f\n",i,v);
    }

}

void    Pulse_wave(int harm,float Vmax)
{
float   Duty,v;
int     i;

    puts("Enter duty cycle (0->1)");
    scanf("%f",&Duty);

    v=(Vmax*Duty);
    printf("DC %.3f\n",v);

    for (i=1;i<=harm;i++)
    {
        v=(2*Vmax*Duty) * sin(i*PI*Duty) / (i*PI*Duty);
        printf("Harmonic %d Amplitude %.3f\n",i,v);
    }

}

int     SelectOption(void)
{
int     Select;

    do {
        puts("Do you wish");
        puts("1- Square wave");
        puts("2- Pulse train");
        puts("3- Exit");
        scanf("%d",&Select);

    } while ( (Select<0) || (Select>3) );

    return(Select);
}
```

Test run 5.5 shows a sample run.

⌨ **Test run 5.5**

```
Do you wish
1- Square wave
2- Pulse train
3- Exit
1

Enter number of harmonics required
10

Enter max voltage
4

Harmonic 1 Amplitude 1.274
Harmonic 3 Amplitude 0.425
Harmonic 5 Amplitude 0.255
Harmonic 7 Amplitude 0.182
Harmonic 9 Amplitude 0.142
**************************

Do you wish
1- Square wave
2- Pulse train
3- Exit
2
Enter number of harmonics required
10
Enter max voltage
1
Enter duty cycle (0->1)
0.2
DC 0.200000
Harmonic 1 Amplitude  0.374
Harmonic 2 Amplitude  0.303
Harmonic 3 Amplitude  0.202
Harmonic 4 Amplitude  0.094
Harmonic 5 Amplitude  0.000
Harmonic 6 Amplitude -0.062
Harmonic 7 Amplitude -0.086
Harmonic 8 Amplitude -0.076
Harmonic 9 Amplitude -0.042
Harmonic 10 Amplitude -0.000
****************************
Do you wish
1- Square wave
2- Pulse train
3- Exit
3
```

### 5.5.5  Classification of radio waves

Program 5.16 determines in which classification a radio wave is entered into. The function `radiowave()` returns an integer in the range 0 to 10. This relates to the radio wave classification. If the return value is zero the input is INVALID !!! A basic structure chart of this program is given in Figure 5.15.

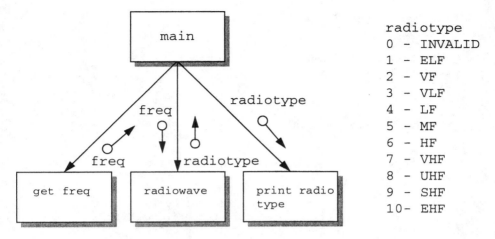

**Figure 5.15:** Structure chart for the radio wave program

📄 **Program 5.16**

```
/*    prog5_16.c                                    */
/*    Program to determine classification of radio  */
/*    wave                                          */
#include <stdio.h>

/* define function returns */
#define    INVALID    -1
#define    ELF        0
#define    VF         1
#define    VLF        2
#define    LF         3
#define    MF         4
#define    HF         5
#define    VF         6
#define    SHF        7
#define    UHF        8
#define    SHF        9
#define    EHF        10

void    print_radio_type(int type);
int     radiowave(float f);
float   get_freq(void);

int     main(void)
{
float   freq;
int     radiowave_type;

    freq=get_freq();

    radiowave_type=radiowave(freq);
    print_radio_type(radiowave_type);
    return(0);
}
```

```
float   get_freq(void)
{
float   f;
   printf("Enter frequency of radio wave>>");
   scanf("%f",&f);
   return(f);
}

void    print_radio_type(int type)
{
/* Print radio wave type */
   printf("Electromagnetic wave is ");
   switch (type)
   {
      case ELF:       puts("Extralow frequency");    break;
      case VF:        puts("Voice frequency");       break;
      càse VLF:       puts("Very low frequency");    break;
      case LF:        puts("Low frequency");         break;
      case MF:        puts("Medium frequency");      break;
      case HF:        puts("High frequency");        break;
      case VHF:       puts("Very high frequency");   break;
      case UHF:       puts("Ultra high frequency");  break;
      case SHF:       puts("Super high frequency");  break;
      case EHF:       puts("Extra high frequency");  break;
      case TOOLARGE:  puts("Input wave too large");  break;
      default:        puts("INVALID");
   }
}
int   radiowave(float f)
{
/* determine classification of radiowave */
   if (f<0)            return(INVALID);
   else if (f<300)     return(ELF);
   else if (f<3e3)     return(VF);
   else if (f<30e3)    return(VLF);
   else if (f<300e3)   return(LF);
   else if (f<3e6)     return(MF);
   else if (f<30e6)    return(HF);
   else if (f<300e6)   return(VHF);
   else if (f<3e9)     return(UHF);
   else if (f<30e9)    return(SHF);
   else if (f<300e9)   return(EHF);
   else                return(TOOLARGE);
}
```

A sample test is given in test run 5.6.

---

🖥 **Test run 5.6**

```
Enter frequency of radio wave>> 1e-3
Electromagnetic wave is Voice frequency
```

### 5.5.6 Impedance of a transmission line

A transmission line is used to transmit digital or analogue signals from a transmitter to a receiver. It can be a coaxial cable, twisted pair, etc. From a circuit point of view, it is made up of series resistance and inductance, which go to make up the series impedance of the conducting wires, and a shunt conductance and capacitance of the dielectric between the conductors, which makes up the shunt impedance of the line. If a given length of this transmission line were divided into more and more sections, the ultimate case would be an infinitesimal section of the basic elements: resistance $R$, inductance $L$, conductance $G$, and capacitance $C$. The equivalent circuit that results is given in Figure 5.16.

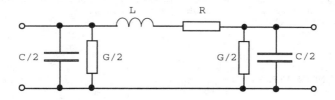

**Figure 5.16:** Equivalent circuit of a transmission line

The parameters R, L, G and C are known as the primary line constants. These are:

- series resistance $R$      $\Omega.\text{m}^{-1}$
- series inductance $L$      Henries.$\text{m}^{-1}$
- shunt conductance $G$      Siemens.$\text{m}^{-1}$
- shunt capacitance $C$      Farads.$\text{m}^{-1}$

The characteristic impedance, $Z_0$, is the ratio of the voltage to current for each wave propagated along a transmission line, which is given by:

$$Z_0 = \frac{V}{I}$$

From this it can be shown that

$$Z_0 = \sqrt{\frac{R + j\omega L}{G + j\omega C}}$$

The magnitude of this impedance will be given by:

$$Z_0 = \sqrt{\frac{R^2 + (2\pi f L)^2}{G^2 + (2\pi f C)^2}}$$

Program 5.17 determines the magnitude of the characteristic impedance for a transmission line with entered primary line constants. One problem that can occur in this program is that there will be a divide-by-zero error when the denominator of the characteristic impedance formula is 0 (when G and ωC are 0). To overcome this the calc_Zo() function determines if the denominator is 0 (value2) and returns an infinity flag (INFINITYFLAG) to the calling routine. If the main program detects this flag then it displays the impedance as INFINITY. A value of −1 has been chosen for this flag as this value cannot occur under normal calculations.

📄 **Program 5.17**

```
/*    prog5_17.c                                                   */
/*    Program to determine impedance of a transmission Line        */
/*    Impedance of TL is   root((R+jwL)/(G+jwC))                   */
#include <stdio.h>
#include <math.h>

#define MILLI         1e-3
#define MICRO         1e-6
#define INFINITYFLAG  -1
#define PI            3.14159

float   calc_Zo(float r,float l,float g,float c,float f);
float   calc_mag(float x,float y);
float   calc_imp(float f, float val);

int     main(void)
{
float   Zmag,R,L,G,C,f;

    puts("Program to determine impedance of a transmission line");

    printf("Enter R,L(mH),G(mS),C(uF) and freq.>>");

    scanf("%f %f %f %f %f",&R,&L,&G,&C,&f);

    Zmag=calc_Zo(R,L*MILLI,G*MILLI,C*MICRO,f);

    if (Zmag==INFINITYFLAG)printf("Magnitude is INFINITY ohms\n");
    else                   printf("Magnitude is %.2f ohms\n",Zmag);
    return(0);
}

float   calc_Zo(float r,float l,float g,float c,float f)
{
float   value1,value2;

    value1=calc_mag(r,calc_imp(f,l));
    value2=calc_mag(g,calc_imp(f,c));
    /* Beware if dividing by zero */
    if (value2==0)   return(INFINITYFLAG);
    else             return(sqrt(value1/value2));
}

float   calc_mag(float x,float y)
{
```

```
   return(sqrt((x*x)+(y*y)));
}

float   calc_imp(float f, float val)
{
   return(2*PI*f*val);
}
```

Test run 5.7 shows a sample test run.

```
Program to determine impedance of a transmission line
Enter R, L (mH), G (mS), C (uF) and freq.>> 0 40 0 7 1000
Magnitude is 75.59 ohms
```

## 5.6 Tutorial

Q5.1   Program 5.18 has an error in it. A sample run from this program is given in test run 5.8 (the error has caused the output to be unpredictable and may give a different output on a different machine). Determine the error and correct it so that it runs correctly.

📄 **Program 5.18**
```
/*    prog5_18.c                                          */
/*    Program to determine impedance of a capacitor       */

#include <stdio.h>
#include <math.h>

#define   PI 3.14159

int     main(void)
{
float   f,C,Xc;

   puts("Program to determine impedance of a capacitor");
   printf("Enter f and C >>> ");

   scanf("%f %f",&f,&C);

   Xc=calc_Xc(f,C);

   printf("Impedance is %f ohms\n",Xc);
   return(0);
}

calc_Xc(float f,float l)
{
   return(1/(2*PI*f*l));
}
```

⌨ **Test run 5.8**

```
Program to determine impedance of a capacitor
Enter f and C >>> 1e3 1e-6
Floating point error: Divide by 0.
```

Q5.2    Program 5.19 has an error in it; determine the error and correct it. Test run 5.9 shows a sample run (as in Q5.1, the program will give an unpredictable output).

📄 **Program 5.19**

```
/*    prog5_19.c                                    */
/*    Program to determine impedance of an inductor  */
#define   PI    3.14159

#include <stdio.h>
#include <math.h>

float   calc_Xl(int f,int l);

int     main(void)
{
float   f,L,Xl;

   puts("Program to determine impedance of an inductor");
   printf("Enter f and L >>> ");

   scanf("%f %f",&f,&L);

   Xl=calc_Xl(f,L);
   printf("Impedance is %f ohms\n",Xl);
   return(0);
}

float   calc_Xl(int f,int l)
{
   return(2*PI*f*l);
}
```

⌨ **Test run 5.9**

```
Program to determine impedance of an inductor
Enter f and L >>>   1e3 1e-3
Impedance is 0.000000 ohms
```

Q5.3    Repeat Q4.12 using functions to determine the noise voltage and signal-to-noise ratio (SNR). Use these to determine the SNR for bandwidths from 1 Hz up to 10 GHz in decade steps.

Q5.4    Write a program which will determine the impedance of an RC series circuit for a an entered frequency. Refer to program 5.12.

Q5.5    Repeat Q5.4 with an LC series circuit.

Q5.6    Write Boolean logic functions for the following four digital gates:

AND3 (A,B,C)
OR3 (A,B,C)
NAND3 (A,B,C)
NOR3 (A,B,C)

Add these functions to the library of Boolean functions already generated (i.e. boolean.h). Refer to program 5.9.

Q5.7    Using the functions generated in Q5.6 determine the truth table for the following equations.

$$Z = \overline{A + B + C} + (\overline{B}.C.D) + A$$

$$Z = \overline{A.C.D.(\overline{C}.D).B}$$

$$Z = \overline{A.B.\overline{C}.(A + B + C).(\overline{B}.C.D)}$$

Q5.8    Repeat Q4.3 using the functions generated in Q5.6.

Q5.9    Generate a function which will implement a two input exclusive-OR gate. Test run 5.10 is a sample test run.

---
💻  **Test run 5.10**
```
A  B  Z
0  0  0
0  1  1
1  0  1
1  1  0
```
---

Q5.10   Using the function generated in Q5.9, write a program that will convert 4-bit binary code into Gray code. Figure 5.17 gives a schematic of a 4-bit Gray code converter, and test run 5.11 is a sample run.

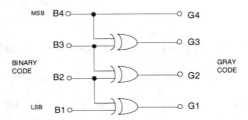

**Figure 5.17:** Binary to Gray code converter

**Test run 5.11**

| BINARY | | | | GRAY | | | |
|---|---|---|---|---|---|---|---|
| B4 | B3 | B2 | B1 | G4 | G3 | G2 | G1 |
| 0 | 0 | 0 | 0 | 0 | 0 | 0 | 0 |
| 0 | 0 | 0 | 1 | 0 | 0 | 0 | 1 |
| 0 | 0 | 1 | 0 | 0 | 0 | 1 | 1 |
| 0 | 0 | 1 | 1 | 0 | 0 | 1 | 0 |
| 0 | 1 | 0 | 0 | 0 | 1 | 1 | 0 |
| 0 | 1 | 0 | 1 | 0 | 1 | 1 | 1 |
| 0 | 1 | 1 | 0 | 0 | 1 | 0 | 1 |
| 0 | 1 | 1 | 1 | 0 | 1 | 0 | 0 |
| 1 | 0 | 0 | 0 | 1 | 1 | 0 | 0 |
| 1 | 0 | 0 | 0 | 1 | 1 | 0 | 1 |

Q5.11  Write a function which will determine the truth table for a 3-input exclusive-OR gate.

Q5.12  Modify program 5.17 so that invalid values of components and the frequency value cannot be entered. The valid ranges of values are given next.

| Parameter | Minimum | Maximum |
|---|---|---|
| R | 0 Ω | 1 MΩ |
| C | 1 pF | 100 mF |
| L | 0 H | 100 mH |
| f | 1 Hz | 10 GHz |

Q5.13  Rewrite program 5.17 so that the characteristic impedance is given as a magnitude and a phase angle. The angle of the impedance (in radians) can be found by:

$$\langle Z \rangle = \frac{1}{2} \cdot \left[ \tan^{-1}\left[ \frac{\omega L}{R} \right] - \tan^{-1}\left[ \frac{\omega C}{G} \right] \right]$$

Q5.14  Write a macro using #define which will determine the larger of two integer numbers. For example

```
#define _max(_A,_B)  ......
```

Check the macro by calling it from a program. For example

```
printf("Maximum is %d",_max(c,d) );
```

When this function has been tested put it into a header file (e.g. *main.h*) and include this file in the program.

Q5.15  Repeat Q5.14 for a minimum function.

# CHAPTER 6

# Pointers

If a company were to send a form to a person and they neglected to inform the person of the correct return address then it will not be possible for the recipient to send back the modified form (unless the person already knows the address). Variables sent to functions operate in a similar manner. If the function does not know where a variable *lives* (its address in memory) then the function cannot change its contents.

A program uses data which is stored by variables. These are assigned to a unique space in memory, the number of bytes they use depends on their data type. For example, a char uses 1 byte, an int will typically take 2 or 4 bytes, and a float, typically, 4 or 8 bytes. Each memory location contains one byte and has a unique address associated with it (i.e. its binary address). This address is normally specified as a hexadecimal value as this can be easily converted to the actual binary address. The memory map in Figure 6.1 shows how three variables value1, value2 and ch could be allocated in memory. This diagram assumes that a float uses 4 bytes, and an int 2 bytes. The compiler, in this case, has allocated value1 from addresses 100h to 103h, value2 at 104h and 105h, and ch is allocated to 106h. The start of the variable's address in memory can be described as a memory pointer to the variable. A pointer variable is used to store a memory address.

Variables sent to a function can have their contents changed by passing a pointer in the argument list. This method involves sending a memory *address* rather than a copy of the variable's value. A preceding ampersand (&) specifies a pointer. This can be thought of as representing *the address of*:

&variable_name    {address of variable_name}

A pointer to a variable will store the address to the first byte of the area allocated to the variable. An asterisk (*) preceding a pointer is used to access the contents of the location pointed to. The number of bytes accessed will depend on the data type of the pointer. The * operator can be thought of representing *at address*:

*ptr   {value stored at address specified by ptr}

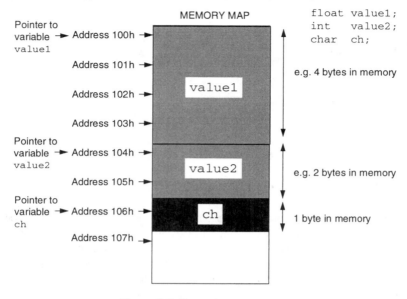

**Figure 6.1:** Example memory map

Figure 6.2 shows an example memory map. A variable `resistance_1` has the value of `310.0` and is stored at a memory location starting at `107h`. If the data type is a short integer then it will take up 2 bytes in memory (i.e. `107h` and `108h`), if it is a float it may take up 4 bytes in memory (i.e. `107h` to `110h`). The memory map also shows that a pointer `ptr` points to memory location `102h`. The value stored at this location is 15; `*ptr` accesses its contents. The declaration of the pointer defines the data type of the pointer and thus the number of bytes used to store the value at the address pointed to by the pointer.

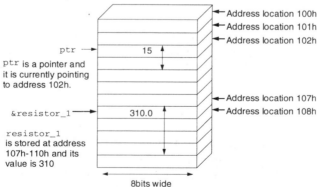

**Figure 6.2:** Example memory map

## 6.1 Pointers with functions

In the previous chapter it was shown that a single value is passed out of a function through the function header. In order pass to values out through the argument list the address of the variable is passed; that is referred to as *'call by reference'*. To declare a pointer the data type is specified and the pointer name is preceded by an asterisk. The following is the general format.

```
type_def *ptr_name;
```

In this case `ptr_name` is the name of the pointer. The contents of the variable at this address can be accessed using `*ptr_name`. When a function is to modify a variable then a pointer to its address is sent. For example, if the variable to be modified is `value` then the argument passed is `&value`.

Program 6.1 shows an example of a function that swaps the contents of two variables (a and b). Figure 6.3 shows how the compiler checks the parameters passed to the function and the return type. The function prototype, in this case, specifies that the parameters sent are pointers to integer values and the return type is `void`. The compiler checks that the parameters sent to the function are integer pointers and that nothing is assigned to the return value from the function.

**Program 6.1**
```c
/*    prog6_1.c     */
#include <stdio.h>


void    swap(int *ptr1,int *ptr2);


int     main(void)
{
int     a,b;

   a=5; b=6;
   swap(&a,&b); /* send addresses of a and b */
   printf("a= %d b = %d \n",a,b);
   return(0);
}


void    swap(int *ptr1,int *ptr2)
{
   /* ptr1 and ptr2 are pointers (addresses). */
int     temp;

   temp = *ptr1;
   *ptr1 = *ptr2;
   *ptr2 = temp;

}
```

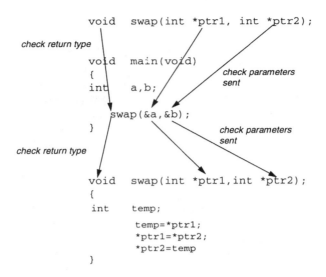

**Figure 6.3:** Compiler checking for program 6.1

An example of a standard C function that uses call by reference is `scanf()` where a pointer is passed for each variable. This allows the function to change its contents.

## 6.2  Examples

### 6.2.1  Quadratic equations

Program 6.2 determines the roots of a quadratic equation. The function `get_values()` gets variables a, b and c; these variables are passed as pointers. Within the `get_values()` function the `scanf()` do not require a preceding ampersand; the variable arguments are already pointers.

The function to determine the root(s) of a quadratic equation is `quadratic_equ()`. This returns the root type (e.g. singular, real or complex) through the function header and passes the equation root(s) through the argument list using pointers. The root type returned can be referred to as a return flag; this flag is set up using an `enum` declaration. There are three possible states for this: SINGULAR (a value of 0), REAL_ROOTS (a value of 1) and COMPLEX_ROOTS (a value of 2). The program then uses the flag to determine how the root(s) are to be displayed. If the root is singular then `print_results()` prints a single value of `root1`; else, if the roots are real, then two values `root1` and `root2` are printed; and if the roots are complex the function will print the roots in the form `root1 +/-j root2`.

Figure 6.4 gives a basic structure chart of this program. The return flag from the `quadratic_equ()` function is represented by an arrow with a circle on the end.

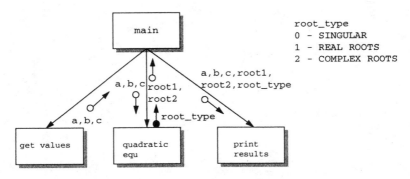

**Figure 6.4:** Structure chart for program 6.2

📄 **Program 6.2**

```
/*    prog6_2.c                          */
#include <stdio.h>
#include <math.h>d
enum    {SINGULAR, REAL_ROOTS,COMPLEX_ROOTS } quad_roots;

void    get_values(float *ain,float *bin,float *cin);
int     quadratic_equ(float a,float b,float c, float *r1,float *r2);
void    print_results(int r_type,float a,float b,float c, float r1,
            float r2);

int     main(void)
{
float   a,b,c,root1,root2;
int     root_type;

   get_values(&a,&b,&c);
   root_type=quadratic_equ(a,b,c,&root1,&root2);
   print_results(root_type,a,b,c,root1,root2);
   return(0);
}

void    get_values(float *ain,float *bin,float *cin)
{
   printf("Enter a, b and c >>");
   scanf("%f %f %f",ain,bin,cin); /*ain,bin and cin are pointers*/
}

int     quadratic_equ(float a,float b,float c, float *r1,float *r2)
{
   if (a==0)
   {
      *r1=-c/b;
      return(SINGULAR);
   }
   else if ((b*b)>(4*a*c))
   {
      *r1=(-b+sqrt(b*b-4*a*c))/(2*a);
      *r2=(-b-sqrt(b*b-4*a*c))/(2*a);
      return(REAL_ROOTS);
   }
```

```
   else if ((b*b)<(4*a*c))
   {
      *r1=-b/(2*a);
      *r2=sqrt(4*a*c-b*b)/(2*a);
      return(COMPLEX_ROOTS);
   }
   else
   {
      *r1=-b/(2*a);
      return(SINGULAR);
   }
}

void   print_results(int r_type,float a,float b,float c,
               float r1,float r2)
{
   printf("Quadratic equation %8.3f x^2 + %8.3f x +
%8.3f\n",a,b,c);
   if (r_type==SINGULAR)
      printf("Singular root of %8.3f\n",r1);
   else if (r_type==REAL_ROOTS)
      printf("Real roots of %8.3f and %8.3f\n",r1,r2);
   else
      printf("Complex root of %8.3f +/-j %8.3f\n",r1,r2);
}
```

Test run 6.1 shows tests for each of the root types.

---

🖥 **Test run 6.1**
```
Enter a, b and c >>  2 1 1

Quadratic equation     2.000 x^2 +    1.000 x +    1.000
Complex root of   -0.250 +/-j     0.661

Enter a, b and c >>  1 -2 -3

Quadratic equation     1.000 x^2 +   -2.000 x +   -3.000
Real roots of     3.000 and   -1.000

Enter a, b and c >>  1 2 1

Quadratic equation     1.000 x^2 +    2.000 x +    1.000
Singular root of    -1.000
```

---

### 6.2.2  Equivalent parallel resistance

Program 6.3 uses pointers to determine the equivalent parallel resistance of two resistors. A basic structure chart, given in Figure 6.5, shows that get_values() returns the variables R1 and R2; in order to change their values they are sent as pointers. It also shows that the variables sent to calc_parallel_res() are R1, R2 and R_equ is returned. Variables R1, R2 and R_equ are then passed into print_results().

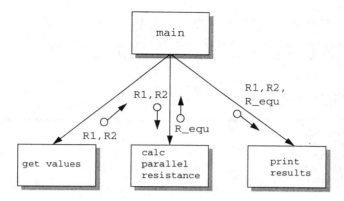

**Figure 6.5:** Structure chart for program 6.3

📖 **Program 6.3**

```
/*    prog6_3.c    */

#include <stdio.h>

void    get_values(float *r1,float *r2);
void    get_parallel_res(float r1,float r2,float *r_e);
void    print_results(float r1,float r2,float r_e);

int     main(void)
{
float   R1,R2,R_equ;

   get_values(&R1,&R2);
   get_parallel_res(R1,R2,&R_equ);
   print_results(R1,R2,R_equ);
   return(0);
}

void    get_values(float *r1,float *r2)
{
   do
   {
      printf("Enter R1 >>");
      scanf("%f",r1); /*r1 is already a pointer no need for &r1 */
      if (*r1<0) puts("INVALID: re-enter");
   } while (*r1<0);

   do
   {
      printf("Enter R2 >>");
      scanf("%f",r2);
      if (*r2<0) puts("INVALID: re-enter");
   } while (*r2<0);
}
void    get_parallel_res(float r1,float r2,float *r_e)
{
   *r_e=1/(1/r1+1/r2);
}
```

```
void    print_results(float r1,float r2,float r_e)
{
   printf("Parallel resistors %8.3f and %8.3f ohm\n",r1,r2);
   printf("Equivalent resistance is %8.3f ohm\n",r_e);
}
```

Test run 6.2 shows a sample run.

🖳 **Test run 6.2**
```
Enter R1 ·>> 1000
Enter R2 >> 800
Parallel resistors 1000.000 and  800.000 ohm
Equivalent resistance is  444.444 ohm
```

### 6.2.3 Impedance of an RL circuit

Program 6.4 calculates the input impedance of an RL series circuit for a sweep of frequencies.

📄 **Program 6.4**
```
/* prog6_4.c    */
#include <stdio.h>
#include <math.h>

#define   PI    3.14159

void    get_values(float *fe,int *fn,float *r,float *l);
void    calc_impedance_XL(float f,float r,float l,float *zmag,
                          float *zang);

int     main(void)
{
float   f,fend,R,L,Zmag,Zangle;
int     fsteps;

   get_values(&fend,&fsteps,&R,&L);

   for (f=0;f<fend;f+=fend/fsteps)
   {
      calc_impedance_XL(f,R,L,&Zmag,&Zangle);
      printf("%8.2f %8.3f %8.3f\n",f,Zmag,Zangle);
   }
   printf("Press ENTER to continue >>");
   getchar();
   return(0);
}

void    get_values(float *fe,int *fn,float *r,float *l)
{
   printf("Enter end frequency >>");
   scanf("%f",fe);
   printf("Enter number of frequency steps >>");
   scanf("%d",fn);
   printf("Enter resistance >>");
```

```
    scanf("%f",r);
    printf("Enter inductance >>");
    scanf("%f",l);
}

void   calc_impedance_XL(float f,float r,float l,float *zmag,
                              float *zang)
{
float  Xl;

    Xl=2*PI*f*l;
    *zmag=sqrt( (Xl*Xl)+(r*r));
    *zang=atan(Xl/r);
}
```

Test run 6.3 shows a sample run.

**Test run 6.3**
```
Program to determine impedance of an RL circuit
Enter fmax and number of freq steps >> 1e6 20
Enter R and L >> 1000 1e-3
```

| Frequency | Impedance Magnitude | Angle |
|---|---|---|
| 0.00 | 1000.00 | 0.00 |
| 50000.00 | 1048.19 | 17.44 |
| 100000.00 | 1181.01 | 32.14 |
| 150000.00 | 1374.14 | 43.30 |
| 200000.00 | 1605.97 | 51.49 |
| 250000.00 | 1862.10 | 57.52 |
| 300000.00 | 2133.79 | 62.05 |
| 350000.00 | 2415.80 | 65.55 |
| 400000.00 | 2704.91 | 68.30 |
| 450000.00 | 2999.06 | 70.52 |
| 500000.00 | 3296.91 | 72.34 |
| 550000.00 | 3597.53 | 73.86 |
| 600000.00 | 3900.29 | 75.14 |
| 650000.00 | 4204.72 | 76.24 |
| 700000.00 | 4510.48 | 77.19 |
| 750000.00 | 4817.32 | 78.02 |
| 800000.00 | 5125.06 | 78.75 |
| 850000.00 | 5433.52 | 79.39 |
| 900000.00 | 5742.61 | 79.97 |
| 950000.00 | 6052.21 | 80.49 |
```
Press any key to continue >>>
```

### 6.2.4 Memory viewer

Program 6.5 displays the contents of the RAM while the program is being executed. Each address in memory contains one byte, so that a `char` pointer is set up to point to each location; the declaration `char *ptr` is used for this purpose. This pointer does not have a memory allocated to it when it is declared, so that at the start of the program it is set to the first memory location `0x00` (`ptr=0x00`).

After the contents of each memory location have been read, the pointer is incremented to the next address in memory. As the declaration is a character pointer it will be incremented by one byte (this will be discussed in more detail in the next chapter).

The program reads 64 bytes from memory and displays these as ASCII characters. It then waits for the user to enter the character. If the entered character is an 'x' then the program will quit; any other character causes the program to continue displaying the memory contents. Some special control characters for line-feeds, new lines, form-feed, etc., are non-printing. For this purpose some of these characters are displayed with a '?'. Macros such as CR (carriage return) , VT (vertical tab) and BS (backspace), etc., are used to define these characters.

**Program 6.5**

```
/* prog6_5.c    */
#include <stdio.h>
#define   BELL        7
#define   BS          8
#define   HT          9
#define   LF          10
#define   VT          11
#define   FF          12
#define   CR          13
int     main(void)
{
char    *ptr,ch=NULL;
int     i;

    puts("Memory viewer program Ver 1.00");
    puts("Enter an 'x' to exit the program");
    ptr=0x00;

    do
    {
        printf("%4p >> ",ptr); /* display memory pointer     */
        for (i=0;i<64;i++)
        {
            if ((*ptr!=BELL) && (*ptr!=CR) && (*ptr!=VT) &&
                    (*ptr!=BS) && (*ptr!=FF) && (*ptr!=LF))
                putchar(*ptr);
            else putchar('?'); /* display control character   */

            ptr++;      /* move one byte in memory   */
        }
        printf("\n");
        ch=getchar();

    } while (ch!='x'); /* enter an 'x' to exit */
    return(0);
}
```

Program 6.6 contains several enhancements. It displays 24 lines of memory contents before the user is prompted to continue (the number of lines is set up by the constant SCREEN_SIZE and the number of characters on a single line by COLUMN_SIZE).

## Program 6.6

```c
/* prog6_6.c    */
#include <stdio.h>
#include <ctype.h> /* required for tolower() function    */

#define    BELL            7
#define    BS              8
#define    HT              9
#define    LF              10
#define    VT              11
#define    FF              12
#define    CR              13
#define    SCREEN_SIZE     24
#define    COLUMN_SIZE     64

int    main(void)
{
char    *ptr,ch=NULL; /* initialise ch as a NULL character */
int     i,j;
  puts("Memory viewer program Ver 1.01");
  ptr=0;

  do
  {
    for (j=0;j<SCREEN_SIZE;j++)
    {
      printf("%4p >> ",ptr);

      for (i=0;i<COLUMN_SIZE;i++)
      {

          if ((*ptr!=BELL) && (*ptr!=CR) && (*ptr!=VT)
                && (*ptr!=BS) && (*ptr!=FF) && (*ptr!=LF))
            putchar(*ptr);
          else {
            putchar('?');
          }

          ptr++;
      }

      printf("\n");
    }

    printf("Do you wish to continue (y/n) >> ");
    ch=tolower(getchar());

  } while (ch=='y');

  return(0);

}
```

Figure 6.6 shows a sample run taken from an IBM compatible Personal Computer (PC). The '?' character has replaced the special control characters, such as line-feed, horizontal tab, etc.

```
000 >>     Turbo-C - Copyright (c) 1988 Borland Intl. Null pointer assi
0040 >> gnment??Divide error??Abnormal program termination??%@|&|#p )!#@
0080 >> Cs ?@ ; .?o@ëz( #z# ...
00C0 >>
0100 >>
0140 >>                        %4p >>  ? Do you wish to continue (y/n) >>
0180 >>
01C0 >>
0200 >>
0240 >>
0280 >>
02C0 >>
0300 >>
0340 >>
0380 >>
03C0 >>
0400 >>
0440 >>
0480 >>                        @ print scanf : floating point formats not l
04C0 >> inked?? ? (null) 0123456789ABCDEF
0500 >>
0540 >>
0580 >>                                    (?    y@  COMSPEC=C:\C
05C0 >> OMMAND.COM CPAV=C:\PCTOOLS\DATA\CPAV.INI PCTOOLS=C:\PCTOOLS\DATA
Do you wish to continue (y/n) >>
```

**Figure 6.6:** Test run for program 6.6

### 6.2.5  Accessing PC video text memory

***Programs in this section will only work on a PC-based system.***

A PC uses a specific area of memory to store all the characters which appear on the screen. For a colour monitor this starts at the address B800:0000. Each character has a text attribute associated with it. This attribute defines the text foreground and background colours, and whether it is to blink or not (to flash on and off). A typical monitor has 80 columns and 25 rows. Thus, a total of 4000 bytes are used to store all the characters (80*25 characters and 80*25 attributes). Figure 6.7 shows how the characters and attributes are arranged in memory. Attribute bit definitions are given in Figure 6.8.

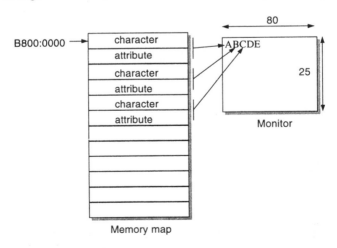

**Figure 6.7:** Video text memory map

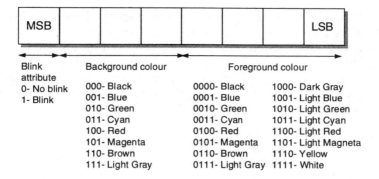

**Figure 6.8:** Character attributes

In program 6.7 the user is prompted for a text string. The characters in this string are then written to display memory starting at the top left position on the screen. The attribute the characters are given is 0x21 (0 010 0001b). This gives a foreground colour of blue, a background colour of green and no blink. After each character and attribute has been written to memory the pointer is incremented by 2 to move onto the next character in memory. The strlen() function determines the number of characters in the string (this will be covered in more detail in Chapter 8).

The PC defaults to a 16-bit address pointer (in most cases). In order to access the upper reaches of the PC memory a 32-bit address pointer is required. The pointer is then declared as a far pointer. This is achieved by declaring it as char far *ptr.

📄 **Program 6.7**

```c
/* prog6_7.c    */
#include <stdio.h>
#include <string.h>
int  main(void)
{
char far  *ptr;
char       str[BUFSIZ];
int        i;

   ptr=(char far *)0xb8000000; /* memory address B800:0000 */

   printf("\nEnter string for direct memory access >>");
   gets(str);

   for (i=0;i<strlen(str);i++)
   {
      *ptr=str[i];      /* write character                        */
      *(ptr+1)=0x21;    /* character attribute 0 010 0001         */
      /* B XXX YYYY B - Blink, XXX - B/G Colour YYYY - F/G Colour*/
      /* Colour 0-Black, 1 Blue, 2 Green, etc.                  */
      ptr+=2;
   }
   puts("");
   return(0);
}
```

When this program is run the entered string should appear at the top left-hand corner of the screen. The character colour is blue on a green background.

Program 6.8 fills the text video memory with a single character. The character used in this case is 'X' and the text attribute is 0x70 (0  111  0000b). This gives a white background colour and a black text colour. The number of rows and columns is set up with the macros COLUMNS and ROWS. A sample run is given in test run 6.4.

**Program 6.8**

```
/* prog6_8.c    */
#define   COLUMNS   80
#define   ROWS      25

#include <stdio.h>

int  main(void)
{
char far *ptr;
int      i;

    ptr=(char far *)0xb8000000; /* memory address B800:0000 */

    for (i=0;i<COLUMNS*ROWS;i++)
    {
        *ptr='X';              /* fill with an 'X'                        */
        *(ptr+1)=0x70;         /* 0 111 0000                              */
        ptr+=2;                /* move onto next character in memory      */
    }
    getchar();
    puts("");
    return(0);
}
```

**Test run 6.4**

```
XXXXXXXXXXXXXXXXXXXXXXXXXXXXXXXXXXXXXXXXXXXXXXXXXXXXXXXXXXXXXXXXXXXXXXXXXXXXXXXXXX
XXXXXXXXXXXXXXXXXXXXXXXXXXXXXXXXXXXXXXXXXXXXXXXXXXXXXXXXXXXXXXXXXXXXXXXXXXXXXXXXXX
XXXXXXXXXXXXXXXXXXXXXXXXXXXXXXXXXXXXXXXXXXXXXXXXXXXXXXXXXXXXXXXXXXXXXXXXXXXXXXXXXX
XXXXXXXXXXXXXXXXXXXXXXXXXXXXXXXXXXXXXXXXXXXXXXXXXXXXXXXXXXXXXXXXXXXXXXXXXXXXXXXXXX
XXXXXXXXXXXXXXXXXXXXXXXXXXXXXXXXXXXXXXXXXXXXXXXXXXXXXXXXXXXXXXXXXXXXXXXXXXXXXXXXXX
XXXXXXXXXXXXXXXXXXXXXXXXXXXXXXXXXXXXXXXXXXXXXXXXXXXXXXXXXXXXXXXXXXXXXXXXXXXXXXXXXX
XXXXXXXXXXXXXXXXXXXXXXXXXXXXXXXXXXXXXXXXXXXXXXXXXXXXXXXXXXXXXXXXXXXXXXXXXXXXXXXXXX
XXXXXXXXXXXXXXXXXXXXXXXXXXXXXXXXXXXXXXXXXXXXXXXXXXXXXXXXXXXXXXXXXXXXXXXXXXXXXXXXXX
XXXXXXXXXXXXXXXXXXXXXXXXXXXXXXXXXXXXXXXXXXXXXXXXXXXXXXXXXXXXXXXXXXXXXXXXXXXXXXXXXX
XXXXXXXXXXXXXXXXXXXXXXXXXXXXXXXXXXXXXXXXXXXXXXXXXXXXXXXXXXXXXXXXXXXXXXXXXXXXXXXXXX
XXXXXXXXXXXXXXXXXXXXXXXXXXXXXXXXXXXXXXXXXXXXXXXXXXXXXXXXXXXXXXXXXXXXXXXXXXXXXXXXXX
XXXXXXXXXXXXXXXXXXXXXXXXXXXXXXXXXXXXXXXXXXXXXXXXXXXXXXXXXXXXXXXXXXXXXXXXXXXXXXXXXX
XXXXXXXXXXXXXXXXXXXXXXXXXXXXXXXXXXXXXXXXXXXXXXXXXXXXXXXXXXXXXXXXXXXXXXXXXXXXXXXXXX
XXXXXXXXXXXXXXXXXXXXXXXXXXXXXXXXXXXXXXXXXXXXXXXXXXXXXXXXXXXXXXXXXXXXXXXXXXXXXXXXXX
XXXXXXXXXXXXXXXXXXXXXXXXXXXXXXXXXXXXXXXXXXXXXXXXXXXXXXXXXXXXXXXXXXXXXXXXXXXXXXXXXX
XXXXXXXXXXXXXXXXXXXXXXXXXXXXXXXXXXXXXXXXXXXXXXXXXXXXXXXXXXXXXXXXXXXXXXXXXXXXXXXXXX
XXXXXXXXXXXXXXXXXXXXXXXXXXXXXXXXXXXXXXXXXXXXXXXXXXXXXXXXXXXXXXXXXXXXXXXXXXXXXXXXXX
XXXXXXXXXXXXXXXXXXXXXXXXXXXXXXXXXXXXXXXXXXXXXXXXXXXXXXXXXXXXXXXXXXXXXXXXXXXXXXXXXX
XXXXXXXXXXXXXXXXXXXXXXXXXXXXXXXXXXXXXXXXXXXXXXXXXXXXXXXXXXXXXXXXXXXXXXXXXXXXXXXXXX
XXXXXXXXXXXXXXXXXXXXXXXXXXXXXXXXXXXXXXXXXXXXXXXXXXXXXXXXXXXXXXXXXXXXXXXXXXXXXXXXXX
XXXXXXXXXXXXXXXXXXXXXXXXXXXXXXXXXXXXXXXXXXXXXXXXXXXXXXXXXXXXXXXXXXXXXXXXXXXXXXXXXX
XXXXXXXXXXXXXXXXXXXXXXXXXXXXXXXXXXXXXXXXXXXXXXXXXXXXXXXXXXXXXXXXXXXXXXXXXXXXXXXXXX
XXXXXXXXXXXXXXXXXXXXXXXXXXXXXXXXXXXXXXXXXXXXXXXXXXXXXXXXXXXXXXXXXXXXXXXXXXXXXXXXXX
XXXXXXXXXXXXXXXXXXXXXXXXXXXXXXXXXXXXXXXXXXXXXXXXXXXXXXXXXXXXXXXXXXXXXXXXXXXXXXXXXX
XXXXXXXXXXXXXXXXXXXXXXXXXXXXXXXXXXXXXXXXXXXXXXXXXXXXXXXXXXXXXXXXXXXXXXXXXXXXXXXXXX
```

## 6.3 Tutorial

Q6.1   Write a program which determines the impedance, for an entered frequency range, for the following circuits:

    (a)   series RC circuit;
    (b)   parallel RC circuit;
    (c)   parallel RL circuit.

Figure 6.9 gives a basic structure chart for the series RC circuit. Refer to program 6.4.

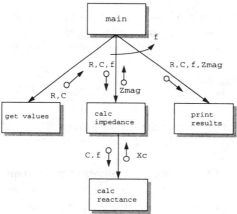

**Figure 6.9:** Structure chart for Q6.1

Q.6.2   Repeat Q6.1, but determine the magnitude and the phase angle of the circuit. Figure 6.10 gives a top-level structure chart for this program.

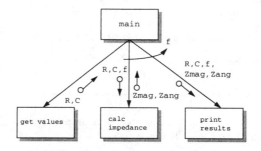

**Figure 6.10:** Structure chart for Q6.2

Q6.3   Write a program that determines the resistance values for the simple base resistor biased transistor circuit given in Q4.11. Figure 6.10 gives a structure chart for this program.

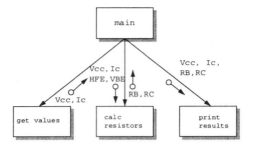

**Figure 6.11:** Structure chart for Q6.3

Q6.4    Modify the following programs from Chapter 5 to create an improved structure. Typically, get_values() and print_results() functions can be added. Also modify these programs so that an invalid zero frequency cannot be entered.

    (a)    program 5.17;
    (b)    program 5.14.

Q6.5    Modify program 6.8 so that the user is prompted for the starting address of the memory viewer.

**If you have a PC complete the following tutorial questions:**

Q6.6    Write a program which fills the text screen with a single character 'z' with a white background and a blue foreground colour using direct video access.

Q6.7    Write a program which fills a screen with an entered character and entered background and foreground colours. A sample run is given in test run 6.5.

---
⌨ **Test run 6.5**
```
Enter a character to be displayed >> c
Select foreground colour
(0)- BLACK (1)- BLUE (2)- GREEN (3)- CYAN (4)- RED
>> 4
Select background colour
(0)- BLACK (1)- BLUE (2)- GREEN (3)- CYAN (4)- RED
>> 3
```
---

Q6.8    The ROM BIOS date on a PC is stored at an address starting at F000:FFF5 (0xF000FFF5) and uses 8 bytes. Write a program which reads this date. A sample run is shown in test run 6.6 (in this case the 8 characters read are 11/11/92.

---
⌨ **Test run 6.6**
```
BIOS RAM Date is 11/11/92
```
---

# CHAPTER 7

# Arrays

An array stores more than one value, of a common data type, under a collective name. Each value has a unique slot and is referenced using an indexing technique. Figure 7.1 shows a circuit with 5 resistors, which could be declared with a program with 5 simple float declarations. If these resistor variables were required to be passed into a function all 5 would have to be passed through the parameter list. A neater method uses arrays to store all of the values under a common name (in this case R). Thus a single array variable can then be passed into any function that uses it.

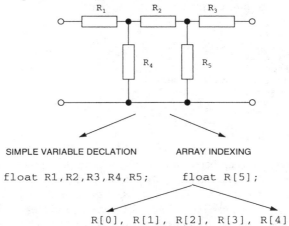

**Figure 7.1:** Simple variables against array indexing

The declaration of an array specifies the data type, the array name and the number of elements in the array in brackets ([ ]). The following gives the standard format for an array declaration.

```
data_type array_name[size];
```

Figure 7.2 shows that the first element of the array is indexed 0 and the last element as size-1. The compiler allocates memory for the first element array_name[0] to the last array element array_name[size-1]. The number of bytes allocated in memory will be the number of elements in the array multiplied by the number of bytes used to store the data type of the array.

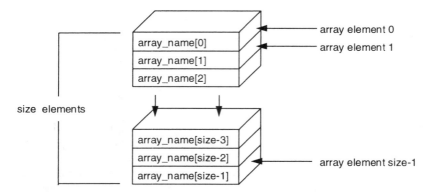

**Figure 7.2:** Array elements

The following gives some example array declarations.

```
int circuit[10];
     /* allocates space for circuit[0]    */
     /* to circuit[9]                      */
float impedance[50];
     /* allocates for impedance[0] to      */
     /* impedance[49]                      */
```

## 7.1 Pointers and arrays

There is a strong relationship between pointers and arrays. A pointer variable stores a memory address which can be modified, whereas an array name stores a fixed address, set to the first element in the array. The address of the first element of an array named arrname is thus &arrname[0]. Table 7.1 shows examples of how arrays and pointers use different indexing notations and how it is possible to interchange them.

**Table 7.1:** Relationship between arrays and pointers

| Using arrays | Using pointers |
|---|---|
| float arr[10]; | float *arr; |
| | arr=(float *) malloc(10*sizeof(float)); |
| arr[0] | *(arr) |
| arr[1] | *(arr+1) |
| arr[2] | *(arr+2) |
| arr[9] | *(arr+9) |

Figure 7.3 shows two array declarations for `arrname`. Each has five elements; the first is `arrname[0]` and the last `arrname[4]`. The number of bytes allocated to each element depends on the data type declaration. A `char` array uses one byte for each element, whereas an `int` array will typically take 2 or 4 bytes. The array name `arrname` is set to the address of the first element of the array. Each element within the array is referenced with respect to this address.

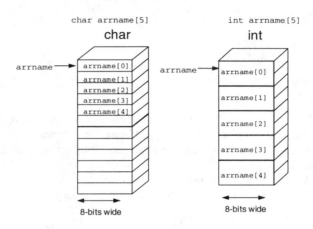

**Figure 7.3:** Array elements

Table 7.2 gives some examples of array and pointer statements.

**Table 7.2:** Examples of array and pointer statements

| Statements | Description |
|---|---|
| `int tmp[100];` | declare an array named `tmp` with 100 elements |
| `tmp[1]=5;` | assign 5 to the second element of array `tmp` |
| `*(tmp+1)=5;` | equivalent to previous statement |
| `ptr=&tmp[2];` | get address of third element |

## 7.2 Passing arrays to functions

At compilation the compiler reserves enough space for all elements in an array and initializes the array name to the start of it. In order for a function to modify the array the base address is passed through the parameter list. The function itself does not know the maximum number of elements in the array; unless a parameter relating to the maximum number of elements in the array is also passed. It is thus possible to run off the end of an array and access memory not allocated to the array.

The notation used to signify that an array is being passed in a function is square brackets (this signifies that it is a fixed address and not a pointer variable). The following gives an example of array passing.

```
float maximum(int number_of_elements,float arrayname[])
{
float max;
/* number_of_elements maximum number of elements in the array*/
/* this function determines maximum value in an    array      */

   max=arrayname[0];
   for (i=1;i<number_of_elements;i++)
     if (max<arrayname[i]) max=arrayname[i];
   return(max);
}
```

Program 7.1 is a 3-point running average program. This type of program has a low-pass filter response and can filter data samples. Figure 7.4 illustrates how the output is a function of the average of three elements in the input array; this is achieved by generating a running average.

The first and last values of the processed array will take on the same values as the input array as there are not three values over which to take an average.

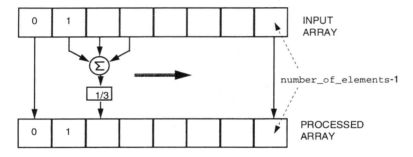

**Figure 7.4:** Array elements

📄 **Program 7.1**
```
/* prog7_1.c          */
#include <stdio.h>

#define    MAX  150   /* maximum values in the array */
#define    TRUE 1
#define    FALSE  0

void    filter(int n,float array_in[],float array_out[]);
void    get_values(int *n,float array[]);
void    print_values(int n,float array_in[],float array_out[]);

int     main(void)
{
float   input[MAX],output[MAX];/*input values, processed values */
```

```
int     nvalues;

    get_values(&nvalues,input);
    filter(nvalues,input,output);
    print_values(nvalues,input,output);
    return(0);
}


void    filter(int n,float array_in[],float array_out[])
{
int     i;
    array_out[0]=array_in[0];
    array_out[n-1]=array_in[n-1];

    for (i=1;i<n-1;i++)
       array_out[i]=(array_in[i-1]+array_in[i]+array_in[i+1])/3;
}


void    get_values(int *n,float array[])
/* *n is the number of elements in the array */
{
int     i,rtn,okay;

    do
    {
       printf("Enter number of values to be processed >>");
       rtn=scanf("%d",n);
       if ((rtn!=1) || (*n<0) || (*n>MAX))
       {
          printf("Max elements are %d, re-enter\n",MAX);
          okay=FALSE;
       }
       else okay=TRUE;
    } while (!okay);

    for (i=0;i<*n;i++)
    {
       puts("Enter value >> ");
       scanf("%f",&array[i]);
    }
}

void    print_values(int n,float array_in[],float array_out[])
{
int     i;
    printf("Input     Output\n");
    for (i=0;i<n;i++)
       printf(" %6.3f %6.3f \n",array_in[i],array_out[i]);
}
```

Test run 7.1 shows a sample run with 10 entered values.

🖥 **Test run 7.1**

```
Enter number of values to be processed >> 10
Enter value >> 3
Enter value >> -2
Enter value >> 4
Enter value >> 10
Enter value >> 3
Enter value >> 2
Enter value >> 1
Enter value >> 0
Enter value >> 19
Enter value >> 14
Input     Output
   3.000    3.000
  -2.000    1.667
   4.000    4.000
  10.000    5.667
   3.000    5.000
   2.000    2.000
   1.000    1.000
   0.000    6.667
  19.000   11.000
  14.000   14.000
```

Program 7.2 is an example of a sorting program where an array is passed to the sort() function, which then orders the values from smallest to largest. The algorithm initially checks the first value in an array with all the other values. If the value in the first position is greater than the sampled array value then the two values are swapped.

Figure 7.5 shows an example of how a 6-element array can be sorted to determine the smallest value. In the first iteration the value of 20 is compared with 22. Since 20 is smaller than 22 the values are not swapped. Next, the value of 20 is compared with 12 (the third element), as this is smaller the values are swapped. This now makes 12 the first element. This continues until the last value (15) is tested. At the end of these iterations the smallest value (3) will be the first element in the array. As the first element now contains the smallest value the operation can now continue onto the second element. This is tested against the third, fourth, fifth and sixth elements and so on. The number of iterations required to complete this process will therefore be 15 (5+4+3+2+1).

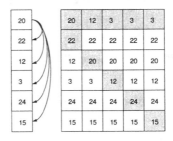

**Figure 7.5:** Array elements

📄 **Program 7.2**

```c
/* prog7_2.c          */
#include <stdio.h>

#define   MAX     150
#define   TRUE    1
#define   FALSE   0

void    get_values(int *n,float array[]);
void    print_values(int n,float array_in[]);
void    sort(int n,float input[]);
void    order(float *val1,float *val2);

int     main(void)
{
float   array[MAX];
int     nvalues;

   get_values(&nvalues,array);
   sort(nvalues,array);
   print_values(nvalues,array);
   return(0);
}

void    get_values(int *n,float array[])
/* *n stores the number of value in the array */
{
int     i,rtn,okay;

   do
   {
      printf("Enter number of values to be processed >>");
      rtn=scanf("%d",n);
      if ((rtn!=1) || (*n<0) || (*n>MAX))
      {
         printf("Max elements is %d, re-enter\n",MAX);
         okay=FALSE;
      }
      else okay=TRUE;
   } while (!okay);

   for (i=0;i<*n;i++)
   {
      printf("Enter value >>");
      scanf("%f",&array[i]);
   }
}

void    print_values(int n,float array_in[])
{
int     i;

   printf("Ordered values\n");
   for (i=0;i<n;i++)
      printf("%8.3f ",array_in[i]);
}
```

```
void    sort(int n,float input[])
/* order array input to give smallest to largest */
{
int     i,j;

   for (i=0;i<n-1;i++)
     for (j=n-1;i<j;j--)
        order(&input[i],&input[j]);
}

void    order(float *val1,float *val2)
/* val1 is the smallest */
{
float   temp;

   if (*val1 > *val2)
   {
      temp = *val1;
      *val1 = *val2;
      *val2 = temp;
   }
}
```

Test run 7.2 shows a sample run with 10 entered values.

---

🖥  **Test run 7.2**
```
Enter number of values be entered >> 10
Enter value >> 3
Enter value >> -2
Enter value >> 4
Enter value >> 10
Enter value >> 3
Enter value >> 2
Enter value >> 1
Enter value >> 0
Enter value >> 19
Enter value >> 14
Ordered values
   -2.000     0.000    1.000     2.000     3.000     3.000
4.000    10.000   14.000    19.000
```

---

## 7.3  Array initialization

The initialization of an array with values (or characters) is defined between a set of braces ({ }). The following gives the standard format for initializing an array:

```
type arrname[nvalues]={val_0,val_1,  .... val_n-1};
```

Program 7.3 determines the nearest preferred resistor value in the range 10 to 100 Ω. An initialized array pref_values[] contains normalized preferred values of 10, 12, 15, 18, 22, 27, 33, 39, 47, 56, 68, 82 and 100 Ω.

The find_nearest_pref() function determines the nearest preferred value. Its operation uses the difference between the entered value and an index value in the preferred value array. If the difference is less than the difference between the previous nearest value and the entered value then the current preferred value will take on the current indexed array value. Figure 7.6 shows a basic structure chart for this program.

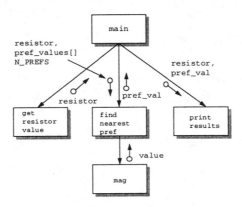

**Figure 7.6:** Structure chart for program 7.3

📄 **Program 7.3**

```c
/* prog7_3.c   */
#define    TRUE    1
#define    FALSE   0

#include <stdio.h>

#define    N_PREF     13

void    get_resistor_value(float *r);
void    find_nearest_pref(float r,float pref_arr[],int n_prf,
            float *p_val);
void    print_results(float r,float pref_r);
float   mag(float val);

int     main(void)
{
float
   pref_values[N_PREF]={10,12,15,18,22,27,33,39,47,56,68,82,100};
float   resistor,pref_val;

   get_resistor_value(&resistor);
   find_nearest_pref(resistor,pref_values,N_PREF,&pref_val);
   print_results(resistor,pref_val);
   return(0);
}

void    get_resistor_value(float *r)
{
int     rtn,okay;
   /* get a value between 10 and 100 ohms   */
```

```
      do
      {
        printf("Enter a resistance (10-100 ohm) >> ");
        rtn=scanf("%f",r);
        if ((rtn!=1) || (*r<10) || (*r>100))
        {
          puts("Invalid value, re-enter");
          okay=FALSE;
        }
        else okay=TRUE;
      } while (!okay);
    }

    void    find_nearest_pref(float r,float pref_arr[],int n_prf,
                              float *p_val)
    {
    int    i;

      *p_val=pref_arr[0];
      for (i=1;i<n_prf;i++)
      {
        if (mag(r-pref_arr[i])<mag(*p_val-pref_arr[i]))
          *p_val=pref_arr[i];
      }
    }

    void    print_results(float r,float pref_r)
    {
      printf("Value entered %8.3f ohm, pref value is %8.3f ohm\n",
                  r,pref_r);
    }

    float   mag(float val)
    { /* Determine the magnitude of val   */
      if (val<0.0) return(-val);
      else return(val);
    }
```

Test run 7.3 shows a sample run.

---

🖳  **Test run 7.3**
```
Enter a resistance (10-100 ohm) >> 3
Invalid value, re-enter
Enter a resistance (10-100 ohm) >> 45
Value entered   45.000 ohm, pref value is   47.000 ohm
```

---

## 7.4  Multidimensional arrays

The array declarations used up to this point have been linear or one-dimensional arrays. Many applications require the indexing of data in a multidimensional form. Figure 7.7 shows how rows and columns make up a 2-dimensional array. The first array index term specifies the row number, the second the column.

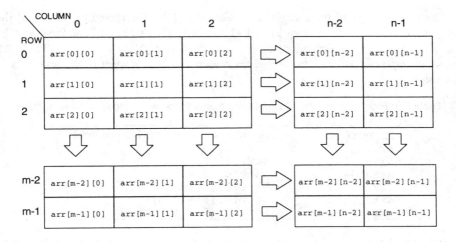

type arr[m][n];

**Figure 7.7:** Array elements

Figure 7.8 shows how a 2-dimensional array is arranged in memory. In this case an array arr is set-up with m columns and n rows. The compiler allocates space for m*n values. A contiguous area of memory is allocated and the array base pointer points to the start of the allocation (this area of memory is known as the heap).

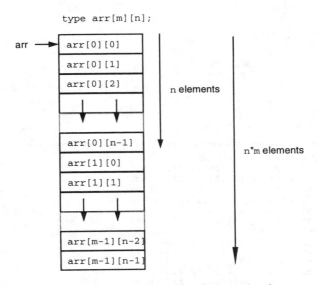

**Figure 7.8:** Memory allocation for a 2-dimensional array

The base address of the array will be &arr[0][0]; the memory location of the second element will be &arr[0][0]+1; element arr[1][0] address will be &arr[0][0]+n; element arr[2][0] will be &arr[0][0]+2*n+3. Table 7.3 shows examples of array elements and their addresses with respect to the array's base address.

**Table 7.3:** Examples of array elements and their address with respect to base address

| Array element | Address with respect to base address |
|---|---|
| arr[0][0] | &arr[0][0] |
| arr[0][1] | &arr[0][0]+1 |
| arr[0][n-1] | &arr[0][0]+(n-1) |
| arr[1][0] | &arr[0][0]+n |
| arr[3][5] | &arr[0][0]+(3*n)+5 |
| arr[m-1][n-1] | &arr[0][0]+(m-1)*n+(n-1) |

Program 7.4 displays the memory allocation of a 3 by 4 array. Test run 7.4 shows that the base address of the array is FFAEh. Since the array is of type float each element takes 4 bytes in memory (this may differ on various systems). The offset address of the second element [0][1] will thus be 4 bytes away from the base address. Figure 7.9 outlines the memory allocation for this test run.

▤  **Program 7.4**
```
/* prog7_4.c       */
#include  <stdio.h>
#define   ROWS      3
#define   COLUMNS   4
int       main(void)
{
float     arr[ROWS][COLUMNS];
int       row,col;

   for (row=0;row<ROWS;row++)
     for (col=0;col<COLUMNS;col++)
       printf("Address of element [%d][%d] is %p(hex)\n",
          row,col,&arr[row][col]);
   return(0);
}
```

🖳  **Test run  7.4**
```
Address of element [0][0] is ffae(hex)
Address of element [0][1] is ffb2(hex)
Address of element [0][2] is ffb6(hex)
Address of element [0][3] is ffba(hex)
Address of element [1][0] is ffbe(hex)
Address of element [1][1] is ffc2(hex)
Address of element [1][2] is ffc6(hex)
Address of element [1][3] is ffca(hex)
Address of element [2][0] is ffce(hex)
Address of element [2][1] is ffd2(hex)
Address of element [2][2] is ffd6(hex)
Address of element [2][3] is ffda(hex)
```

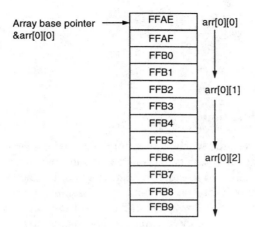

**Figure 7.9:** Array elements

In passing a 2-dimensional array into a function, the size of the columns must be specified. This gives information on the offset address for each row (see Figure 7.8). The sample code given next shows how the column size is specified within brackets and that there is also no need to specify the row size.

```
void    pass_arr(float a[][6]);

void    main(void)
{
float   arr[4][6];

    pass_arr(arr);
}

void    pass_arr(float a[][6])
{
}
```

Larger-dimensional arrays are uncommon but can be set up using a method similar to that used for 2-dimensional arrays. Extra indexing terms are added for each dimension. The following examples use 3- and 4-dimensional arrays.

```
void    pass_arr1(float a[][5][6]);
void    pass_arr2(int a[][5][5][5]);

int     main(void)
{
float   arr_3d[4][5][6];
int     temp[5][5][5][5];

    pass_arr1(arr_3d);
    pass_arr2(temp);
    return(0);
}
```

```
void    pass_arr1(float a[][5][6])
{
}
void    pass_arr2(float a[][5][5][5])
{
}
```

## 7.5  Dynamic allocation

When a variable is declared within a program the compiler assigns memory to it. There is no guarantee that this memory is available at run-time. It can also occur that the amount of memory required to store the data may not be known until the program is run. To overcome these problems a technique of assigning memory at run-time, known as dynamic memory allocation, is used. This involves declaring a pointer and then allocating memory to it when the program is run. The pointer initially has no memory allocated and a memory allocation function, such as malloc(), is used to allocate the required memory.

To declare a pointer the data type is specified and the pointer name is preceded by an asterisk. The following is the general format:

```
type_def *ptr_name;
```

Program 6.5 shows how a pointer is declared using the statement int  *b. The compiler will not reserve space for the integer variable. To dynamically assign memory at run-time malloc() is used; this is prototyped in the *stdlib.h*.

A type-casting operation (int *) informs the compiler that the starting address of the memory allocation is to point to a type int. The sizeof() function returns the number of bytes of the data type, e.g. two or four bytes for an integer. This allows portability between different systems that use a different number of bytes to store a specific data type.

▤  **Program 7.5**
```
/* prog7_5.c    */
#include <stdio.h>
#include <stdlib.h>

int  main(void)
{
int  a,*b;

   b=(int *) malloc(sizeof(int)); /*allocate space for integer */

   a=5;
   *b=6;

   printf("Address of variable a is %x, value is %d\n",&a,a);
   printf("Address of pointer  b is %x, value pointed to is %d\n",b,*b);
   return(0);
}
```

Test run 7.5 shows a sample run. In this case, the compiler has assigned a to the address FFDAh (1111 1111 1101 1010b) and the integer stored at the locations pointed to by its starting address is 5. Pointer b has been assigned the address 061Eh by the malloc() function and the integer value stored at this address is 6. Pointer b has an initial address of NULL (a null, or unallocated pointer).

---

🖥 **Test run 7.5**

```
Address of variable a is ffda, value is 5
Address of pointer  b is 61e, value pointed to is 6
```

---

When using pointers care must be taken that there is enough memory assigned to them to store all the required data, otherwise data can be written to memory that has not been assigned for that purpose.

## 7.6 Pointer arithmetic

A pointer can be operated on arithmetically. The number of locations to which a pointer is moved or referenced will depend on the data type of the pointer. Figure 7.10 shows an example of a pointer named resistors with five allocated values. If this pointer is defined as a float pointer then each variable will occupy 4 bytes in memory (this will vary on different systems). Incrementing the pointer will move the pointer on 4 bytes in memory. Values stored in memory can also be referenced with respect to the base pointer resistors. The contents will be referenced as follows:

| Reference pointer | Value stored |
|-------------------|--------------|
| *resistors | value1 |
| *(resistors+1) | value2 |
| *(resistors+2) | value3 |
| *(resistors+3) | value4 |
| *(resistors+4) | value5 |

Program 7.6 determines the equivalent resistance of a number of resistors in parallel and contains an example of incrementing a pointer. It uses dynamic memory allocation to assign memory for all entered resistances. If there is not enough memory available then the malloc() function will return a NULL (a null pointer). This signifies that the function was not able to allocate memory for the required data. If there is enough memory then the get_values() function prompts the user for each resistance. The resistors pointer is incremented after each value is entered.

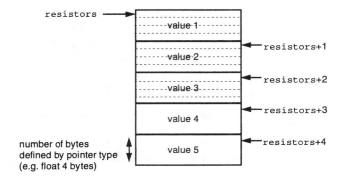

**Figure 7.10:** Array elements

📄 **Program 7.6**

```
/* prog7_6.c    */
#include <stdio.h>
#include <stdlib.h>

void    get_resistors(int n,float *res);
void    calc_resistance(int n,float *res,float *r_e);

int     main(void)
{
float   *resistors,R_equ;
int     nres;

   printf("How many resistors in parallel >>");
   scanf("%d",&nres);

   resistors=(float *) malloc(nres*sizeof(float));

   if (resistors==NULL)
     puts("Cannot allocate enough memory");
   else
   {
     get_resistors(nres,resistors);
     calc_resistance(nres,resistors,&R_equ);
     printf("Equivalent resistance is %8.3f ohm\n",R_equ);
   }
   return(0);
}

void    get_resistors(int n,float *res)
{
int     i;

   for (i=1;i<=n;i++)
   {
     printf("Enter resistor %d >>",i);
     scanf("%f",res);
     res++;   /* increment pointer to next value */
   }
}
```

```
void    calc_resistance(int n,float *res,float *r_e)
{
float   r=0;
int     i;
   for (i=0;i<n;i++)
   {
      r+=1/(*res);
      res++; /* increment pointer to next value */
   }
   *r_e=1/r;
}
```

Sample run 7.6 shows a run for three resistors in parallel.

---

🖳 **Test run 7.6**
```
How many resistors in parallel >> 3
Enter resistor 1 >> 100
Enter resistor 2 >>  75
Enter resistor 3 >>  30
Equivalent resistance is    17.647 ohm
```

---

## 7.7 Arrray of pointers

An array of pointers can be set up using dynamic memory allocation. This is useful in applications where the amount of memory required at compilation is not known. Each element in the array is a pointer to an area of memory which is allocated at run-time using a memory allocation function, such as malloc(). Figure 7.11 shows an array of 5 pointers; each of these pointers points to an array of 8 floats.

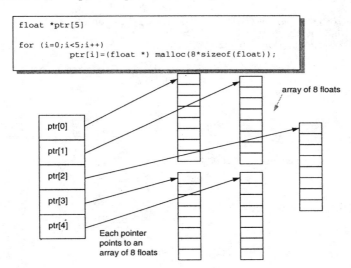

**Figure 7.11:** Array of pointers

Program 7.7 uses an array of pointers to store a number of binary sequences. Each sequence is a fixed length of 5 binary digits; this is set up by the constant SEQ_LENGTH. There can be a maximum of 100 sequences stored, if there is enough memory, as this is the maximum number of pointers in the array bin_seq[] This maximum value is set up by the constant MAXSEQUENCES.

The malloc() function allocates memory to one of the pointers in the array each time the user requests the program to store another sequence. The get_seq() function uses this pointer and operates on it as if it were a linear array.

The array of pointers sent into show_seq() is *seq[]. A pointer *s_ptr is initialized to the start of each of the sequences and the binary digits printed using array indexing.

### Program 7.7

```
/* prog7_7.c       */
#include   <stdio.h>
#include   <stdlib.h>
#define    TRUE          1
#define    FALSE         0
#define    MAXSEQUENCES  100   /* max no of sequences    */
#define    SEQ_LENGTH    5     /* sequence length        */

void     get_seq(int seq[]);
void     show_seq(int n_seq,int *seq[]);

int      main(void)
{
int      n_seq=0;
int      *bin_seq[MAXSEQUENCES];
   do
   {
      printf("Do you wish to add a binary sequence >>");
      fflush(stdin);/* flush keyboard   */
      if (getchar()=='n') break;

      bin_seq[n_seq]=(int *) malloc(SEQ_LENGTH*sizeof(int));

      get_seq(bin_seq[n_seq]);
      n_seq++;

      show_seq(n_seq,bin_seq);
      if (n_seq==MAXSEQUENCES) puts("Maximum sequences reached");

   } while (n_seq!=MAXSEQUENCES);
   return(0);
}

void     get_seq(int seq[])
{
int      in,i,rtn,okay;

   for (i=0;i<SEQ_LENGTH;i++)
   {
      do
      {
```

```
        printf("Enter sequence number %d >>",i);
        rtn=scanf("%d",&in);
        if ((rtn!=1) || ( (in!=0) && (in!=1)))
        {
            puts("INVALID re-enter 1 or 0");
            okay=FALSE;
        }
        else okay=TRUE;

    } while (!okay);
    seq[i]=in;
    }
}
void    show_seq(int n_seq,int *seq[])
{
int     *s_ptr,n,i;

    /* s_ptr points to the start of each of the sequences */

    for (n=0;n<n_seq;n++)
    {
    s_ptr=seq[n]; /* initialise array to start of sequence */
    printf("Binary seq %d >>",n);

    for (i=0;i<SEQ_LENGTH;i++)
    {
        printf("%d",s_ptr[i]);
    }
    puts("");
    }
}
```

Test run 7.7 shows a sample run.

---

🖳 **Test run 7.7**
```
Do you wish to add a binary sequence >>y
Enter sequence number 0 >>1
Enter sequence number 1 >>0
Enter sequence number 2 >>1
Enter sequence number 3 >>0
Enter sequence number 4 >>1
Binary seq 0 >>10101
Do you wish to add a binary sequence >>y
Enter sequence number 0 >>1
Enter sequence number 1 >>1
Enter sequence number 2 >>1
Enter sequence number 3 >>1
Enter sequence number 4 >>1
Binary seq 0 >>10101
Binary seq 1 >>11111
Do you wish to add a binary sequence >>n
```

---

Note that there is no test within the program to determine if there was enough memory for each of the elements. The following modified section of the program determines the result of the memory allocation and displays an error message if it cannot allocate the required memory.

```
int  okay=TRUE;
   do
   {
      printf("Do you wish to add a binary sequence >>");
      fflush(stdin);

      if (getchar()=='n') break;

      bin_seq[n_seq]=(int *) malloc(SEQ_LENGTH*sizeof(int));

      if (bin_seq[n_seq]==NULL)
      {
         puts("Cannot allocate memory");
         okay=FALSE;
      }
   } while (okay);
```

## 7.8 Examples

### 7.8.1 Boolean circuit

Program 7.8 uses a 2-dimensional array to set up a 3-bit input sequence applied to a digital circuit. The Boolean equation used is:

$$Z = (in_1 . in_2) + in_3$$

Figure 7.12 shows the initialized `input_states[]` array showing groups of binary digits arranged into rows. Initialization of these digits is achieved by grouping them together within braces.

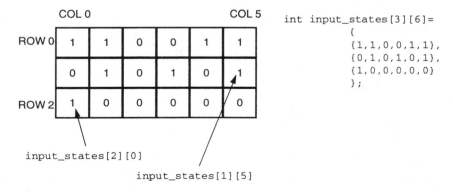

**Figure 7.12:** Array elements

📄 Program 7.8

```
/* prog7_8.c    */
#include  <stdio.h>
#define  NO_STATES   6

void   process_states(int nstates,int in[][NO_STATES],int out[]);
void   print_results(int nstates,int in[][NO_STATES],int out[]);

int    main(void)
{
int    input_states[3][NO_STATES]= {
       {1,1,0,0,1,1},{0,1,0,1,0,1},{1,0,0,0,0,0}};
int    output_state[NO_STATES];

   process_states(NO_STATES,input_states,output_state);
   print_results(NO_STATES,input_states,output_state);
   return(0);
}

void   process_states(int nstates,int in[][NO_STATES],int out[])
{
int    i;
   for (i=0;i<nstates;i++)
     out[i]=(in[0][i] & in[1][i]) | in[2][i];
}

void   print_results(int nstates,int in[][NO_STATES],int out[])
{
int    i;
   puts(" A  B  C  Z");
   for (i=0;i<nstates;i++)
     printf("%3d%3d%3d%3d\n",in[0][i],in[1][i],in[2][i],out[i]);
}
```

Test run 7.8 shows a sample run.

```
💻  Test run  7.8
   A   B   C   Z
   1   0   1   1
   1   1   0   1
   0   0   0   0
   0   1   0   0
   1   0   0   0
   1   1   0   1
```

## 7.8.2  Impedance of an RL circuit

Program 7.9 uses an array to generate the impedance of an RL circuit for a range of frequencies.

📄 **Program 7.9**

```
/* prog7_9.c          */
#include    <math.h>
#include    <stdio.h>
/* maximum array size */
#define    MAXVALUES    30
#define    TRUE         1
#define    FALSE        0
#define    PI           3.14159

/* define prototypes */
void    get_param(float *r,float *l,int *fn,float *f1, float *f2);
void    generate_imp(float r,float l,int fn,float f1, float f2,
                        float imp[]);
float   calc_Zrl(float f,float r,float l);
void    print_imp(int f_points,float f1,float f2,float imp[]);

int     main(void)
{
float   R,L,start_f,end_f,impedance[MAXVALUES];
int     freq_points;

/* start_f and end_f are the start and end freq points     */
/* freq_points is the number of freq pointsto sweep         */
/* impedance[] is an array containing the impedance values */

    get_param(&R,&L,&freq_points,&start_f,&end_f);
    generate_imp(R,L,freq_points,start_f,end_f,impedance);
    print_imp(freq_points,start_f,end_f,impedance);
    return(0);
}

void    get_param(float *r,float *l,int *fn,float *f1, float *f2)
{
int     rtn, okay;

    printf("Enter r and l >> ");
    scanf("%f %f",r,l);
    do
    {
      printf("Enter number of frequency points>>");
      rtn=scanf("%d",fn);
      if ((rtn!=1) || (*fn<0) || (*fn>MAXVALUES))
      {
        puts("Invalid input");
        okay=FALSE;
      }
      else okay=TRUE;
    } while (!okay);

    printf("Enter start and end frequencies >> ");
    scanf("%f %f",f1,f2);
}

void    generate_imp(float r,float l,int fn,float f1, float f2,
                                float imp[])
{
float   fstep,f;
```

```
int     i;

   fstep=(f2-f1)/fn;
   f=f1;
   for (i=0;i<fn;f+=fstep,i++)
      imp[i]=calc_Zrl(f,r,l);
}

float   calc_Zrl(float f,float r,float l)
{
float   Xl;

   Xl=2*PI*f*l;
   return(sqrt(r*r+Xl*Xl));
}

void    print_imp(int fn,float f1,float f2,float imp[])
{
float   fstep,f;
int     i;

   f=f1;
   fstep=(f2-f1)/fn;

   puts("Frequency       Impedance");

   for (i=0;i<fn;i++,f+=fstep)
      printf("%10.3f %10.3f\n",f,imp[i]);
}
```

Test run 7.9 shows a sample run.

---

🖥  **Test run 7.9**

```
Enter r and l >> 1000 1e-3
Enter number of frequency points >> 20
Enter start and end frequencies >> 1 10e5

Frequency       Impedance
      0.000    1000.000
  50000.000    1048.187
 100000.000    1181.010
 150000.000    1374.141
 200000.000    1605.969
 250000.000    1862.096
 300000.000    2133.790
 350000.000    2415.803
 400000.000    2704.912
 450000.000    2999.063
 500000.000    3296.908
 550000.000    3597.530
 600000.000    3900.286
 650000.000    4204.715
 700000.000    4510.479
 750000.000    4817.324
 800000.000·   5125.055
 850000.000    5433.522
 900000.000    5742.606
 950000.000    6052.212
```

---

### 7.8.3 DC circuit analysis

The DC circuit, shown in Figure 7.13 will be analyzed to determine the circulating currents $I_1$, $I_2$ and $I_3$. This is a simple circuit to analyze as the currents could be found simply by determining $I_1$ to be $V_1/R_1$ and $I_3$ to be $V_3/R_3$. It will be used to test the matrix manipulation technique used in the program.

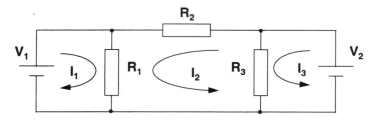

**Figure 7.13:** DC circuit

The following equations are then generated:

$$R_1 I_1 + R_1 I_2 + 0 I_3 - V_1 = 0$$
$$R_1 I_1 + (R_1 + R_2 + R_3) I_2 - R_3 I_3 = 0$$
$$0 I_1 - R_3 I_2 + R_3 I_3 - V_2 = 0$$

This is in the form of a 3-variable simultaneous equation:

$$a_1 x + b_1 y + c_1 z + d_1 = 0$$
$$a_2 x + b_2 y + c_2 z + d_2 = 0$$
$$a_3 x + b_3 y + c_3 z + d_3 = 0$$

A solution can be found using the determinants of matrices. It can be shown that:

$$x = -\frac{\begin{vmatrix} b_1 & c_1 & d_1 \\ b_2 & c_2 & d_2 \\ b_3 & c_3 & d_3 \end{vmatrix}}{\begin{vmatrix} a_1 & b_1 & c_1 \\ a_2 & b_2 & c_2 \\ a_3 & b_3 & c_3 \end{vmatrix}}$$

$$y = -\frac{\begin{vmatrix} a_1 & c_1 & d_1 \\ a_2 & c_2 & d_2 \\ a_3 & c_3 & d_3 \\ b_1 & a_1 & c_1 \\ b_2 & a_2 & c_2 \\ b_3 & a_3 & c_3 \end{vmatrix}}{}$$

$$z = -\frac{\begin{vmatrix} b_1 & a_1 & d_1 \\ b_2 & a_2 & d_2 \\ b_3 & a_3 & d_3 \\ c_1 & b_1 & a_1 \\ c_2 & b_2 & a_2 \\ c_3 & b_3 & a_3 \end{vmatrix}}{}$$

In this case

$$a_1 = R_1$$
$$b_1 = R_1$$
$$c_1 = 0$$
$$d_1 = -V_1$$
$$a_2 = R_1$$
$$b_2 = R_1 + R_2 + R_3$$

$$c_2 = -R_3$$
$$d_2 = 0$$
$$a_3 = 0$$
$$b_3 = -R_3$$
$$c_3 = R_3$$
$$d_3 = -V_2$$

Program 7.10 determines the current in the circuit using the determinant method.

📄 **Program 7.10**
```
/* prog7_10.c   */

#include    <stdio.h>
#define    TRUE    1
#define    FALSE   0
void    fill_matrix(float,float,float,float,float, float [][4]);
void    getvalues(float *,float *,float *, float *,float *);
void    solve_soln(float [][4],float *,  float *,float *);
```

```
void    get_column(int ,float [][4],float []);
float   deter(float [],float [],float []);
void    print_values(float i1,float i2,float i3);

int     main(void)
{
float   R1,R2,R3,V1,V2,I1,I2,I3;
float   matrix[3][4];

   getvalues(&R1,&R2,&R3,&V1,&V2);
   fill_matrix(R1,R2,R3,V1,V2,matrix);
   solve_soln(matrix,&I1,&I2,&I3);
   print_values(I1,I2,I3);
   return(0);
}

void    getvalues(float *r1,float *r2,float *r3,float *v1,
                         float *v2)
{
int     rtn,okay;
   do
   {
      printf("\nEnter R1, R2 and R3 >>");
      rtn=scanf("%f %f %f",r1,r2,r3);
      if (rtn!=3 || (*r1<0) || (*r2<0) || (*r3<0))
      {
         okay=FALSE;
         puts("Invalid values, re-enter");
      }
      else   okay=TRUE;
   } while (!okay);

   do
   {
      printf("Enter V1, V2  >>");
      rtn=scanf("%f %f",v1,v2);
   } while (rtn!=2);
}

void    fill_matrix(float r1,float r2,float r3,float v1,
            float v2, float mat[][4])
{
/*fills matrix with required values(see notes)*/
   mat[0][0]=r1;
   mat[0][1]=r1;
   mat[0][2]=0;
   mat[0][3]=-v1;

   mat[1][0]=r1;
   mat[1][1]=r1+r2+r3;
   mat[1][2]=-r3;
   mat[1][3]=0;

   mat[2][0]=0;
   mat[2][1]=-r3;
   mat[2][2]=r3;
   mat[2][3]=-v2;
}
```

```
void    solve_soln(float mat[][4],float *i1,float *i2,float *i3)
{
float   a_col[3],b_col[3],c_col[3],d_col[3];

    get_column(0,mat,a_col);
      /*scan matrix for column */
    get_column(1,mat,b_col);
    get_column(2,mat,c_col);
    get_column(3,mat,d_col);

    *i1=-deter(b_col,c_col,d_col)/deter(a_col,b_col,c_col);
    *i2=-deter(a_col,c_col,d_col)/deter(b_col,a_col,c_col);
    *i3=-deter(b_col,a_col,d_col)/deter(c_col,b_col,a_col);
}

void    get_column(int col,float mat[][4],float column[])
{
int     row;

    for (row=0;row<3;row++)
      column[row]=mat[row][col];
}

float   deter(float col1[],float col2[], float col3[])
{
float   det;
    /* calculate the determinant of a matrix of the form:  */
    /*    | col1[0] col2[0] col3[0] |                       */
    /*    | col1[1] col2[1] col3[1] |                       */
    /*    | col1[2] col2[2] col3[3] |                       */
    det=col1[0]*(col2[1]*col3[2]-col2[2]*col3[1])-
        col2[0]*(col1[1]*col3[2]-col1[2]*col3[1])+
        col3[0]*(col1[1]*col2[2]-col1[2]*col2[1]);
    return(det);
}

void    print_values(float i1,float i2,float i3)
{
    printf("I1 = %6.2fA I2 = %6.2fA I3 = %6.2fA\n",i1,i2,i3);
}
```

Test run 7.10 shows a sample run.

---

🖳 **Test run 7.10**
```
Enter R1, R2 and R3 >> 10 5 10
Enter V1, V2  >> 5 10

I1 =    0.50A I2 =    0.50A I3 =    2.50A
```

---

This shows that the current in $R_1$ is 1 A $(I_1 + I_2)$, in $R_2$ is 0.5 A and in $R_3$ is 2 A $(I_3 - I_2)$. These currents could have been predicted using Ohm's law, and therefore the program passes the first test.

### 7.8.4  Logic simulation

The example in this section simulates a clocked logic circuit with feedback from the output. An applied sequence of bits are set up and the resultant output determined. The Boolean equation is given by

$$Z_n = \overline{A + B} + (\overline{C + Z_{n-1}})$$

where $Z_n$ is the current output state and $Z_{n-1}$ is the previous output state. Figure 7.14 gives a  schematic representation of this equation.

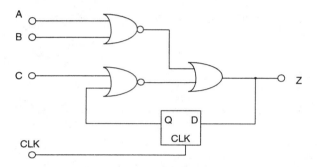

**Figure 7.14:** Schematic representation of Boolean function

Figure 7.15 illustrates the simulated input sequence.

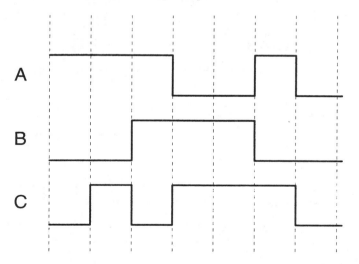

**Figure 7.15:** Timing diagram

▤ **Program 7.11**

```
/* prog7_11.c        */

#include  <stdio.h>

#define   NO_STATES   7

void     print_table(int [],int [],int [],int []);
void     process_states(int [],int [],int [],int []);

int      main(void)
{
int      A[NO_STATES]={1,1,1,0,0,1,0};
int      B[NO_STATES]={0,0,1,1,1,0,0};
int      C[NO_STATES]={0,1,0,1,1,1,0};
int      Q[NO_STATES];

   process_states(A,B,C,Q);
   print_table(A,B,C,Q);
   return(0);
}

void     process_states(int a[],int b[],int c[],int q[])
{
int      i;

   q[0]=!(a[0] | b[0]) | (c[0] & 0);
            /* initial state Zn-1=0*/

   for (i=1;i<NO_STATES;i++)
     q[i]=!(a[i] | b[i]) | !(c[i] | q[i-1]);
}

void     print_table(int a[],int b[],int c[],int q[])
{
int      i;

   printf("\n  A  B  C  Q\n");
   for (i=0;i<NO_STATES;i++)
     printf("%3d%3d%3d%3d\n",a[i],b[i],c[i],q[i]);
}
```

Test run 7.11 shows a sample run.

🖳 **Test run 7.11**

| A | B | C | Q |
|---|---|---|---|
| 1 | 0 | 0 | 0 |
| 1 | 0 | 1 | 0 |
| 1 | 1 | 0 | 1 |
| 0 | 1 | 1 | 0 |
| 0 | 1 | 1 | 0 |
| 1 | 0 | 1 | 0 |
| 0 | 0 | 0 | 1 |

Note that the number of states could be passed as a parameter to the `process_states()` and `print_table()` functions, as shown next.

```
      :         :
   process_states(NO_STATES,A,B,C,Q);
   print_table(NO_STATES,A,B,C,Q);
}
void    process_states(int n,int a[],int b[],
          int c[],  int q[])
{
int  i;
     for (i=1;i<n;i++)
        q[i]=!(a[i] | b[i]) | !(c[i] | q[i-1]);
```

## 7.9 Tutorial

Q7.1    Write a function that will return the largest value in an array.

Q7.2    Repeat Q7.1 for a minimum function.

Q7.3    Modify program 7.9 so that it determines the phase angle of the impedance and stores it in an array.

Q7.4    Modify program 7.9 so that it determines the impedance of an RC series circuit.

Q7.5    Write a function that will arrange an array in descending values. Refer to program 7.2.

Q7.6    Modify program 7.10 so that it determines the currents of the circuit given in Figure 7.16.

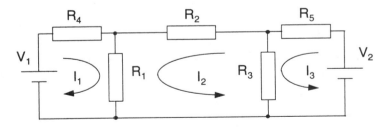

**Figure 7.16:** DC circuit

Q7.7    Modify program 7.10 so that it determines the solution to the following simultaneous equations which were determined by Kirchoff's laws.

(a)

$$2i_1 + i_2 + i_3 = 1.67$$
$$3i_1 + 4.5i_2 - 1.5i_3 = 0$$
$$2.25i_1 + 1.5i_2 + 5.23i_3 = 0$$
$$[ANS: i_1 = 3.94A, i_2 = -3.54A, i_3 = -2.71A]$$

(b)

$$14i_1 - 5i_2 - 6i_3 = 10$$
$$-5i_1 + 14i_2 - 2i_3 = 3$$
$$-6i_1 - 2i_2 + 18i_3 = 5$$
$$[ANS: i_1 = 1.358A, i_2 = 0.816A, i_3 = 0.821A]$$

Q7.8    For the digital circuit given in Figure 7.17 determine the Boolean state table for the given sequence (assume that initially $Z$ is 0). Refer to program 7.11.

Sequence:

         start of sequence
           ⇓
    A    100111010011110101000
    B    000101011000111110100
    C    111010101010101010001

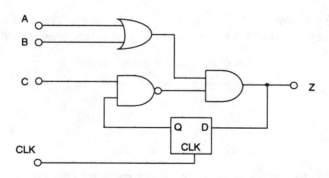

**Figure 7.17:** Digital circuit

Q7.9    Modify the program in Q7.8 so that the user can enter the A, B and C sequences from the keyboard. Use a function to get the entered sequence. Program 7.12 gives an outline of the program.

📄 **Program 7.12**
```
#define    MAX_STATES   100

        :              :

int     main(void)
{
int   A[MAX_STATES],B[MAX_STATES],C[MAX_STATES],
  Q[MAX_STATES];

   get_sequence(&n_sequence,A,B,C);

   process_sequence(A,B,C,Q);

   print_sequence(A,B,C,Q);

   return(0);
}

void    get_sequence(....)
{
   get_seq(n,"Enter A sequence",a);

   get_seq(n,"Enter B sequence",b);

   get_seq(n,"Enter C sequence",c);

}
    :  :  :  :
    :  :  :  :
```

Q7.10    Modify program 7.3 so that it determines the nearest preferred resistor value between 10 and 100 $\Omega$ for the set of preferred values given in Table 7.4.

**Table 7.4:** Preferred resistor values

| | | | | |
|---|---|---|---|---|
| 10 | 16 | 27 | 43 | 68 |
| 11 | 18 | 30 | 47 | 76 |
| 12 | 20 | 33 | 51 | 82 |
| 13 | 22 | 36 | 56 | 91 |
| 15 | 24 | 39 | 62 | 100 |

Q7.11    Modify the program in Q7.10 so the user can enter any value of resistance and the program will determine the nearest preferred resistor value. Test run 7.12 gives a sample run. Hint: write a function which scales the entered value between 10 and 100 $\Omega$, then pass the scaled value to the preferred value's function.

💻 **Test run 7.12**
```
Enter resistor value >> 42130
Nearest preferred value is 43000 ohms
```

Q7.12   Write a program with a 5 × 3 array and determine the addresses of each of the elements in the array. Refer to program 7.4. Repeat the procedure for a 3 × 4 × 2 array.

Q7.13   Write a program that determines the input impedance of a number of inductors in parallel given an operating frequency. Use dynamic memory allocation. Refer to program 7.6.

Q7.14   Repeat Q7.13 for capacitors in parallel.

# CHAPTER 8

# Strings

Strings are one-dimensional arrays containing characters. They tend to be variable in length so it is necessary to declare the string with the maximum number of required characters. Examples of strings are:

- computer names, e.g. "IBM PC", "Apple Mac", "MicroVAX";
- microprocessor names, e.g. "Intel i80386", "Motorola MC68000";
- electronic component names, e.g. "Resistor 1", "Phased Locked Loop", "Differential Amplifier".

Of course, the number of characters used in these names will vary. Figure 8.1 shows that a single character is stored using 8 bits. A string can be variable in its size and contains a number of single characters. The ASCII Null or termination character ('\0') defines the end of a string. In Figure 8.1 the string "XYZ" is terminated in a Null character (i.e. 0000 0000b).

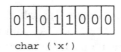

char ('x')

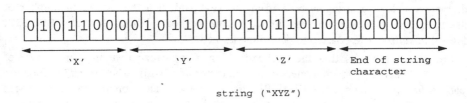

**Figure 8.1:** Example storage of differing data types

If double quotes are used to define a string, e.g. "Cap1", then a Null character is automatically appended onto it. If the string is loaded, as an array, with single characters then the Null character must be inserted after the last character. For example, if the string to be loaded is "Cap1" then the array elements would be `'C','a','p','1','\0'`.

## 8.1 String input

Strings are character arrays with maximum size. The string name is the memory address for the first character in the string. For a declared string of `char name[SIZE]`, the array name `name` is a fixed address at the start of the string and `SIZE` the number of characters reserved in memory for the string. Figure 8.2 shows a sample string allocation in memory; the declared string contains a maximum of 11 characters. The maximum number of displayable characters in the stored string will only be 10 as the Null character terminates the string.

```
char str1[11];
```

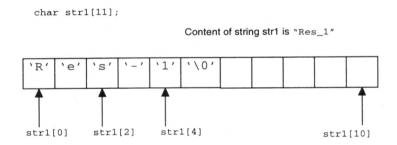

**Figure 8.2:** Example of string allocation

The first character of a string declared as `char  str1[SIZE]` is indexed as `str1[0]` and the last as `str1[SIZE-1]`. As with arrays, it is possible to overrun the end of a string (especially if the termination character is not present). This can cause data to be read from or written to areas of memory not assigned for this purpose. The dimensioned string should always contain at least the maximum number of entered characters + 1. If a string is read from the keyboard then the maximum number of characters that can be entered is limited by the keyboard buffer. A macro `BUFSIZ`, defined in *stdio.h*, can be used to determine its size.

Program 8.1 shows that the declared string `instr` can contain a maximum of `BUFSIZ-1` displayable characters (one character for Null). The `gets()` function reads a line of text until the RETURN key is pressed. This function accepts spaces between words, whereas `scanf()` delimits each string by spaces (see program 2.12 and test run 2.9). The program will continue prompting for text strings until the first character of the entered string is an 'X'.

📄 **Program 8.1**
```
/* prog8_1.c  */
#include <stdio.h>

int    main(void)
{
char    instr[BUFSIZ];

   do
   {
      printf("Enter a name (enter 'X' to exit )>>");
      gets(instr);
      printf("Name entered is %s\n",instr);
   } while (instr[0]!='X');
   return(0);
}
```

Test run 8.1 shows a sample run.

🖥 **Test run 8.1**
```
Enter a name (enter X to exit )>> resistor_1
Name entered is resistor_1
Enter a name (enter X to exit )>> inverting amplifier
Name entered is inverting amplifier
Enter a name (enter X to exit )>> X
Name entered is X
```

## 8.2 String assignment

As with arrays, strings can be loaded with characters using array indexing, as follows:

```
name[0] = 'R';
name[1] = 'e';
name[2] = 's';
name[3] = '_';
name[4] = '1';
name[5] = '\0'/* Terminate string with a Null */
```

This will load an 'R' into the first location, 'e' into the second and so on. Program 8.2 shows an example of how individual characters are loaded into a character array. The address passed to the first printf() points to the start of this string. It is possible to print part of the string by passing a different base address. For example, to print "s_1" the address passed to printf() is &instr[2].

The strcpy() function is contained in the standard library. It copies the second argument string into the first argument string.

📄 **Program 8.2**

```
/* prog8_2.c   */
#include  <stdio.h>
#include  <string.h>

int     main(void)
{
char    instr[BUFSIZ];

   instr[0]='R';
   instr[1]='e';
   instr[2]='s';
   instr[3]='_';
   instr[4]='1';
   instr[5]= '\0'; /* terminate string with a null */

   printf("String is %s\n",instr);

   printf("Part of string is %s\n",&instr[2]);

   strcpy(instr,"Res_2");
   printf("String is %s\n",instr);
   return(0);
}
```

Test run 8.2 shows a sample test run.

🖥 **Test run  8.2**

```
String is Res_1
Part of string is s_1
String is Res_2
```

Program 8.3 shows an example of how `malloc()` allocates memory for a string. It assigns a number of bytes of free space and returns a pointer to the start of the allocated memory. The `strcat()` function concatenates (appends) the second argument string onto the first argument string and puts the result into the first argument.

📄 **Program 8.3**

```
/* prog8_3.c   */

#include  <stdio.h>
#include  <stdlib.h>
#include  <string.h>

int     main(void)
{
char    *str1,*str2;
    /* dynamic string allocation */
   str1=(char *)malloc(BUFSIZ*sizeof(char));
   str2=(char *)malloc(BUFSIZ*sizeof(char));

   printf("Enter a string of text >>");
   gets(str1);
```

```
    printf("Enter a second string of text >>");
    gets(str2);

    printf("STR1: %s\n",str1);
    printf("STR2: %s\n",str2);

    strcat(str1,str2);

    printf("STR1+STR2: %s",str1);
    return(0);
}
```

Test run 8.3 shows a sample run.

---

🖥 **Test run 8.3**
```
Enter a string of text >> resistor 1 is 43 ohms
Enter a second string of text >> resistor 2 is 56 ohms
STR1: resistor 1 is 43 ohms
STR2: resistor 2 is 56 ohms
STR1+STR2: resistor 1 is 43 ohms resistor 2 is 56 ohms
```

---

Program 8.4 contains a function (nochars()) which scans a string and determines the number of occurrences of a given character. It uses gets() to read the string as it accepts spaces between words.

The function nochars() uses pointer arithmetic to read each of the characters in the passed string until a Null character. The getchar() function is used to get the search character.

📄 **Program 8.4**
```
/* prog8_4.c   */
#include <stdio.h>

/* Find the number of occurrences in a string */

int  nochars(char *str,char ch);

int  main(void)
{
char str1[BUFSIZ],ch;

    printf("Enter a string >>");
    gets(str1);

    printf("Enter character to find >>");
    ch=getchar();

    printf("Number of occurrences is %d\n", nochars(str1,ch));
    return(0);
}

int  nochars(char *string,char c)
{
int no_occ=0;
```

```
/* repeat until end of string (Null) */
while (*string!='\0')
{
   if (c== *string) no_occ++;
   string++; /* increment pointer to the next character */
}
return(no_occ); /* no. of characters found */
}
```

Test run 8.4 shows a sample run.

The following function implements nochars() using array indexing notation. The number of characters in the string is determined using strlen(). A for() loop is then used to index each of the characters in the array and these are tested against the search character.

```
int  nochars(char str[],char c)
{
int  i=0,no_occ=0,size;
   size=strlen(str);
   for (i=0;i<size;i++)
      if (str[i]==c) no_occ++;

   return(no_occ);
}
```

## 8.3  Standard string functions

There are several string handling functions in the standard library; most are prototyped in *string.h*. Table 8.1 lists these. All the string functions return a value; for example, strlen() returns an integer value relating to the length of a string and the functions strcat(), strupr(), strlwr() and strcpy() return pointers to the resultant string. This pointer can be used, if required, but the resultant string is also passed back as the first argument of these functions. The strcmp() function returns a 0 (zero) only if both strings are identical.

**Table 8.1:** The main string handling functions

| Conversion functions | Header file | Description |
|---|---|---|
| `int`<br>`  strcmp(char *str1,char *str2);` | string.h | Function: Compares two strings `str1` and `str2`.<br>Return: A 0 (zero) is returned if the strings are identical, a negative value if `str1` is less than `str2`, or a positive value if `str1` is greater than `str2`. |
| `int  strlen(char *str);` | string.h | Function: Determines the number of characters in `str`.<br>Return: Number of characters in `str`. |
| `char  *strcat(char *str1,`<br>`        char *str2);` | string.h | Function: Appends `str2` onto `str1`. The resultant string `str1` will contain `str1` and `str2`.<br>Return: A pointer to the resultant string. |
| `char  *strlwr(char *str1);` | string.h | Function: Converts uppercase letters in a string to lowercase<br>Return: A pointer to the resultant string |
| `char  *strupr(char *str1);` | string.h | Function: Converts lowercase letters in a string to uppercase.<br>Return: A pointer to the resultant string. |
| `char`<br>`  *strcpy(char *str1, char *str2);` | string.h | Function: Copies `str2` into `str1`.<br>Return: A pointer to the resultant string. |
| `int sprintf(char *str,`<br>`     char *format_str,arg1,....);` | stdio.h | Function: Similar to `printf()` but output goes into string `str`.<br>Return: Number of characters output. |
| `int sscanf(char *str,`<br>`     char *format_str,arg1,...);` | stdio.h | Function: Similar to `scanf()` but input is from string `str`.<br>Return: Number of fields successfully scanned. |

Program 8.5 shows how `sscanf()` scans a string with different data types. In this case, the user enters a string of text. The first word of the string is read as a string (`res_name`) and the second as a float (`res_values`). The `sscanf()` returns the number of fields sucessfully scanned; if the number of fields scanned is equal to 2 the variable `okay` is set to TRUE and the `do{}while()` loop will thus end. If it is not equal to 2 the `okay` variable is set to FALSE and an error message is displayed, the user will then be prompted to re-enter the values.

📄 **Program 8.5**

```
/* prog8_5.c   */
#define   TRUE      1
#define   FALSE     0
#include  <stdio.h>
#include  <string.h>

int     main(void)
{
char    res_name[BUFSIZ],instr[BUFSIZ],outstr[BUFSIZ];
float   res_value;
int     rtn,okay;

   do
   {
      printf("Enter resistor identifier and the value >>");
      gets(instr);

      rtn=sscanf(instr,"%s %f",res_name,&res_value);
      if (rtn!=2)
      {
         okay=FALSE;
         printf("Invalid input <%s>\n",instr);
      }
      else okay=TRUE;
   } while (!okay);

   printf("Resistor name is %s, value is %8.3f ohm\n",
            res_name,res_value);

   sprintf(outstr,"Resistor name is %s, value is %8.3f ohm\n",
            res_name,res_value);
   puts(outstr);
   return(0);
}
```

Test run 8.5 shows a sample run.

💻 **Test run 8.5**

```
Enter resistor identifier and the value >> resistor_1 1430
Resistor name is resistor_1, value is 1430.000 ohm
Resistor name is resistor_1, value is 1430.000 ohm
```

Program 8.6 uses the string function strcmp(). The do{}while() loop continues until the user enters the word "exit".

📄 **Program 8.6**

```c
#include <stdio.h>
#include <string.h>

int     main(void)
{
char    str1[BUFSIZ],str2[BUFSIZ],instr[BUFSIZ];

   do
   {
      printf("Enter a string >> ");
      gets(str1);

      printf("Enter a string >> ");
      gets(str2);

      if (!strcmp(str1,str2))puts(">>>Strings are identical<<<");
      else puts(">>>Strings differ<<<");

      printf("Do you wish to continue (type 'exit' to quit)>>");
      gets(instr);

   } while (strcmp(instr,"exit"));
   return(0);
}
```

Test run 8.6 shows a sample run.

🖥 **Test run 8.6**
```
Enter a string >> this is a string
Enter a string >> this is another string
>>>Strings differ<<<
Do you wish to continue (type 'exit' to quit)>>
Enter a string >> input is zero
Enter a string >> input is zero
>>>Strings are identical<<<
Do you wish to continue (type 'exit' to quit)>> exit
```

## 8.4 Impedance of a parallel RC circuit

The program in this section determines the impedance of a parallel RC circuit. Figure 8.3 gives a schematic of this circuit.

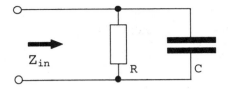

**Figure 8.3:** Parallel RC circuit

The impedance of this circuit can be found using the product of the impedances over the sum. Thus

$$Z = \frac{R.\dfrac{1}{j\omega C}}{R+\dfrac{1}{j\omega C}} = \frac{R}{j\omega C(R+\dfrac{1}{j\omega C})} = \frac{R}{j\omega CR+1}$$

The magnitude of the impedance is thus:

$$|Z| = \frac{R}{\sqrt{1+(\omega RC)^2}}$$

A structure chart for a program which determines this magnitude is given in Figure 8.4. The get_parameters() function gets three variables (Res, Cap and freq); parallel_impedance() determines the input impedance and returns it back into the variable Zin. Finally, print_impedance() displays the input parameters and calculated impedance.

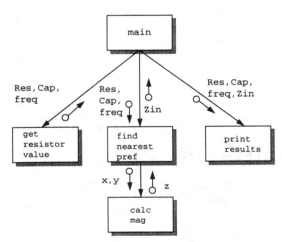

**Figure 8.4:** Structure chart for program 8.7

In previous programs values were entered into the program using scanf(). This function can be unreliable when the format of the entered data is different from the required format. For example, the user may have entered a string of characters or a real value when an integer value is required. An improved method of entering values involves reading the input as a string (with gets()) and scanning it for the required parameters (with sscanf() ). A section of code which achieves this is given next.

In this case, the user is prompted for a value of resistance and the string entered from the keyboard is loaded into inline. This is then scanned for a floating point value and put into the pointer variable r. If a single floating point value is scanned, then rtn will be 1 and the entered value is not negative, so that the loop will end, else the user will be re-prompted for a value.

```
void    get_parameters(float *r,float *c,float *f)
{
char    inline[BUFSIZ];
int     rtn,okay;

   do
   {
      printf("Enter resistance >>");
      gets(inline);
      rtn=sscanf(inline,"%f",r);
      if ((rtn!=1) || (*r<0))
      {
         printf("Invalid input <%s>\n",inline);
         okay=FALSE;
      }
      else okay=TRUE;
   } while (!okay);
```

The completed program is given in program 8.7.

📄 **Program 8.7**
```
/* prog8_7.c   */
#include <stdio.h>
#define   TRUE       1
#define   FALSE      0
#define   PI         3.14159

void    get_parameters(float *r,float *c,float *f);
void    parallel_impedance(float r,float c,float f,float *Z);
void    print_impedance(float r,float c,float f,float Z);
float   calc_mag(float x,float y);

int     main(void)
{
float   Res,Cap,freq,Zin;

   get_parameters(&Res,&Cap,&freq);
   parallel_impedance(Res,Cap,freq,&Zin);
   print_impedance(Res,Cap,freq,Zin);
   return(0);
}
```

```c
void    get_parameters(float *r,float *c,float *f)
{
char    inline[BUFSIZ];
int     rtn,okay;

   do
   {
     printf("Enter resistance  >>");
     gets(inline);
     rtn=sscanf(inline,"%f",r);
     if ((rtn!=1) || (*r<0))
     {
       printf("Invalid input <%s>\n",inline);
       okay=FALSE;
     }
     else okay=TRUE;
   } while (!okay);
   do
   {
     printf("Enter capacitance >>");
     gets(inline);
     rtn=sscanf(inline,"%f",c);
     if ((rtn!=1) || (*c<0))
     {
       printf("Invalid input <%s>\n",inline);
       okay=FALSE;
     }
     else okay=TRUE;
   } while (!okay);
   do
   {
     printf("Enter frequency   >>");
     gets(inline);
     rtn=sscanf(inline,"%f",f);
     if ((rtn!=1) || (*f<0))
     {
       printf("Invalid input <%s>\n",inline);
       okay=FALSE;
     }
     else okay=TRUE;
   } while (!okay);
}

void    print_impedance(float r,float c,float f,float Z)
{
   printf("R=%f ohms C=%f uF f=%f Hz\n",r,c,f);
   printf("Zin = %f ohms\n",Z);
}
void    parallel_impedance(float r,float c,float f,float *Z)
{
   *Z=r/(calc_mag(1,2*PI*f*r*c));
}
float   calc_mag(float x,float y)
{
   return(x*x+y*y);
}
```

Test run 8.7 shows that the user can enter a value in the incorrect format and the program will re-prompt for another. Notice that the user has entered the strings "none" and "fred"; the program copes with these and re-prompts for an input. If scanf() had been used instead of gets() and sscanf() the program may act unprecidably. For example, a run of this program on a PC system using scanf() caused the prompt Enter resistance >> to be displayed recursively when a string of characters was entered instead of a real value.

---

🖥 **Test run 8.7**
```
Enter resistance   >>none
Invalid input <none>
Enter resistance   >>fred
Invalid input <fred>
Enter resistance   >>-100
Invalid input <-100>
Enter resistance >>1000
Enter capacitance  >>1e-6
Enter frequency    >>1e3
R=1000.000 ohms C=   1.00 uF f=1000.000 Hz
Zin = 24.704565 ohms
```

---

The get_parameters() function contains code which is repeated three times. An improved program replaces the repeated code with single function calls. A function named get_float() gets a floating point value within a specified range. A prototype of this function is given next. The first argument is the message prompt, the next two are the minimum and maximum values, and the final argument is a pointer to the value.

```
void    get_float(char msg[],float min,float max,float *val);
```

Program 8.8 contains this function. The get_parameters() function now contains three calls to the get_float().

📄 **Program 8.8**
```
/* prog8_8.c   */
#include <stdio.h>
#define   TRUE    1
#define   FALSE   0
#define   PI      3.14159
#define   MICRO   1e-6

void    get_parameters(float *r,float *c,float *f);
void    parallel_impedance(float r,float c,float f,float *Z);
void    print_impedance(float r,float c,float f,float Z);
float   calc_mag(float x,float y);
void    get_float(char msg[],float min,float max,float *val);

int    main(void)
{
float   Res,Cap,freq,Zin;

   get_parameters(&Res,&Cap,&freq);
```

```
      parallel_impedance(Res,Cap,freq,&Zin);
      print_impedance(Res,Cap,freq,Zin);
      return(0);
}

void    get_parameters(float *r,float *c,float *f)
{
   get_float("Enter resistance  >> ",0,10e6,r);
   get_float("Enter capacitance >> ",0,1,c);
   get_float("Enter frequency   >> ",0,1e7,f);
}

void    get_float(char msg[],float min,float max,float *val)
{
char    inline[BUFSIZ];
int     rtn,okay;

   do
   {
      printf("%s",msg);
      gets(inline);
      rtn=sscanf(inline,"%f",val);
      if ((rtn!=1) || (*val<min) || (*val>max))
      {
         okay=FALSE;
         printf("Invalid input <%s>\n",inline);
      }
      else okay=TRUE;

   } while (!okay);
}

void    print_impedance(float r,float c,float f,float Z)
{
   printf("R=%f ohms C=%f uF f=%f Hz\n",r,c/MICRO,f);
   printf("Zin = %f ohms\n",Z);
}
void    parallel_impedance(float r,float c,float f,float *Z)
{
   *Z=r/(calc_mag(1,2*PI*f*r*c));
}
float   calc_mag(float x,float y)
{
   return(x*x+y*y);
}
```

## 8.5  Circuit selection

Program 8.9 displays a basic menu system which can be used in a program to display a Boolean truth table. An array of strings is set up to store the menu options. The declaration char *menu_options[5] declares an array of 5 pointers; each of these pointers points to one of the menu options. The first pointer menu_options[0] points to the string "1-AND function", the second pointer `menu_options[1]` to `"2-OR function"` and so on. The following gives a list of strings in the pointer array.

```
menu_options[0]    "1-AND function"
menu_options[1]    "2-OR function"
menu_options[2]    "3-NOR function"
menu_options[3]    "4-NAND function"
menu_options[4]    "5-EXIT"
```

An array of pointers is set up and initialized to the menu options.

### Program 8.9

```c
/* prog8_9.c */
#define    LOGIC_FUNCTIONS   5
#define    TRUE              1
#define    FALSE             0

#include <stdio.h>

int     display_menu(char *menu[LOGIC_FUNCTIONS]);
void    get_int(int *opt,int min,int max,char msg[]);

enum    logic {AND=1,OR,NOR,NAND,EXIT};

int     main(void)
{
char    *menu_options[LOGIC_FUNCTIONS]={
        "1-AND function","2-OR function","3-NOR function",
        "4-NAND function","5-EXIT"};
enum    logic   option;

   do
   {
      option=display_menu(menu_options);
      printf("Option selected is %d (%s)\n",
                  option,menu_options[option-1]);
   } while (option!=EXIT);
   return(0);
}

int  display_menu(char *menu[LOGIC_FUNCTIONS])
{
int  i,opt;

   /* display menu and get circuit option   */
   for (i=0;i<LOGIC_FUNCTIONS;i++)
      puts(menu[i]);

   get_int(&opt,AND,EXIT,"Enter logic device >>");
   return(opt);
}

void    get_int(int *opt,int min,int max,char msg[])
{
char    inline[BUFSIZ];
```

```
int    rtn,okay;
   /* get an integer value between min and max */
   do
   {
      printf("%s",msg);
      gets(inline);
      rtn=sscanf(inline,"%d",opt);
      if ((rtn!=1) || (*opt<min) || (*opt>max))
      {
         okay=FALSE;
         printf("Invalid input <%s>\n",inline);
      }
      else okay=TRUE;

   } while (!okay);
}
```

Test run 8.8 gives a sample run.

---

🖳  **Test run 8.8**
```
1-AND function
2-OR function
3-NOR function
4-NAND function
5-EXIT
Enter logic device >>1
Option selected is 1 (1-AND function)
1-AND function
2-OR function
3-NOR function
4-NAND function
5-EXIT
Enter logic device >>3
Option selected is 3 (3-NOR function)
1-AND function
2-OR function
3-NOR function
4-NAND function            .
5-EXIT
Enter logic device >>5
Option selected is 5 (5-EXIT)
```

---

## 8.6  Setting up an array of strings

The simplest way of setting up an array of strings is to define a new string data type. In program 8.10 a new data type named string is defined using the statement typedef char string[BUFSIZ]. An array of strings is then set up using the declaration string database[MAX_COMP_NAMES]. Each string in the array can contain a maximum of BUFSIZ characters (note this can be changed to any size if required) and can be accessed using normal array indexing.

### Program 8.10

```c
/* prog8_10.c   */
#include <stdio.h>
#include <string.h>

#define   MAX_COMP_NAMES   100

typedef char string[BUFSIZ];

void   get_component_name(int *comp, string data[]);
void   print_component_names(int comp, string data[]);


int    main(void)
{
int    components=0;
string database[MAX_COMP_NAMES];

   do
   {
     get_component_name(&components,database);

     if (strcmp(database[components-1],"exit")) break;

     print_component_names(components,database);
   } while (components<MAX_COMP_NAMES);
   return(0);
}


void   get_component_name(int *comp, string data[])
{
int    i;

   printf("Enter component name >>");

   gets(data[*comp]);

   (*comp)++;

}

void   print_component_names(int comp, string data[])
{
int    i;

   puts("Component Names");

   for (i=0;i<comp;i++)
     printf("%d          %s\n",i,data[i]);

}
```

A sample run is given in test run 8.8. Note that the string "exit" quits the program.

---

⌨ **Test run 8.9**
```
Enter component name >>resistor 1
0              resistor 1
Enter component name >>resistor 2
Component Names
0              resistor 1
1              resistor 2
Enter component name >>capacitor 1
Component Names
0              resistor 1
1              resistor 2
2              capacitor 1
Enter component name >>capacitor 4
Component Names
0              resistor 1
1              resistor 2
2              capacitor 1
3              capacitor 4
Enter component name >>inductor 5
Component Names
0              resistor 1
1              resistor 2
2              capacitor 1
3              capacitor 4
4              inductor 5
Enter component name >>exit
```

---

A array of strings can also be initialized using braces. Program 8.11 and test run 8.10 show how this is set up.

📄 **Program 8.11**
```c
#include <stdio.h>
#define     MAX_COMP_NAMES   5

typedef   char string[BUFSIZ];

int  main(void)
{
string database[MAX_COMP_NAMES]={"Res 1","Res 2","Res 3",
                                 "Res 4","Cap 1"};
int    i;

   for (i=0;i<MAX_COMP_NAMES;i++)
     printf("%s\n",database[i]);
   return(0);
}
```

---

⌨ **Test run 8.10**
```
Res 1
Res 2
Res 3
Res 4
Cap 1
```

## 8.7  Tutorial

Q8.1    Write a program which will accept a string of text and determine the values of two entered resistors. The format of the entered string is:

```
RES_NAME1    COMPONENT_VALUE1    RES_NAME2    COMPONENT_VALUE2
```

The program should determine the equivalent series resistance of the resistors. Test run 8.11 shows a sample run.

---

💻  **Test run 8.11**
```
Enter string: R1 244 R2 300
Two resistors are R1=244, R2=300, total is 544 ohms
Enter string: R15   3000 R20 534
Two resistors are R15=3000, R20=535, total is 3534 ohms
Enter string: quit
```

---

Q8.2    Write a program that declares the following seven strings.

```
"RL series", "RC series","LC series","RL parallel",
"RC parallel", "LC parallel","EXIT"
```

Store these strings as a single array of strings named menu by declaring an array of strings. The program should display these strings as menu options using a for() loop. Test run 8.12 shows a sample run.

---

💻  **Test run 8.12**
```
Menu Options
   RL series
   RC series
   LC series
   RL parallel
   RC parallel
   LC parallel
   QUIT
```

---

Q8.3    Modify the program in Q8.2 so that the user can enter the menu option. The program will display a message on the option selected. Test run 8.13 shows a sample run.

---

⌨ **Test run 8.13**

```
Menu Options
   RL series
   RC series
   LC series
   RL parallel
   RC parallel
   LC parallel
   QUIT
Enter option >> RL series
   >>> RL series circuit selected
Menu Options
   RL series
   RC series
   LC series
   RL parallel
   RC parallel
   LC parallel
   QUIT
Enter option >> QUIT
```

---

Q8.4    Write a function named get_int() which will read a string from the keyboard. This is then scanned for an integer value within a defined mimimum and maximum range.

Q8.5    Modify some programs in previous chapters so that program parameters are entered using the get_float() function.

Q8.6    Write a function that will capitalize all the characters in a string.

Q8.7    Repeat Q8.6 but make the characters lowercase.

Q8.8    Write a function that will determine the number of words in a string.

# CHAPTER 9

# Structures

A structure is an identifiable object that contains items which define it. These items are linked under a common grouping. For example, an electrical circuit has certain properties that define it. These could be:

- a circuit title;
- circuit components with identifiable names;
- circuit components with known values.

Figure 9.1 shows a basic RC filter circuit. The title of this circuit is "RC Filter Circuit", the circuit components are named "R1", "R2" and "C1" and the values of these are 4320 $\Omega$, 1200 $\Omega$ and 1 $\mu$F, respectively. The title and the component names are character strings, whereas the component values are floating point. A structure groups these properties into a single entity. These grouping are referred to as fields and each field is made up of members.

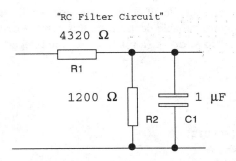

**Figure 9.1:** RC filter circuit

Figure 9.2 shows how the circuits fields can be joined to create a single structure. In this case, there are three fields: the circuit title, component names and component values.

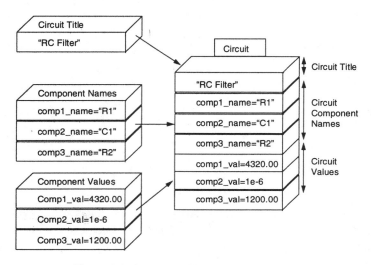

**Figure 9.2:** Grouping of fields within a structure

A structure is a type that is a composite of elements that are distinctive and perhaps of different data types. The following gives an example of a structure declaration (in this case the strings have been declared with a maximum of 100 characters).

```
struct
{
   char    title[100];
   char    comp1_name[100], comp2_name[100], comp3_name[100];
   float   comp1_val, comp2_val, comp3_val;
} circuit;
```

The following is an example of a structure which will store a single electrical component. The structure variable declared, in this case, is `Component`. It has three fields of differing data types; `cost` (a float), `code` (an integer) and `name` (a character string).

```
struct
{
   float   cost;
   int     code;
   char    name[BUFSIZ];
} Component;
```

The dot notation (`.`) accesses each of the members within the structure. For example:

```
Component.cost=12.3
Component.code=31004;
strcpy(Component.name,"Resistor 1");
```

Program 9.1 is a simple database program. The database stores a record of a single electrical component which includes its name (Component.name), its cost (Component.cost) and its code number (Component.code). The name is a string, the code a signed integer and the cost a floating point value.

📄 **Program 9.1**
```
/*       prog9_1.c       */
#include <stdio.h>
#include <string.h>

int main(void)
{
struct
{
   float   cost;
   int     code;
   char    name[BUFSIZ];
} Component;

   Component.cost=30.1;
   Component.code=32201;
   strcpy(Component.name,"Resistor 1");

   printf("Name %s Code %d Cost %f\n",
           Component.name,Component.code,Component.cost);
   return(0);
}
```

Test run 9.1 shows a sample run.

💻 **Test run 9.1**

```
Name Resistor 1 Code 32201 Cost 30.100000
```

Note that the structure could have been set up at initialization using the following:

```
struct
{
   float   cost;
   int     code;
   char    name[BUFSIZ];
} Component={30.1, 32201, "Resistor 1"};
```

Program 9.2 contains a function to print the structure (print_component()). To pass a structure into a function the data type of parameter passed must be defined. For the purpose the typedef keyword is used to define a new data type, in this case, it is named CompType. The program also uses braces to initialize the fields within the structure.

**Program 9.2**

```
/*    prog9_2.c      */
#include <stdio.h>
#include <string.h>

typedef struct
{
   float   cost;
   int     code;
   char    name[BUFSIZ];
} CompType;

void    print_component(CompType Comp);

int     main(void)
{
CompType Component={30.1,32201,"Resistor 1"};

   print_component(Component);
   return(0);
}

void    print_component(CompType Comp)
{
   printf("Name %s Code %d Cost %f\n",
           Comp.name,Comp.code,Comp.cost);
}
```

Test run 9.2 shows a sample run.

**Test run 9.2**
```
Name Resistor 1 Code 32201 Cost 30.100000
```

Program 9.3 uses a function to get data into the structure (get_component()). The parameter passed into this function will be a pointer to the base address of the structure. For this purpose, an ampersand is inserted before the structure name. The structure pointer operator (->) is used with the structure pointer to access a member of a field.

**Program 9.3**

```
/*      prog9_3.c      */
#include <stdio.h>
#include <string.h>

typedef struct
{
   float cost;
   int    code;
   char   name[BUFSIZ];
} CompType;

void    get_component(CompType *Comp);
void    print_component(CompType Comp);
```

```
int     main(void)
{
CompType Component;

   get_component(&Component);
   print_component(Component);
   return(0);
}

void    get_component(CompType *Comp)
{
   Comp->cost=30.1;
   Comp->code=32201;
   strcpy(Comp->name,"Resistor 1");
}

void    print_component(CompType Comp)
{
   printf("Name %s Code %d Cost %f\n",
                 Comp.name,Comp.code,Comp.cost);
}
```

Test run 9.3 shows that the results are identical to the previous run.

---

🖳 **Test run 9.3**
Name Resistor 1 Code 32201 Cost 30.100000

---

## 9.1 Array of structures

An array of structures can be set up in a way similar to normal array indexing. When an array is declared the compiler assigns enough memory to hold all its elements. If there is enough memory the structure array name is assigned to the starting address of the array (the base address). This memory is contiguous and only one pointer is used to reference all array elements within the structure.

Program 9.4 is similar to program 9.3, but uses an array of structures to store up to 5 electrical components. Figure 9.3 shows how this structure is arranged in memory. In this program the structure is not passed with a preceding ampersand as the structure name is the base address of the structure (similar to array passing). Each of the functions that use the structure Components can determine how each element within the structure is accessed as the data type of each of the members is known (i.e. the number of bytes they take up in memory). For example, referring to Figure 9.3, the second structure array element will be 4+2+BUFSIZ bytes away from the base pointer (Comp[1] or Comp+1), the third 2*(4+2+BUFSIZ) bytes away from the base pointer (Comp[2] or Comp+2), etc.

Figure 9.4 shows a structure chart of this program. It uses get_float() and get_int() to filter any invalid inputs for the cost and code of a component. These functions were developed in Chapter 8 and have been reused as they have been well tested and are easily ported into any program. The cost of the electrical components is

now limited between 0 and 1,000 and the component code from 0 to 32,767. A
get_string() function has also been added to get the name of the component.

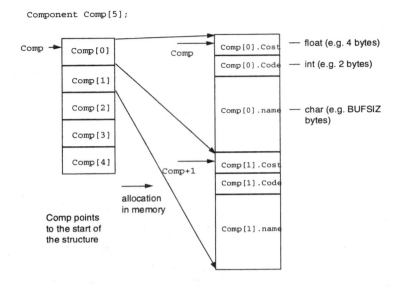

**Figure 9.3:** Arrangement of an array of structures

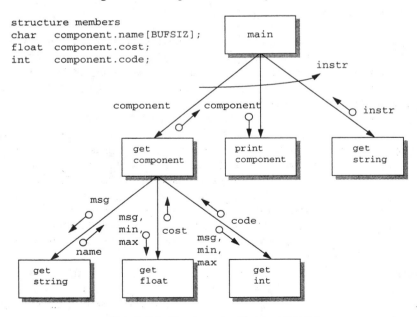

**Figure 9.4:** Structure chart for program 9.4

📄 **Program 9.4**

```c
/*    prog9_4.c      */
#include          <string.h>
#include          <stdio.h>

#define    TRUE               1
#define    FALSE              0
#define    MAXCOMPONENTS      5

typedef struct
{
   float   cost;
   int     code;
   char    name[BUFSIZ];
} CompType;

void    get_component(int *n,CompType Comp[]);
void    print_component(int n,CompType Comp[]);
void    get_int(char msg[],int min,int max,int *val);
void    get_float(char msg[],float min,float max,float *val);
void    get_string(char msg[],char ins[]);

int     main(void)
{
int        NumComponents=0;
char       instr[BUFSIZ];
CompType   Component[MAXCOMPONENTS];

   do
   {
     get_component(&NumComponents,Component);
     print_component(NumComponents,Component);
     get_string("Do you wish to continue (type 'exit' to leave)",
                instr);
   } while (strcmp(instr,"exit")!=0);
   return(0);
}

void    get_component(int *n,CompType Comp[])
{
int    i;

   i=*n;
   get_string("Enter name of component >> ",Comp[i].name);
   get_float("Enter cost of component >> ",0.0,1000.0,
             &Comp[i].cost);
   get_int("Enter component code >> ",0,32767,&Comp[i].code);
   (*n)++;
}

void    print_component(int n,CompType Comp[])
{
int    i;

   for (i=0;i<n;i++)
     printf("Name %12s Code %8d Cost %8.2f\n",
              Comp[i].name,Comp[i].code,Comp[i].cost);
}
```

```
void    get_string(char msg[],char ins[])
{
   printf("%s",msg);
   gets(ins);
}

void    get_float(char msg[],float min,float max,float *val)
{
char    inline[BUFSIZ];
int     rtn,okay;

   do
   {
      printf("%s",msg);
      gets(inline);
      rtn=sscanf(inline,"%f",val);
      if ((rtn!=1) || (*val<min) || (*val>max))
      {
         okay=FALSE;
         printf("Invalid input <%s>\n",inline);
      }
      else okay=TRUE;

   } while (!okay);
}

void    get_int(char msg[],int min,int max,int *val)
{
char    inline[BUFSIZ];
int     rtn,okay;
   /*get an integer value between min and max*/
   do
   {
      printf("%s",msg);
      gets(inline);
      rtn=sscanf(inline,"%d",val);
      if ((rtn!=1) || (*val<min) || (*val>max))
      {
         okay=FALSE;
         printf("Invalid input <%s>\n",inline);
      }
      else okay=TRUE;

   } while (!okay);
}
```

Test run 9.4 shows a sample run.

🖳 **Test run 9.4**

```
Enter name of component >> resistor 1
Enter cost of component >> 1.23
Enter component code >> 32455
Name    resistor 1 Code    32455 Cost       1.23
Do you wish to continue (type 'exit' to leave)y
Enter name of component >> capacitor 1
Enter cost of component >> 2.68
```

```
Enter component code >> 32456
Name    resistor 1 Code     32455 Cost     1.23
Name    capacitor 1 Code    32456 Cost     2.68
Do you wish to continue (type 'exit' to leave)y
Enter name of component >> inductor 2
Enter cost of component >> 6.32
Enter component code >> 32457
Name    resistor 1 Code     32455 Cost     1.23
Name    capacitor 1 Code    32456 Cost     2.68
Name    inductor 2 Code     32457 Cost     6.32
Do you wish to continue (type 'exit' to leave)exit
```

Program 9.4 has several flaws. One of the main flaws is that it will accept more than 5 electrical components. This could cause problems as there is only enough memory for 5 components causing the program to eventually crash or act unpredictably. This problem is dealt with in the next program.

Program 9.5 uses get_component() to check the number of components in the array structure. If there are more components than the number declared then it will return DB_FULL, else it will return !DB_FULL. This return value is tested in main(). If the return is DB_FULL the message Database is full, now exiting will be displayed, else it will print the contents of the database.

📄 **Program 9.5**
```c
/*      prog9_5.c           */
#include          <string.h>
#include          <stdio.h>

#define  TRUE           1
#define  FALSE          0
#define  DB_FULL        1
#define  MAXCOMPONENTS  5

typedef struct
{
   float  cost;
   int    code;
   char   name[BUFSIZ];
} CompType;

int    get_component(int *n,CompType Comp[]);
void   print_component(int n,CompType Comp[]);
void   get_int(char msg[],int min,int max,int *val);
void   get_float(char msg[],float min,float max,float *val);
void   get_string(char msg[],char ins[]);

int    main(void)
{
int    NumComponents=0;
char   instr[BUFSIZ];
CompType Component[MAXCOMPONENTS];
   do
   {
      if (get_component(&NumComponents,Component)==DB_FULL)
      {
```

```
         puts("Database is now full");
         break;
      }
      print_component(NumComponents,Component);
      get_string("Do you wish to continue (type 'exit' to leave)",
                instr);
   } while (strcmp(instr,"exit")!=0);
   return(0);
}

int  get_component(int *n,CompType Comp[])
{
int  i;

   i=*n;
   if (i>=MAXCOMPONENTS) return(DB_FULL);

   get_string("Enter name of component >> ",Comp[i].name);
   get_float("Enter cost of component >> ",0.0,1000.0,&Comp[i].cost);
   get_int("Enter component code >> ",0,1000,&Comp[i].code);
   (*n)++;
   return(!DB_FULL);
}

void    print_component(int n,CompType Comp[])
{
:::: see Program 9.4
}
void    get_string(char msg[],char ins[])
{
:::: see Program 9.4
}
void    get_float(char msg[],float min,float max,float *val)
{
:::: see Program 9.4
}

void    get_int(char msg[],int min,int max,int *val)
{
:::: see Program 9.4
}
```

Program 9.6 shows an example of how an array of structures can be initialized at the point it is declared. A macro MAXSTRING has been set up to define the maximum string size (BUFSIZ is normally used when the input is from the keyboard).

📄 **Program 9.6**
```
/* prog9_6.c   */
#include  <stdio.h>

#define    MAXSTRING    100
#define    COMPONENTS   5

typedef struct
{
   char name[MAXSTRING];
```

```
    float   value;
    char unit[MAXSTRING];
} Compname;

int  main(void)
{
Compname  comp[COMPONENTS]={
        {"R1",43,"Kohm"},{"C2",1.02,"uF"},
        {"R2",100,"Mohm"},{"C1",2.6,"uF"},
        {"R3",1.2,"Kohm"}};
    int       i;

    for (i=0;i<COMPONENTS;i++)
      printf("%10s %8.2f %10s\n",
             comp[i].name,comp[i].value,comp[i].unit);

    return(0);
}
```

Test run 9.5 shows a sample run.

☐ **Test run 9.5**

| | | |
|---|---|---|
| R1 | 43.00 | Kohm |
| C2 | 1.02 | uF |
| R2 | 100.00 | Mohm |
| C1 | 2.60 | uF |
| R3 | 1.20 | Kohm |

## 9.2 Allocating structures dynamically

Once a new data type has been created for a structure it is simple to allocate memory to it dynamically. This is achieved by declaring the structure name as a pointer, and then memory is allocated using a memory allocation function such as malloc(). The return from this function is then assigned to the structure pointer. If the return from malloc() is a NULL there is not enough memory for the structure. Program 9.7 shows an example of how an array of structures is dynamically allocated.

📄 **Program 9.7**
```
/* prog9_7.c   */
#include <string.h>
#include <stdio.h>
#include <alloc.h>/* required for malloc()   */

#define   TRUE            1
#define   FALSE           0
#define   DB_FULL         1
#define   MAXCOMPONENTS   5

typedef struct
{
   float   cost;
   int     code;
```

```
        char    name[BUFSIZ];
   } CompType;

   int    get_component(int *n,CompType Comp[]);
   void   print_component(int n,CompType Comp[]);
   void   get_int(char msg[],int min,int max,int *val);
   void   get_float(char msg[],float min,float max,float *val);
   void   get_string(char msg[],char ins[]);

   int    main(void)
   {
   int       num_components=0,max_comp;
   char      instr[BUFSIZ];
   CompType *component;

      do
      {
        get_int("Enter maximum number of components >>",0,32000,
                   &max_comp);
        component=(CompType *) malloc(max_comp*sizeof(CompType));
        if (component==NULL)
        {
          puts("Cannot allocated memory for components");
          break;
        }
        if (get_component(&num_components,component)==DB_FULL)
        {
          puts("Database is now full");
          break;
        }
        print_component(num_components,component);
        get_string("Do you wish to continue (type 'exit' to leave)",
                   instr);
      } while (strcmp(instr,"exit")!=0);
      return(0);
   }

   void   get_component(int *n,CompType Comp[])
   {
      get_string("Enter name of component >> ",Comp[i].name);
      get_float("Enter cost of component >> ",0.0,1000.0,&Comp[i].cost);
      get_int("Enter component code >> ",0,1000,&Comp[i].code);
      (*n)++;
   }

   void   print_component(int n,CompType Comp[])
   {
   :::: see Program 9.4
   }

   void   get_string(char msg[],char ins[])
   {
   :::: see Program 9.4
   }

   void   get_float(char msg[],float min,float max,float *val)
   {
   :::: see Program 9.4
```

```
}

void    get_int(char msg[],int min,int max,int *val)
{
::.: see Program 9.4
}
```

## 9.3 Bit fields

A structure can be used to define bit fields within an integer (signed or unsigned). These
bit fields can vary from 1 to 16 bits wide (or more depending on compiler
implementation). The identifier of the bit field is defined after the data type and the
width of the bit field is specified after a colon. This is shown in the following example.
If there is no bit field identifier then the bits defined in that field are unused.

```
struct
{
   int  limit      :2;
                    /*Bit fields 0 and 1 used for limit    */
   int  sensors    :2;
                    /*Bit fields 2 and 3 used for sensors   */
   int             :4;
                    /*Bit fields 4,5,6 and 7 are unused     */
   unsigned int  motors   :3;
                    /*Bit fields 8,9 and 10 are used for motors*/
} in_out;
```

The layout of the bits within the structure in_out is given in Figure 9.5.

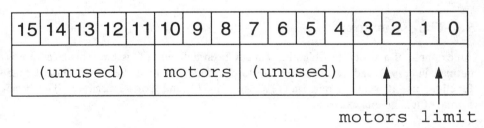

**Figure 9.5:** Bit field arrangement for in_out structure

The bit fields are accessed using the dot operator, e.g. bit fields 8-10 are accessed by
in_out.motors. If the bit field type is signed then the most significant bit of the
field is a sign flag as signed integers are stored in 2's complement notation. For
example, in a 3-bit signed integer bit field a value of -1 (decimal) will be stored as 111
(binary), whereas a 3-bit unsigned field 111 (binary) would correspond to 7 (decimal).

Thus, the range of a 3-bit signed field is from 011 (3) to 100 (-4) and that of an unsigned 3-bit field from 111 (7) to 000 (0). Table 9.1 shows the different decimal ranges for a 3-bit binary format.

**Table 9.1:** 3-bit signed and unsigned decimal values

| 3-bit binary format | Signed decimal value (int) | Unsigned decimal value (unsigned int) |
|---|---|---|
| 011 | 3 | 3 |
| 010 | 2 | 2 |
| 010 | 1 | 1 |
| 000 | 0 | 0 |
| 111 | -1 | 7 |
| 110 | -2 | 6 |
| 101 | -3 | 5 |
| 100 | -4 | 4 |

Table 9.2 shows an example of a sequence of operations on the bit fields of in_out. It is assumed that all the bit fields are set initially to 0.

**Table 9.2:** Sample operations on in_out structure

| Statement | Bit pattern of in_out after statement |
|---|---|
| in_out.limit=1; | 000000 000 000 00 01 |
| in_out.sensors=-2; | 000000 000 000 10 01 |
| in_out.motors=7; | 000000 111 000 10 01 |

Programs 9.10 and 9.11 give examples of programs which use bit fields.

## 9.4 Time structure

An example of a structure which has already been defined in C is tm. This structure is defined in *time.h* and can be used to store a date and time. Several standard time functions use it, such as gmtime(), asctime() and localtime(). The basic format of it is given next.

```
struct tm
{
    int  tm_sec;   /* seconds (0-59)                      */
    int  tm_min;   /* minutes (0-59)                      */
    int  tm_hour;  /* hours   (0-23)                      */
    int  tm_mday;  /* day of the month (1-31)             */
    int  tm_wday;  /* day of week (0-6) Sunday is 0       */
    int  tm_mon;   /* month of the year   (0-11)          */
    int  tm_year;  /* calendar year (year minus 1990)     */
    int  tm_yday   /* day of the year (0-364)             */
}
```

Program 9.8 is a simple program in which the user enters a month as an integer (i.e. 1 to 12) and the current day of the month. The program will then display the date in a DD–MMM format, where MMM is 3-character representation of the month (i.e. JAN, FEB, etc.). The program checks the number of days in the entered month and will display an error message if the entered day of the month exceeds the number of days in the specified month. It will also display an error if the entered day value is less than 1. The number of days in each month is set up using an array days_in_month[] (i.e. 31 for January, 28 for February, etc.). Note that the program assumes that the year is not a leap year.

📄 **Program 9.8**

```
/*    prog9_8.c                                          */
#include  <stdio.h>
#include  <time.h>

#define   NMONTHS   12    /* Number of months in a year   */
#define   TRUE      1
#define   FALSE     0

void    get_int(char msg[],int min,int max,int *val);

int     main(void)
{
struct tm    t;
int     days_in_month[NMONTHS]={31,28,31,30,31,
                                30,31,31,30,31,30,31};

char    *months[NMONTHS]={"JAN","FEB","MAR","APR","MAY",
                "JUN","JUL","AUG","SEP","OCT","NOV","DEC"};

  get_int("Enter current month (1-12) >>",1,12,&t.tm_mon);

  get_int("Enter day of the month >>",
             1,days_in_month[t.tm_mon-1],&t.tm_mday);

  printf("Date is %02d-%s\n",t.tm_mday,months[t.tm_mon-1]);

  return(0);
}

void    get_int(char msg[],int min,int max,int *val)
{
:::: see Program 9.4
}
```

Test run 9.6 shows a sample test run. The user has entered a value of 2 for the month (i.e. February) and then entered the day of the month as 31. This is invalid, since February does not have 31 days, and the user is then re-prompted for another day of the month. The program is able to test for the number of days in the month as the value max sent to get_int() is set by the days_in_month[] array. Since the entered value is 2 then the maximum value sent will be 28 (Note that 1 is subtracted from the entered month as 0 is taken as the first month).

⌨ **Test run 9.6**

```
Enter current month (1-12) >> 2
Enter day of the month >>31
Invalid input <31>
Enter day of the month >>-3
Invalid input <-3>
Enter day of the month >>23
Date is 23-FEB
```

Program 9.9 contains standard C functions which can be used to generate a tm structure, these are time() and gmtime(). The function time() determines the current system time and gmtime() converts this time into a tm structure format. The syntax of these functions is given next.

```
time_t      time(time_t *timer)
struct  tm  *gmtime(time_t *timer)
```

The time() function determines the number of seconds that have passed since 00:00:00 GMT on January 1 1970. The return value is returned as a pointer (*timer) and also through the function header (the data type of the return value is time_t, which is also defined in *time.h*). This returned value is then passed to gmtime() which fills the ttt structure. The variable ttt is declared as a pointer to a tm structure and the gmtime() function reserves enough space in memory for the structure and returns a pointer to the start of it.

📄 **Program 9.9**
```
/*    prog9_9.c                              */
#define   MAXSTRING    30
        /* Format of string is Current Date is XX-YY-ZZ */

#include <stdio.h>
#include <time.h>

int  main(void)
{
time_t      timer;
struct tm   *ttt;
char        str[MAXSTRING];

   time(&timer);    /* get number of seconds since 0:0:0 1/1/70 */
   ttt=gmtime(&timer); /* convert seconds into tm format        */

   sprintf(str,"Current Date is %02d-%02d-%02d",
      ttt->tm_mday,ttt->tm_mon,ttt->tm_year);
   puts(str);

   return(0);
}
```

Test run 9.7 shows a sample test run; in this case the current date is 5 September 1994.

```
Current Date is 05-09-94
```

## 9.5 Examples

### 9.5.1 Traffic light sequence

Program 9.10 generates a basic traffic light sequence with pedestrian control lights. A structure named `traffic_bit_field` stores the bits for the RED, AMBER and GREEN traffic light status (0 - OFF or 1 - ON) and the pedestrian status (0 - DONT WALK, 1 - WALK). The traffic light bit fields are shown in Figure 9.6. Bits 0-2 are used for the traffic light colours and bit 3 for the pedestrian status.

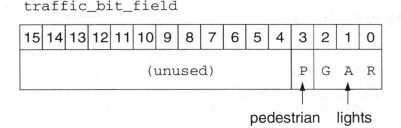

**Figure 9.6:** Bit field arrangement for `traffic_bit_field` structure

A function `show_sequence()` is used to mask each of the bits within the structure and display their status. Four bit masks have been set up, these are RED, AMBER and GREEN. The RED bitmask operates on the first bit of the lights field, AMBER the second and GREEN the third. For example, if `traff.lights & RED` is TRUE then the RED bit is set, else it will be FALSE (a 0 is FALSE while a TRUE is any other value). Table 9.3 shows the required sequence.

**Table 9.3:** Traffic light and pedestrian control sequence

| Traffic Light   | Pedestrian  |
|-----------------|-------------|
| RED             | DONT WALK   |
| RED and AMBER   | DONT WALK   |
| GREEN           | DONT WALK   |
| AMBER           | DONT WALK   |
| RED             | WALK        |
| RED and AMBER   | DONT WALK   |
| GREEN           | DONT WALK   |
| *etc.*          |             |

**Program 9.10**

```c
/*    prog9_10.c                                        */
#include <stdio.h>

#define    RED     1   /* 1st bit field */
#define    AMBER   2   /* 2nd bit field */
#define    GREEN   4   /* 3rd bit field */

#define    FALSE   0
#define    TRUE    1

typedef struct
{
   unsigned int  lights       :3;  /* GAR    */
   unsigned int  pedestrian    :1;  /* P      */
} traffic_bit_field; /* XXXX XXXX XXXX PGAR    */

void    show_sequence(traffic_bit_field traf);

int     main(void)
{
traffic_bit_field  traffic;
char    ch;

   do
   {
      traffic.lights=RED;
      traffic.pedestrian=FALSE;     /* 0 001 */
      show_sequence(traffic);
      ch=getchar(); /* press any key to continue */

      traffic.lights=RED+AMBER;     /* 0 011 */
      show_sequence(traffic);
      ch=getchar(); /* press any key to continue */

      traffic.lights=GREEN;         /* 0 100 */
      show_sequence(traffic);
      ch=getchar(); /* press any key to continue */

      traffic.lights=AMBER;         /* 0 010 */
      show_sequence(traffic);
      ch=getchar(); /* press any key to continue */

      traffic.lights=RED;
      traffic.pedestrian=TRUE;      /* 1 001 */
      show_sequence(traffic);
      printf("Press 'x' to exit >> "); ch=getchar();
   } while (ch!='x');
   return(0);
}

void    show_sequence(traffic_bit_field traff)
{
   if (traff.lights & RED)      printf("RED ");
   if (traff.lights & AMBER)    printf("AMBER ");
   if (traff.lights & GREEN)    printf("GREEN ");

   if (traff.pedestrian==FALSE) puts("<DONT WALK>");
```

```
       else puts("<WALK>");
}
```

Test run 9.8 shows a sample run.

---

🖥 **Test run 9.8**

```
RED <DONT WALK>
RED AMBER <DONT WALK>
GREEN <DONT WALK>
AMBER <DONT WALK>
RED <WALK>
Press 'x' to exit >>
RED <DONT WALK>
RED AMBER <DONT WALK>
GREEN <DONT WALK>
AMBER <DONT WALK>
RED <WALK>
Press 'x' to exit >> x
```

---

Program 9.11 has an improved structure and uses an array to store the traffic light and pedestrian sequences.

📄 **Program 9.11**

```
/*    prog9_11.c                                       */
/*    program to display a traffic light sequence      */
/*    with a pedestrian crossing                       */

#include <stdio.h>

#define    RED      1
#define    AMBER    2
#define    GREEN    4

#define    NO_SEQ   6

#define    FALSE    0
#define    TRUE     1

typedef struct
{
   unsigned int  lights       :3;
   unsigned int  pedestrian   :1;
} traffic_bit_field;

void    show_sequence(traffic_bit_field traf);

int     main(void)
{
traffic_bit_field  traffic;
char ch;
int  lights_seq[NO_SEQ]={RED,RED+AMBER,GREEN,AMBER,RED,RED};
int  pedestrian_seq[NO_SEQ]={FALSE,FALSE,FALSE,FALSE,FALSE,TRUE};
int  i;

   puts("Traffic lights sequence program");
```

```
      puts("Enter 'x' to exit the program");

      do
      {

         for (i=0;i<NO_SEQ;i++)
         {
            traffic.lights=lights_seq[i];
            traffic.pedestrian=pedestrian_seq[i];
            show_sequence(traffic);
            ch=getchar();
            if (ch=='x') break;
         }

      } while (ch!='x');
      return(0);
   }
   void show_sequence(traffic_bit_field traff)
   {
      if (traff.lights & RED)      printf("RED ");
      if (traff.lights & AMBER)    printf("AMBER ");
      if (traff.lights & GREEN)    printf("GREEN ");

      if (traff.pedestrian==FALSE)  puts("<DONT WALK>");
      else                          puts("<WALK>");
   }
```

Test run 9.9 shows a sample test run.

---

🖥  **Test run 9.9**
```
RED <DONT WALK>
RED AMBER <DONT WALK>
GREEN <DONT WALK>
AMBER <DONT WALK>
RED <DONT WALK>
RED <WALK>
RED <DONT WALK>
RED AMBER <DONT WALK>
GREEN <DONT WALK>
AMBER <DONT WALK>
RED <DONT WALK>
RED <WALK>
```
---

### 9.5.2  Input impedance of an RLC circuit

Program 9.12 uses a structure to store the magnitude and angle of the impedance for an RLC series circuit. This strucure is named `polar` and it stores a magnitude and an angle.

📄  **Program 9.12**
```
/*    prog9_12.c                               */
/*    RLC circuit                              */
/*    Program to calculate the input impedance of  */
/*    a series RLC circuit                     */
```

```
typedef struct
{
    float mag,angle;
} polar;


#include <stdio.h>
#include <math.h>

#define   PI               3.14157
#define   TRUE             1
#define   FALSE            0

#define   _calcXL(_f,_L)   (2*PI*(_f)*(_L))
#define   _calcXC(_f,_C)   (1/ (2*PI*(_f)*(_C)))
#define   _calc_mag(_x,_y) (sqrt((_x)*(_x)+(_y)*(_y)))
#define   _calc_angle(_x,_y) atan2((_y),(_x))
#define   _RadToDeg(_rad)  ((_rad)/(PI)*180)
void   get_values(float *f,float *r,float *l, float *c);
void   calc_impedance(float f,float r,float l,float c, polar *z);
void   get_float(char msg[],float min,float max,float *val);

int    main(void)
{
float   R,L,C,freq;
polar   Zin;

   get_values(&freq,&R,&L,&C);
   calc_impedance(freq,R,L,C,&Zin);

   printf("Zin mag is %.2f angle %.2f degrees\n",
         Zin.mag, _RadToDeg(Zin.angle));
   return(0);
}

void   get_values(float *f,float *r,float *l, float *c)
{
   get_float("Enter frequency >>",0,100e6,f);
           /* max freq 100 MHz      */
   get_float("Enter resistance >>",0,100e6,r);
           /* max resistance 100 M   */
   get_float("Enter inductance >>",0,1,l);
           /* max inductance 1 mH    */
   get_float("Enter capacitance >>",0,10e-3,c);
           /* max cap 1 uF           */
}

void   calc_impedance(float f,float r,float l,float c, polar *z)
{
float   reactance;

   reactance=_calcXL(f,l) - _calcXC(f,c);
   z->mag = _calc_mag(r,reactance);
   z->angle = _calc_angle(r,reactance);
}

void get_float(char msg[],float min,float max,float *val)
```

```
{
:::: see Program 9.4
}
```

Test run 9.10 shows a sample run.

---

🖥  **Test run 9.10**

```
Enter frequency >>    10e3
Enter resistance >>   3200
Enter inductance >>   10e-3
Enter capacitance >> 1e-6
Zin mag is 3258.07 angle 10.83 degrees
```

---

### 9.5.3  74-series ICs

The 74-series logic family is a range of TTL digital integrated circuits (ICs). These can be identified with a preceding 74 in the part number, followed by 2 or 3 digits that identify the function of the device. Program 9.13 displays 8 different 74-series ICs. Note that the device numbers are stored as long integers as the maximum value of a 2-byte signed integer is 32,767 and an unsigned integer is 65,535. An L is appended onto a constant value if it is a long integer.

The printf() statement uses the format string "%-6ld  %-20s\n"; the negative sign signifies that the arguments are to be left justified, the default justification is right.

📄  **Program 9.13**

```
/* prog9_13.c          */
#include <stdio.h>

#define   NO_DEVICES    8
#define   MAXSTRING     100

typedef struct
{
   long int  product_no;
   char      name[MAXSTRING];
} Device;

void    show_devices(Device dev[]);

int     main(void)
{
Device device[NO_DEVICES]={
     {7408L,"2-input AND gate"},{7432L,"2-input OR gate"},
     {7400L,"2-input NAND gate"},{7402L,"2-input NOR gate"},
     {7404L,"Inverting buffer"},{7474L,"D-type flip-flop"},
     {7470L,"J-K flip-flop"},{74121L,"Monostable"}};

   show_devices(device);
   return(0);
}
void    show_devices(Device dev[])
```

```
{
int  i;
   for  (i=0;i<NO_DEVICES;i++)
      printf("%-6ld %-20s\n",dev[i].product_no,dev[i].name);
}
```

Test run 9.11 shows a sample run.

---

🖥  **Test run 9.11**

```
7408    2-input AND gate
7432    2-input OR gate
7400    2-input NAND gate
7402    2-input NOR gate
7404    Inverting buffer
7474    D-type flip-flop
7470    J-K flip-flop
74121   Monostable
```

---

## 9.6  Tutorial

Q9.1    Write a program which contains a fixed database containing a list of CMOS 4000 series ICs. Some basic devices are given in Table 9.4. Refer to program 9.13.

**Table 9.4:** 4000-series CMOS ICs

| Device | Function |
| --- | --- |
| 4081 | 2-input AND gate |
| 4011 | 2-input NAND gate |
| 4071 | 2-input OR gate |
| 4001 | 2-input NOR gate |
| 4070 | 2-input EX-OR gate |
| 4013 | D-type flip-flip |
| 4027 | JK flip-flop |
| 4043 | RS flip-flop |

Q9.2    Modify the program in Q9.1 so that the user can enter a device number and the program will display its function. Test run 9.12 shows a sample run.

---

🖥  **Test run  9.12**

```
Enter a 4000 series device >> 4013
>>>> D-type. flip-flop
Enter a 4000 series device >> 4043
>>>> RS 'flip-flop
```

---

Q9.3    Write a database program, based on program 9.5, which gives a menu choice as to whether the user wishes to enter input a new electric component, to list all the components already in the database, or to exit the program. A sample run is given in test run 9.13.

---
🖥 **Test run 9.13**
```
Do you wish to
(1)   Input a component
(2)   List all components
(3)   Exit from program
Enter option >>>
```
---

Q9.4    Modify program 9.8 so that it takes into account leap years. The user should enter the month, the current year and the day of the month. Note that leap years are divisible by 4 (the modulus operator % may be useful as year % 4 yields a 0). A sample test run is given in test run 9.14.

---
🖥 **Test run 9.14**
```
Enter month                >> 2
Enter year (e.g. 1994)  >> 1993
Enter day of month (1-31) >> 29
Invalid input <29>
Enter day of month (1-31) >> 28
Date is 28-FEB-1993
```
---

Q9.5    Modify program in Q9.4 so that it displays the valid range of days when the day of the month is prompted for. For example, if February is entered then the message prompt will display Enter day of month (1-28). A sample test run is given in test run 9.15.

---
🖥 **Test run 9.15**
```
Enter month                >> 4
Enter year (e.g. 1994)  >> 1993
Enter day of month (1-30) >> 31
Invalid input <31>
Enter day of month (1-30) >> 28
Date is 28-APR-1993
```
---

Q9.6    Modify program 9.9 so that the date is printed in the format DD-MMM-YYYY, where DD is the day of the month, MMM is a 3-character representation of the month and YYYY a 4-digit representation of the year. Test run 9.16 shows a sample run. *Hint*: use the array of strings used in program 9.8 to represent the months.

---
🖥 **Test run 9.16**
```
Current Date is 05-OCT-1994
```
---

Q9.7    Modify program 9.11 so that it displays the sequence of two traffic lights with a single pedestrian control. Table 9.5 shows a sample sequence and Figure 9.7 shows a possible bit pattern for the structure.

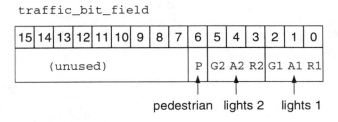

**Figure 9.7:** Bit field arrangement for `traffic_bit_field` structure

**Table 9.5:** Traffic lights and pedestrian control sequence

| Traffic light 1 | Traffic light 2 | Pedestrian |
|---|---|---|
| RED | RED | DONT WALK |
| RED | RED and AMBER | DONT WALK |
| RED | GREEN | DONT WALK |
| RED | AMBER | DONT WALK |
| RED | RED | WALK |
| RED and AMBER | RED | DONT WALK |
| GREEN | RED | DONT WALK |
| AMBER | RED | DONT WALK |
| RED | RED | WALK |
| RED | RED and AMBER | DONT WALK |
|  | etc |  |

Q9.8    Write a program which determines the impedance (magnitude and angle) of a parallel RL circuit. Each impedance should be entered as a magnitude and an angle, and the parallel impedance should be printed in complex form, i.e. as a magnitude and an angle. Refer to programs 6.4 and 9.12.

$$Z = \frac{R.j\omega L}{R + j\omega L}$$

$$= \frac{\omega RL \langle 90° \rangle}{\sqrt{R^2 + (\omega L)^2} \left\langle \tan^{-1} \frac{\omega L}{R} \right\rangle}$$

$$|Z| = \frac{\omega RL}{\sqrt{R^2 + (\omega L)^2}}$$

$$\langle Z \rangle = 90° - \tan^{-1} \frac{\omega L}{R}$$

Q9.9    Write a program using structures with complex impedance values that will determine the parallel impedance of two impedances $Z_1$ and $Z_2$. The formula for the impedances in parallel is given below:

$$Z_{EQ} = \frac{Z_1 Z_2}{Z_1 + Z_2} \quad \Omega$$

# CHAPTER 10

# File Input/Output

Files store data in a permanent form. These files normally have a name followed by a filename extension which identifies the type of file. Some example files could be:

- C, Pascal, FORTRAN, BASIC, COBOL source code (e.g. `file.c`, `file.pas`, `file.ftn`, `file.bas`, `file.cob`);
- Word processor documents (e.g. `temp1.doc`);
- Object code files (e.g. `file1.obj`, `file2.o`);
- Executable file (e.g. `file.exe`, `file1`);
- Input data files (e.g. `in.dat`);
- Output run file (e.g. `out.dat`);
- Help files (e.g. `prog.hlp`);
- etc.

There are two types of files that can be operated on, these are binary and text. A text file uses ASCII characters when reading from and writing to a file; a binary file uses the binary digits which the computer uses to store values. It is not normally possible to view a binary file without a special program, but a text file can be viewed with a text editor. Text files use the functions `fscanf()` and `fprintf()` to read and write, whereas binary files use `fread()` and `fwrite()`.

Figure 10.1 shows an example of two files which contain four integer values. The binary file stores integers using two bytes in 2's complement signed notation, whereas the text file uses ASCII characters to represent the values. For example, the value of $-1$ is represented as `11111111 11111111` in 2's complement. This binary pattern is stored to the binary file. The text file uses ASCII characters to represent $-1$ (these will be '-' and '1'), and the bit pattern stored for the text file will thus be `0010 1101` (ASCII '-') and `0011 0001` (ASCII '1'). If a new line is required after each number then a new-line character is inserted after it. Note, there is no new-line character in ASCII and it is typical to represent a new-line with two characters, a carriage return (CR) and a line feed (LF). In C the new-line character is denoted by '\n'.

The number of bytes used to store each of the elements will depend on the data type of the variable. For example, a long int will be stored as four bytes, whereas a floating point value can be stored as four bytes (on some systems). The floating point format differs from an integer format; the standard floating point format uses a sign-bit, a significand and an exponent. The end of the file is signified by an EOF character.

**Binary file**

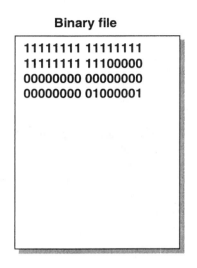

**Text file**

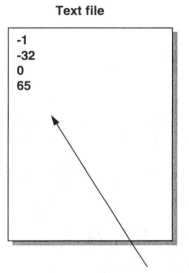

Text file stores the values
as ASCII characters (e.g. -1 is
'-' and '1'). In this example
there is a new line character
at the end of each line.

**Figure 10.1:** Binary and text files

There are 11 main functions used in file input/output (I/O), these are listed below. The fprint() and fscanf() functions are similar to printf() and scanf(), but their output goes to a file.

```
file_ptr=fopen(filename,"attributes");
fclose(file_ptr);
fprintf(file_ptr,"format",arg1,arg2,..);
fscanf(file_ptr,"format",arg1,arg2...);
fgets(str,n,file_ptr);
fputs(str,file_ptr);
fputc(ch,file_ptr);
ch=fgetc(file_ptr);
fwrite(ptr,size,n,file_ptr);
fread(ptr,size,n,file_ptr);
feof(file_ptr);
```

A file pointer stores the current position of a read or write within a file. All operations within the file are made with reference to the pointer. The data type of this pointer is defined in *stdio.h* and is named FILE.

```
#include <stdio.h>


int     main(void)
{
FILE    *fileptr;

}
```

The file pointer moves as each element is read/written. Figure 10.2 shows a file pointer pointing to the current position within the file.

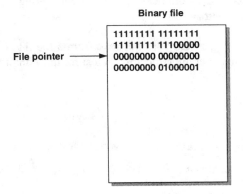

**Figure 10.2:** File pointer

## 10.1 Opening a file (fopen())

A file pointer is assigned using fopen(). The first argument is the file name and the second a string which defines the attributes of the file; these are listed in Table 10.1.

**Table 10.1:** File attributes

| Attribute | Function |
|-----------|----------|
| "r" | open for reading only |
| "w" | create for writing |
| "a" | append; open for writing at the end-of-file or create for writing if the file does not exist |
| "r+" | open an existing file for update (read and write) |
| "w+" | create a new file for update |
| "a+" | open for append: open (or create if the file does not exist) for update at the end of the file) |

The default mode for opening files is text, but a t attribute can be appended onto the attribute string to specify a text file. For example, the attribute "wt" opens a text file for writing. A binary file is specified by appending a b onto the attribute string. For example, "rb" will open a binary file for reading.

The format of the fopen() function is:

```
file_ptr=fopen("Filename","attrib");
```

If fopen() is completed successfully a file pointer will be returned, and this is initialized to the start of the file. If was not able to open the file then a NULL will be returned. There can be many reasons why a file cannot be opened, such as:

- the file does not exist;
- the file is protected from reading from and/or writing to;
- the file is a directory.

It is important that a program does not read from a file that cannot be opened as it may cause the program to act unpredictably. A test for this condition is given next.

```
int     main(void)
{
FILE    *in;

    if ((in=fopen("in.dat","r"))==NULL)
    {
      printf("File IN.DAT could not be opened");
    }
    :::::::::::::::::::::::::::::
    return(0);
}
```

## 10.2 Closing a file (`fclose()`)

Once a file has been used it must be closed before the program is terminated. A file which is not closed properly can cause problems in the file system. The standard format is given next; the return value (rtn) returns a 0 (a zero) on success, otherwise EOF if any errors occur. The macro EOF is defined in *stdio.h*.

```
rtn=fclose(file_ptr)
```

## 10.3 Printing text to a file (`fprintf()`)

The fprintf() function is used with text files and has a similar format to printf() but the output goes to a file. An example of the fprintf() function is given next. The return value (`rtn`) returns the number of bytes sent to the file; in the event of an error it returns EOF.

```
rtn=fprintf(file_ptr,"%s %d",str1,value1);
```

## 10.4 Reading text from a file (`fscanf()`)

The `fscanf()` function is used with text files and has a similar format to `scanf()` but the input is read from a file. An example of the `fscanf()` function is given next.

```
rtn=fscanf(file_ptr,"%s %d %d",str1,&val1,&val2);
```

This function returns the number of fields successfully scanned (`rtn`) or, if there was an attempt to read from the end-of-file, an EOF value is returned.

## 10.5 Finding the end of a file (`feof()`)

The `feof()` function detects the end-of-file character. It returns a non-zero value (i.e. a TRUE) if the file pointer is at the end of a file, else a 0 is returned. The function shown next uses the `feof()` function to detect the end of the file and also tests the return from the `fscanf()` so that an unsuccessful reading from the file is disregarded.

```
int     get_values(int maxval, char fname[],int *n,float arr[])
{
FILE    *in;
int     i=0,rtn;

   if ((in=fopen(fname,"r"))==NULL)
   {
      printf("Cannot open %s\n",fname);
      return(NOFILE);
   }

   while (!(feof(in)))
   {
      rtn=fscanf(in,"%f",&arr[i]);
      if (rtn!=EOF) i++;
      if (i==maxval) break;
   }

   fclose(in);

   *n=i;
   return(!NOFILE);
}
```

## 10.6  Getting a string of text from a file (**fgets()**)

The fgets() function is similar to gets() and is used to get a string of text from a file up to a new-line character. The standard format is given next.

```
rtn=fgets(str,n,file_ptr)
```

It reads from the file specifed by file_ptr into str with a maximum of n characters. The return (rtn) points to a string pointed to by str or will return a NULL if the end-of-file (or an error) is encountered.

## 10.7  Putting a string of text to a file (**fputs()**)

The fputs() function is similar to puts() and is used to write a string of text to a file. It does not append the output with a new line. The standard format is given next.

```
rtn=fputs(str,file_ptr)
```

This outputs str to the file specifed by file_ptr. The return (rtn) returns the last character written; if there is an error it returns EOF.

## 10.8  Putting a character to a file (**fputc()**)

The fputc() function is similar to putchar() and is used to write a single character to a file. The standard format is given next.

```
rtn=fputc(ch,file_ptr)
```

This writes ch to the file specifed by file_ptr. The return (rtn) returns the last character written; if there is an error it will return EOF.

## 10.9  Getting a character from a file (**fgetc()**)

The fgetc() function is similar to getchar() and is used to read a single character from a file. The standard format is given next.

```
ch=fgetc(file_ptr)
```

This reads ch from the file specifed by file_ptr. If there is an error in getting the character an EOF will be returned.

## 10.10 Binary files

### 10.10.1 Reading binary data from a file (`fread()`)

The `fread()` function is used to read data in a binary format. The standard format is:

$$rtn=fread(ptr,size,n,file\_ptr)$$

This will read n items of data into the data block specified by `ptr`, each of length `size` bytes, from the input file specified by `file_ptr`. The value returned `rtn` specifies the number of blocks (or items) which have been successfully read. If no error occurs in the reading then the number of items specified (n) will be the same as the return value (`rtn`). If they differ, an error or end of file has occurred.

The `fread()` function is used in the function given next. In this case, 1 floating point value is read from the file and the return value is tested to see if it has been read properly. The `sizeof()` function is used to determine the number of bytes used to store a `float`.

```
int     read_data(char fname[],float arr[],int *nov)
{
FILE    *in;
int     i;

   *nov=0; /* number of values in the array */

   if ((in=fopen(fname,"rb"))==NULL)
   {
      printf("Cannot open %s\n",fname);
      return(NOFILE);
   }

   while (!feof(in))
   {
      if (fread(&arr[i],sizeof (float),1,in)==1)   /*read 1 value*/
         (*nov)++;
   }

   fclose(in);

   return(!NOFILE);
}
```

### 10.10.2 Writing binary data to a file (`fwrite()`)

The `fwrite()` function is used to write data in binary format. The standard format is:

$$rtn=fwrite(ptr,size,n,file\_ptr)$$

This writes n items of data from the data block specified by `ptr`, each of length `size` bytes, to the output file specified by `file_ptr`. The value returned `rtn` specifies the number of blocks which have been successfully written. The `fwrite()` function is used in the function given next.

```
int     dump_data(char fname[],float arr[],int nov)
{
FILE    *out;
int     i;

   if ((out=fopen(fname,"wb"))==NULL)
   {
      printf("Cannot open %s\n",fname);
      return(NOFILE);
   }

   for (i=0;i<nov;i++)
      fwrite(&arr[i],sizeof (float),1,out);

   fclose(out);
   return(!NOFILE);
}
```

# 10.11  Examples

### 10.11.1  Boolean equation

Program 10.1 uses a text file to store the results of a Boolean circuit simulation. The Boolean equation used is $Z=(A.B)+C$.

📄 **Program 10.1**
```
/* prog10_1.c                                            */
/* Program to determine truth table for boolean         */
/* function Z=(A and B) or C                             */
/* Output truth table is stored to a file               */
/* and then read back from this file                    */

#include <stdio.h>

#define   MAX_STATES    8
#define   STRINGSIZE    100

void   process_eq(int tt[]);
void   dump_table(char fname[],int tt[]);
void   read_table(char fname[]);

int  main(void)
{
int  t_table[MAX_STATES];

   process_eq(t_table);
   dump_table("OUT.DAT",t_table);
```

```
      read_table("OUT.DAT");
      return(0);
}

/* determine truth table */
void    process_eq(int tt[])
{
int     state=0,A,B,C;

   puts("Processing states");

   for (A=0;A<=1;A++)
      for (B=0;B<=1;B++)
         for (C=0;C<=1;C++)
         {
            tt[state]=(A & B) | C;
            state++;
         }
}

/* output truth table to a file */
void    dump_table(char fname[],int tt[])
{
int     state=0,A,B,C;
FILE    *out;

   if ((out=fopen(fname,"w"))==NULL)
   {
      printf("Cannot open %s \n",fname);
      return;
   }

   puts("Writing to file");

   fprintf(out,"A B C Z\n");

   for (A=0;A<=1;A++)
      for (B=0;B<=1;B++)
         for (C=0;C<=1;C++)
         {
            fprintf(out,"%d %d %d %d\n",A,B,C,tt[state]);
            state++;
         }
   fclose(out);
   puts("File written");
}

/* read truth table from a file */
void    read_table(char fname[])
{
int     A,B,C,Z;
FILE    *in;
char    header[STRINGSIZE];

   if ((in=fopen(fname,"r"))==NULL)
   {
      printf("Cannot open %s\n",fname);
      return;
```

```
   }

   puts("Reading from file");

   /* get file header ie "A B C Z" */
   fgets(header,STRINGSIZE,in);
   printf("%s",header);

   while (!feof(in))
   {
      fscanf(in,"%d %d %d %d\n",&A,&B,&C,&Z);
      printf("%d %d %d %d\n",A,B,C,Z);
   }

   fclose(in);
}
```

The output file produced is shown in test run 10.1.

---

🖥  **Test run 10.1**
```
Processing states
Writing to file
File written
Reading from file
A B C Z
0 0 0 0
0 0 1 1
0 1 0 0
0 1 1 1
1 0 0 0
1 0 1 1
1 1 0 1
1 1 1 1
```

---

## 10.11.2  Averages program

Program 10.2 uses text files to determine the average value of a number of floating point values contained in a file. The get_values() function is used to read the values from a file, in this case, *IN.DAT*. This file can be created using a text editor.

📄  **Program 10.2**
```
/* prog10_2.c                                         */
/* Program to determine the average of a file         */
/* containing a number of floating point values       */

#include <stdio.h>

#define   NOVALUES  100 /* max. number of entered values   */
#define   NOFILE    0

int     get_values(int maxvals, char fname[],int *n,float arr[]);
float   calc_average(int nval,float arr[]);
void    display_average(int nval,float arr[],float aver);
```

```
int     main(void)
{
float   values[NOVALUES],average;
int     nvalues;

  if (get_values(NOVALUES,"IN.DAT",&nvalues,values)==NOFILE)
        return(1);
  average=calc_average(nvalues,values);
  display_average(nvalues,values,average);
  return(0);
}

int     get_values(int maxvals, char fname[],int *n,float arr[])
{
FILE    *in;
int     i=0,rtn;

  if ((in=fopen(fname,"r"))==NULL)
  {
    printf("Cannot open %s\n",fname);
    return(NOFILE);
  }

  while (!feof(in))
  {
    rtn=fscanf(in,"%f",&arr[i]);
    if (rtn!=EOF) i++;
    if (i==maxvals) break;
  }
  fclose(in);

  *n=i;
  return(!NOFILE);
}

float   calc_average(int nval,float arr[])
{
int     i;
float   running_total=0;

  for (i=0;i<nval;i++)
    running_total+=arr[i];

  /* note there is no test for a divide by zero */
  return(running_total/nval);
}

void    display_average(int nval,float arr[],float aver)
{
int     i;

  puts("INPUT VALUES ARE:");

  for (i=0;i<nval;i++)
    printf("%8.3f\n",arr[i]);

  printf("Average is %8.3f\n",aver);
}
```

An example of the contents of the *IN.DAT* file are given next.

```
3.240
1.232
6.543
-1.432
```

A sample run using this file is given in test run 10.2.

🖥 **Test run  10.2**
```
INPUT VALUES ARE:
    3.240
    1.232
    6.543
   -1.432
Average is     2.396
```

### 10.11.3  Binary read/write

Program 10.3 is an example of how an array of floating point values is written to a binary file using fwrite() and then read back using fread(). Note that the NOFILE flags returned from dump_data() and read_data() are ignored by main().

📄 **Program 10.3**
```c
/* prog10_3.c                                  */
/* FILEB.C                                      */
/* Writes and reads an array of floats         */
/* to and from a binary file                   */

#include <stdio.h>
#define  NOFILE     0    /* error flag is file does not exist */
#define  MAXSTRING  100  /* max. number of char's in filename */
#define  MAXVALUES  100  /* max. number of floats in array    */

void   get_filename(char fname[]);
void   get_values(int maxvals, float vals[],int *nov);
int    dump_data(char fname[],float arr[],int nov);
int    read_data(char fname[],float arr[],int *nov);
void   print_values(float arr[],int nov);

int    main(void)
{
char   fname[MAXSTRING];
float  values[MAXVALUES];
int    no_values;  /* number of values in the array */

  get_filename(fname);
  get_values(MAXVALUES,values,&no_values);
  dump_data(fname,values,no_values);
  read_data(fname,values,&no_values);
  print_values(values,no_values);
```

```
     return(0);
}
void    get_filename(char fname[])
{
   printf("Enter file name >>");
   scanf("%s",fname);
}

void    get_values(int maxvals, float vals[],int *nov)
{
int     i;

   do
   {
     printf("Number of values to be entered >>");
     scanf("%d",nov);
     if (*nov>maxvals)
          printf("Too many values: MAX: %d\n",MAXVALUES);
   } while (*nov>MAXVALUES);

   for (i=0;i<*nov;i++)
   {
     printf("Enter value %d >>",i);
     scanf("%f",&vals[i]);
   }
}

int     dump_data(char fname[],float arr[],int nov)
{
FILE    *out;
int     i;

        /* open for binary write */
   if ((out=fopen(fname,"wb"))==NULL)
   {
     printf("Cannot open %s\n",fname);
     return(NOFILE); /* unsuccessful file open */
   }

   for (i=0;i<nov;i++)
     fwrite(&arr[i],sizeof (float),1,out);

   fclose(out);
   return(!NOFILE);
}

int     read_data(char fname[],float arr[],int *nov)
{
FILE    *in;

   *nov=0;   /* number of values in the array */

     /* open for binary read */
   if ((in=fopen(fname,"rb"))==NULL)
   {
     printf("Cannot open %s\n",fname);
     return(NOFILE); /* unsuccessful file open */
   }
```

```
    while (!feof(in))
    {
       if (fread(&arr[*nov],sizeof (float),1,in)==1)
          (*nov)++;

    }

    fclose(in);

    return(!NOFILE);
}

void    print_values(float arr[],int nov)
{
int     i;

    printf("Values are:\n");

    for (i=0;i<nov;i++)
       printf("%d %8.3f\n",i,arr[i]);

}
```

A sample test run is given in test run 10.3.

---

🖳 **Test run  10.3**
```
Enter file name >>number.dat
Number of values to be entered >>5
Enter value 0 >>1.435
Enter value 1 >>0.432
Enter value 2 >>-54.32
Enter value 3 >>-1.543
Enter value 4 >>100.01
Values are:
0      1.435
1      0.432
2    -54.320
3     -1.543
4    100.010
```

---

## 10.12  Tutorial

Q10.1    Write a program which will determine the average, the largest and the smallest values of a text file containing floating point values. A sample file is shown next.

---
```
3.24
13.443
100.3
111.02
85.03
43.239
-30.032
```
---

Q10.2 Write a program which will determine the truth table for the following function. The output should be sent to a file (for example *OUT.DAT*).

$$Z = \overline{(A+B)}.(\overline{C}.D)$$

Q10.3 Modify the following programs so that the output is sent to a text file:

(a) program 5.14 (see test run 5.4 for the output file format)
(b) program specified in Q5.7.
(c) program specified in Q5.10 (see test run 5.11 for the output file format)
(d) program 6.4 (see test run 6.3 for the output file format)

Q10.4 Repeat Q10.3, but the input should be read in from a file (e.g. *IN.DAT*) rather than from the keyboard.

Q10.5 Modify program 7.1 so that the program reads values from an input data file and outputs the results to a specified output file.

Q10.6 Write a program which will read a text file containing ASCII characters that represent binary digits (i.e. the characters '0' and '1'). Each line of the file contains five digits. The program should read all sequences and display them in binary format. A sample run is given in test run 10.4.

---

🖥 **Test run 10.4**
```
Input file name > BINARY.DAT
Scanning file .....
Binary sequences
1  10010
2  00011
3  10111
4  11111
5  10010
Program end. BYE
```
===

The contents of *BINARY.DAT* are given next.

---

```
1 0 0 1 0
0 0 0 1 1
1 0 1 1 1
1 1 1 1 1
1 0 0 1 0
```

---

Q10.7 Modify Q10.6 so that it will read in binary sequences of variable lengths. A sample run is given in test run 10.5.

⌨ **Test run 10.5**
```
Input file name > BINARY.DAT
Scanning file .....
Binary sequences
1  100101010001
2  00
3  101110101
4  111110001000
5  1001011
Program end. BYE
```

The contents of *BINARY.DAT* are given next.

```
1 0 0 1 0 1 0 1 0 0 0 1
0 0
1 0 1 1 1 0 1 0 1
1 1 1 1 1 0 0 0 1 0 0 0
1 0 0 1 0 1 1
```

Q10.8  Modify the program in Q10.7 so that only the characters '0' and '1' are displayed for a file which contains other characters.

⌨ **Test run 10.6**
```
Input file name > BINARY.DAT
Scanning file .....
Binary sequences
1  100101010001
2  00
3  101110101
4  111110001000
5  1001011
Program end. BYE
```

The contents of *BINARY.DAT* are given next.

```
1 X 0 0 1 0 1 C 0 1 0 0 0 1
0 P 0
1 0 1 1 1 0 1 0 1
1 1 Q 1 1 1 0 0 0 1 0 0 0
1 0 0 ! 1 0 1 1
```

Q10.9  Write a program which will count the number of characters in a file.

Q10.10 Write a program which will count the occurrences of the letter 'a' in a file. Use either `ch=fgetc()` or `fscanf(in,"%c",&ch)` to read individual characters in the file.

Q10.11 Write a program in which the user enters any character and the program will determine the number of occurrences of that character in the specified file. For example:

---

🖳 **Test run 10.7**
```
Enter filename: fred.dat
Enter character to search for: i
There are 14 occurrences of the character i in the file
fred.dat.
```
---

Q10.12 Write a program which will determine the number of words in a file.

Q10.13 Write a program which will determine the number of lines in a file. A possible method is to count the new-line characters, as given next.

```
ch=getc(in);
if (ch=='\n') no_lines++;
```

Q10.14 Programs 10.4 and 10.5 each have one error in them. Both programs will copy the contents of *IN.DAT* into *OUT.DAT*. Program 10.4 uses `fgetc()` and `fputc()`, whereas 10.5 uses `fgets()` and `fputs()`.

📄 **Program 10.4**
```c
/* prog10_4.c                              */
/* Program to copy from IN.DAT to OUT.DAT  */
#include <stdio.h>

int     main(void)
{
int     ch;
FILE    *in,*out;

    if ((in=fopen("in.dat","r"))==NULL)
    {
       puts("Cannot open IN.DAT");
       return(1);
    }
    if ((out=fopen("out.dat","w"))==NULL)
    {
       puts("Cannot open OUT.DAT");
       return(1);
    }

    while (!feof(in))
    {
       ch=fgetc(in);
       if (ch==EOF) fputc(ch,out);
    }
    fclose(in);
    fclose(out);
    return(0);
}
```

📄 **Program 10.5**

```c
/* prog10_5.c   */
/* Program to copy from IN.DAT to OUT.DAT   */
#include <stdio.h>

int     main(void)
{
char    str[BUFSIZ];
FILE    *in,*out;

  if ((in=fopen("in.dat","r"))==NULL)
  {
   puts("Cannot open IN.DAT");
   return(1);
  }

  if ((out=fopen("out.dat","w"))==NULL)
  {
   puts("Cannot open OUT.DAT");
   return(1);
  }

  while (feof(in))
  {
   fgets(str,BUFSIZ,in);
   fputs(str,out);
  }

  fclose(in);
  fclose(out);
  return(0);
}
```

Q10.15 Write a program which will get rid of blank lines in an input file and writes the processed file to an output file. Example input and output files are given next.

Input file:

| Frequency | Impedance (mag) |
|-----------|-----------------|
| 100       | 101.1           |
|           |                 |
|           |                 |
| 150       | 165.1           |
|           |                 |
| 200       | 300.5           |

Output file:

| Frequency | Impedance (mag) |
|-----------|-----------------|
| 100       | 101.1           |
| 150       | 165.1           |
| 200       | 300.5           |

# CHAPTER 11

# Systems programming

An operating system allows the user to access the hardware in an easy to use manner. It accepts commands from the keyboard and displays them to the monitor. The two most popular operating systems are DOS and UNIX. The Disk Operating System, or DOS, gained its name from its original purpose of providing a controller for the computer to access its disk drives. The language of DOS consists of a set of commands which are entered directly by the user and interpreted to perform file management tasks, program execution and system configuration. DOS is a non-multi-tasking operating system in that it can only run one program at a time, whereas UNIX is multi-tasking.

The main functions of an operating system are to run programs, copy and remove files, create directories, move within a directory structure and to list files.

## 11.1 System calls

A program can call the operating system in a number of ways. One method is to use `system()`, which accepts a command string which gets passed to the operating system. One disadvantage of `system()` is that the control of the program is given over to an operating system program. The program has little control over this called program until it returns from the operating system. Examples of system calls using DOS and UNIX operating systems are given in Table 11.1

**Table 11.1:** System calls

|  | DOS | UNIX |
|---|---|---|
| List a directory | `system("dir")` | `system("ls")` |
| Change current directory | `system("cd temp")` | `system("cd temp")` |
| Move a file | `system("rename file1 file2")` | `system("mv file1 file2")` |
| Copy a file | `system("copy file1 file2")` | `system("cp file1 file2")` |

Another method of calling the operating system is to use standard library routines. The advantages of this method are that extra information can be returned from the operating system and that the program has more control over the operating system calls. It also makes the program more portable as they will work on most operating systems. Some typical functions and their operating system compatibility are given in Table 11.2.

**Table 11.2:** Standard library system function

| Function | Description | Header File | DOS | UNIX | ANSI C | Flags set |
|---|---|---|---|---|---|---|
| chdir(directory) | change directory | *dir.h* | ✓ | ✓ | | EACCES |
| mkdir(directory) | make directory | *dir.h* | ✓ | ✓ | | ENOENT |
| | | | | | | EACESS |
| chmod(path,mode) | change file mode | *io.h* | ✓ | ✓ | | ENOENT |
| | | | | | | EACCES |
| creat(name,mode) | create a file | *io.h* | ✓ | ✓ | | ENOENT |
| | | | | | | EMFILE |
| | | | | | | EACCES |
| rename(from,to) | rename file | *stdio.h* | ✓ | | ✓ | ENOENT |
| | | | | | | EACCES |
| system(command) | issue system command | *stdlib.h* | ✓ | ✓ | ✓ | ENOENT |
| | | | | | | ENOMEM |
| | | | | | | E2BIG |
| | | | | | | ENOEXEC |
| rmdir(directory) | remove a directory | *dir.h* | ✓ | ✓ | | EACESS |
| | | | | | | ENOENT |

A global variable errno is set up in *errno.h* and *stdlib.h* and is set when an error occurs in calling the operating system. The main flags used are:

| ENEXEC | - | execution error; |
|---|---|---|
| EACCES | - | permission denied; |
| ENOEXIST | - | file does not exist; |
| E2BIG | - | too many arguments to function call; |
| ENOMEM | - | not enough memory. |

Program 11.1 uses the chdir() function to change the current directory and uses the DOS command DIR to list the contents of the directory. If an error occurs when the function is executed it will return a -1 value. On an error the errno variable is tested to determine whether the directory exists.

Note that if another type of operating system is used, the DIR command should be replaced with its equivalent (e.g. ls for UNIX).

📄 **Program 11.1**
```
/* prog11_1.c      */
/* program to change directory */

#include <errno.h>
#include <stdio.h>
#include <string.h>      /* required for strcmp()  */
#include <dir.h>         /* required for chdir()   */
```

```c
#include <stdlib.h>       /* required for system()  */
int     main(void)
{
char    directory[BUFSIZ];

  while (1)
  {
    puts("Enter a directory");
    gets(directory);

    if (!strcmp(directory,"exit")) break;
        /* exit program if EXIT is entered */

    if (chdir(directory)==-1)
      if (errno==ENOENT) puts("Pathname not found");
    else
    {
      puts("Contents of this directory are:-");
      system("dir");
    }
  }
  return(0);

}
```

Program 11.2 shows how a directory can be created within a program.

📄 **Program 11.2**
```c
/* prog11_2.c  */
/* program to make a directory */

#include <stdio.h>
#include <errno.h>
#include <dir.h>

int     main(void)
{
char    directory[BUFSIZ];

  puts("Enter a directory");
  gets(directory);

    /*   a -1 returned from mkdir()    */
    /*    indicates an error           */
  if (mkdir(directory)==-1)
  {
    if (errno==EACCES) puts("Permisson not allowed");
    if (errno==ENOENT) puts("Path does not exist");
  }
  else
    puts("Directory made");
  return(0);
}
```

The next program copies one file to another. Again it uses DOS system calls.

📄 **Program 11.3**

```
/* prog11_3.c                          */
/* Program to copy one file to another   */
/* Program uses the system() function    */

#include <stdio.h>
#include <string.h>
#include <stdlib.h>
#include <errno.h>

int     main(void)
{
char    str[2*BUFSIZ],file1[BUFSIZ],file2[BUFSIZ];

   puts("Enter file which is to be copied>>");
   gets(file1);

   puts("Enter file which is to be copied to>>");
   gets(file2);

   strcpy(str,"copy ");
   strcat(str,file1);
   strcat(str," ");
   strcat(str,file2);

   if (system(str)==-1)
   {
      if (errno==ENOENT)    puts("File does not exist");
      if (errno==ENOMEM)    puts("Not enough memory");
      if (errno==ENOEXEC)   puts("Not an executable file");
   }
   return(0);
}
```

The block of code:

```
   strcpy(str,"copy ");
   strcat(str,file1);
   strcat(str," ");
   strcat(str,file2);
```

could have been simply replaced with:

```
sprintf(str,"copy %s %s",file1,file2);
```

## 11.2  Passing arguments

Arguments can be passed into a C program using parameters specified in the `main()` function header. The standard format is given next.

```
main(int argc, char *argv[])
```

argc    contains the number of command line arguments;
argv    is an array of strings which contains all command line arguments.

The first argument contains the command name (argv[0]). Program 11.4 lists the command line arguments.

📄 **Program 11.4**

```
/* prog11_4.c                                                    */
#include <stdio.h>

int     main(int argc,char *argv[])
/* argc contains number of command line                          */
/* arguments. argv[] is a pointer to each argument               */
/* argv[0] points to command name, argv[1] points               */
/* to first string, etc.                                         */
{
int   i;

  for (i=0;i<argc;i++)
    printf("Arg %d is %s\n",i,argv[i]);
  return(0);
}
```

A sample run of this program is given in test run 11.1. The command line prompt is shown as a greater than symbol (>). The program name is stored in argv[0] and the rest of the arguments are stored in argv[1] to argv[argc-1]. All command line arguments are treated as strings. If the program is to operate on them numerically then they must be converted using a string conversion function (such as sscanf()).

🖥 **Test run 11.1**

```
> arg1 list 100 4.31 -f
Arg 0 is C:\TC\ARG1.EXE
Arg 1 is list
Arg 2 is 100
Arg 3 is 4.31
Arg 4 is -f
```

## 11.3 Examples

Program 11.5 determines the impedance of a capacitor. The parameters are passed into the program via arguments.

📄 **Program 11.5**

```
/*    prog11_5.c                                                 */
/*    parameters passed via arguments                            */
/*    Format is calcimp frequency capacitance                    */

#include <stdio.h>
#include <math.h>
```

```
#define    PI    3.14159

float   calc_Xc(float f,float c);

int     main(int argc,char *argv[])
{
float   f,C,Xc;

   if (argc!=3)
   {
      puts("Program to determine impedance of a capacitor");
      puts("Format for data is: ");
      puts("calcimp FREQUENCY CAPACITANCE");
      exit(0);
   }

   sscanf(argv[1],"%f",&f);
   sscanf(argv[2],"%f",&C);

   Xc=calc_Xc(f,C);
   printf("Impedance is %f ohms\n",Xc);
}

float   calc_Xc(float f,float c)
{
   return(1/(2*PI*f*c));
}
```

A sample run is given in test run 11.2.

> 🖥 **Test run 11.2**
> ```
> C:\SRC\ARGS> calcimp
> Program to determine impedance of a capacitor
> Format for data is:
> calcimp FREQUENCY CAPACITANCE
>
> C:\SRC\ARGS> calcimp 1e6 1e-6
> Impedance is 0.159155 ohms
> ```

Program 11.6 determines the magnitude of the impedance of a transmission line. The parameters are passed into the program via command line arguments. These are converted to floating point format using the sscanf() function.

📄 **Program 11.6**
```
/*    prog11_6.c                              */
/*    Program to determine impedance of a     */
/*    Transmission Line                       */
/*    Impedance of TL is                      */
/*        root((R+jwL)/(G+jwC))               */
/*    arguments are passed via program prompt */

#include <stdio.h>
#include <math.h>
#define    MILLI         1e-3
```

```
#define   MICRO       1e-6
#define   BIGVALUE    1e38
#define   PI          3.14159

float   calc_mag(float r,float l,float g,float c,float f);
float   rect_to_polar(float x,float y);
float   calc_imp(float f, float val);

int     main(int argc, char *argv[])
{
float   Zmag,R,L,G,C,f;

   puts("Prog to determine impdepance of a transmission line");

   if (argc!=6)
   {
     puts("Data format is:");
     puts("   trans R L G C freq ");
     return(1);
   }

   sscanf(argv[1],"%f",&R);sscanf(argv[2],"%f",&L);
   sscanf(argv[3],"%f",&G);sscanf(argv[4],"%f",&C);
   sscanf(argv[5],"%f",&f);

   Zmag=calc_mag(R,L*MILLI,G*MILLI,C*MICRO,f);
   printf("Magnitude is %.2f ohms\n",Zmag);
   return(0);
}

float calc_mag(float r,float l,float g,float c,float f)
{
float value1,value2;

   value1=rect_to_polar(r,calc_imp(f,l));
   value2=rect_to_polar(g,calc_imp(f,c));

   /* Beware if dividing by zero */
   if (value2==0) return(BIGVALUE);
   else return(sqrt(value1/value2));
}

float rect_to_polar(float x,float y)
{
   return(sqrt((x*x)+(y*y)));
}

float calc_imp(float f, float val)
{
   return(2*PI*f*val);
}
```

Test run 11.3 gives a sample run.

💻 **Test run 11.3**

```
> trans
Program to determine impdepance of a transmission line
Data format is:
   trans R L G C freq
> trans 10 10 8 5 100
Program to determine impedance of transmission line
Magnitude is 37.07 ohms
```

## 11.4 Tutorial

Q11.1    Write a program which reads a data file containing floating point values and print the average, maximum and minimum values. The name of the file is passed to the program via the command line arguments. A sample run is shown in test run 11.4.

💻 **Test run 11.4**
```
> getaver in.dat
The average value is 43.41
The maximum found is 100.34 and minimum is -4.00
>
```

Q11.2    Write a program for the mathematical functions TAN, COS, SIN, and EXP. The program should receive the value via the command line arguments. Test run 11.5 shows a sample run.

💻 **Test run 11.5**
```
> TAN 3.24
The tan of 3.24 is XXXX
> SIN 3.54
The sin of 3.54 is XXXXX
```

Q11.3    Modify the program in Q11.2 so that the user can specify whether the value is in degrees (/d) or radians (/r) or ask for help (/?). Test run 11.6 shows a sample run.

💻 **Test run 11.6**
```
> TAN 30.24 /d
The tan of 3.24 degrees is XXXX
> SIN 30.54 /r
The sin of 30.54 radians is XXXXX
> SIN /?
 FORMAT: SIN VALUE [EXTENSION]
 This is a program which will determine the
 Sine of a value, where value is in degrees (/d)
 or radians (/r). /? will print this page
```

Q11.4   Modify some programs from previous chapters so that the user can prompt for help on the program using /? in the command line. Test run 11.7 shows a sample run.

---

🖳  **Test run 11.7**

```
C:> RESON_LC /?
FORMAT: RESON_LC R C F [EXTENSION]
This is a program which will determine the
resonant frequency of a parallel RLC circuit
/? will print this page
C:>
```

---

Q11.5   Write a program with command line arguments which will determine a preferred value for a resistor. Test run 11.8 shows a sample run.

---

🖳  **Test run 11.8**

```
C:> R_VALUE 1.43 K
Nearest value is 1.4K
C:>
```

---

# Projects

The objective of this section is to revise the techniques used in C programming by means of project work. Sections 12.1 to 12.5 contain samples of well-structured code. Programs written in the tutorial section should be similarly structured.

## 12.1 Resonant frequency of a series RLC circuit

Refer to program 2.9 for background on this problem. A structure chart of the design is given in Figure 12.1.

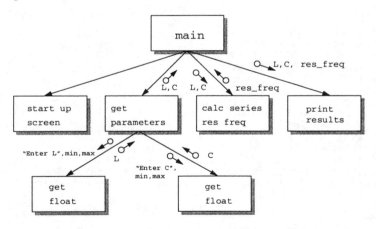

**Figure 12.1:** Structure chart for Program 12.1

Program 12.1 determines the resonant frequency of a series RLC circuit with entered values for inductance and capacitance. The ranges of $L$ and $C$ are limited to 1 nH and 1 pF, respectively, by the parameters passed into get_float(). A program header has been added into the program to give some information on the author of the program, date created, current version number, file name, etc.

📄 **Program 12.1**

```
/*********************************************************/
/* File:        prog12_1.c                             */
/* Title:       Series Resonant Frequency Program      */
/* Function:    To determine the resonant frequency    */
/*              of a series RLC circuit                 */
/* Author(s):              Bill Buchanan               */
/* Version:                1.00                         */
/* Created:                18-JAN-94                    */
/* Last Modified:          18-JAN-94                    */
/* Recent Modifications:   NONE                         */
/*********************************************************/

#define  PI      3.14159265358979323846
#define  MILLI   1e-3
#define  MICRO   1e-6
#define  TRUE    1
#define  FALSE   0

#include <stdio.h>
#include <math.h>
void    start_up_screen(void);
void    get_parameters(float *l, float *c);
float   calc_series_res_freq(float l,float c);
void    print_results(float l,float c,float fres);
void    get_float(char msg[],float min,float max,float *val);

int     main(void)
{
float   L,C,res_freq;

    start_up_screen();
    get_parameters(&L,&C);
    res_freq=calc_series_res_freq(L,C);
    print_results(L,C,res_freq);
    return(0);
}

void    start_up_screen(void)
{
    puts("");
    puts("\tProgram to determine the resonant frequency");
    puts("\tof a series RLC circuit. Note that  values");
    puts("\tfor inductance and capacitance are entered");
    puts("\tas milliHenries and microFarads respectively");
    puts("");
}

void    get_parameters(float *l, float *c)
{
    /* Values of L and C are entered as mH and uF respectively */
    /* and then scaled using the tokens MILLI and MICRO        */
    get_float("Enter inductance(mH) >>",1e-6,1e6,l); /* min 1 nH*/
    get_float("Enter resistance(uF) >>",1e-6,1e6,c); /* min 1 pF*/
    *l=(*l)*MILLI;
    *c=(*c)*MICRO;
}
```

```
float    calc_series_res_freq(float l,float c)
{
float    freq;

   freq=1/(2*PI)*sqrt(1/(l*c));

   return(freq);

}


void    print_results(float l,float c,float fres)
{

   printf("Circuit values are %.2f mH, %.2f uF\n",
                 l/MILLI,c/MICRO);

   printf("Resonant frequency is %.2f Hz\n",fres);
}


void    get_float(char msg[],float min,float max,float *val)
{
char     inline[BUFSIZ];
int      rtn,okay;

   /* get floating point value in the range min to max    */

   do
   {
      printf("%s",msg);
      gets(inline);
      rtn=sscanf(inline,"%f",val);
      if ((rtn!=1) || (*val<min) || (*val>max))
      {
         okay=FALSE;
         printf("Invalid input <%s>\n",inline);
      }
      else okay=TRUE;

   } while (!okay);

}
```

Test run 12.1 shows a sample run.

---

💻 **Test run 12.1**
```
   Program to determine the resonant frequency
   of a series RLC circuit. Note that values
   for inductance and capacitance are entered
   as milliHenries and microFarads respectively
Enter inductance(mH) >> 1
Enter resistance(uF) >> 1
Circuit values are 1.00 mH, 1.0 uF
Resonant frequency is 5032.92 Hz
```

---

## 12.2 Current flow in a diode

Refer to program 4.4 for background on this problem. A first-level structure chart of this problem is given in Figure 12.2. Note that it does not show sub-module calls to get_float() from get_parameters().

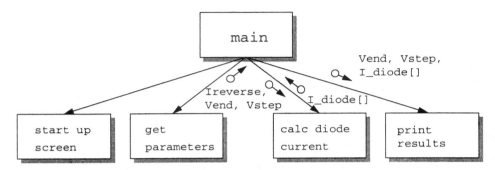

**Figure 12.2:** Structure chart for Program 12.2

Program 12.2 determines the current flow in a diode.

**Program 12.2**
```
/************************************************************/
/* File:        prog12_2.c                              */
/* Title:       Diode Current Program                   */
/* Function:    Program to determine the current flow   */
/*              in a diode given an applied voltage      */
/* Author(s):               Bill Buchanan               */
/* Version:                 1.00                         */
/* Created:                 18-JAN-94                    */
/* Last Modified:           18-JAN-94                    */
/* Recent Modifications:    NONE                         */
/************************************************************/
#include <stdio.h>
#include <math.h>

#define  TEMPERATURE       300 /* Room temperature          */
#define  MICRO             1e-6
#define  MAXCURRENTVALUES  100 /* Maximum values in I_diode */
#define  TRUE    1
#define  FALSE   0

void   start_up_screen(void);
void   get_parameters(float *Io,float *Vend,int *Vn);
void   get_diode_current(float Io,float Vend,int Vn,float I[]);
void   show_diode_current(float Vend,int Vn,float I[]);
void   get_float(char msg[],float min,float max,float *val);

int    main(void)
{
float  I_reverse_sat,Vend;
int    Vsteps;
```

```
float    I_diode[MAXCURRENTVALUES];

   start_up_screen();
   get_parameters(&I_reverse_sat,&Vend,&Vsteps);
   get_diode_current(I_reverse_sat,Vend,Vsteps,I_diode);
   show_diode_current(Vend,Vsteps,I_diode);
        return(0);
}

void    start_up_screen(void)
{
   puts("");
   puts("\tProgram to determine the current flow in a");
   puts("\tdiode given an applied voltage. The program ");
   puts("\tassumes a temperature of 27 degrees C");
   puts("");
}

void    get_parameters(float *Io,float *Vend,int *Vn)
{
float    temp; /* used to get number of voltage steps */

   get_float("Enter reverse saturation current >>",0,1e-6,Io);
   get_float("Enter end voltage                 >>",0,10,Vend);
   get_float("Enter number of voltage steps >>",1,
                         MAXCURRENTVALUES,&temp);
   *Vn=temp;
}

void    get_diode_current(float Io,float Vend,int Vn,float I[])
{
int      i=0;
float    v;

   for (v=0;v<Vend;v+=Vend/Vn,i++)
      I[i]=Io*exp(11600*v/TEMPERATURE-1);
}

void    show_diode_current(float Vend,int Vn,float I[])
{
int      i=0;
float    v;

   puts("VOLTAGE    CURRENT(uA)");
   for (v=0;v<Vend;v+=Vend/Vn,i++)
      printf("%12.2f %12.2f\n",v,I[i]/MICRO);
   puts("");
}
void    get_float(char msg[],float min,float max,float *val)
{
char     inline[BUFSIZ];
int      rtn,okay;

   do
   {
      printf("%s",msg);
      gets(inline);
```

```
        rtn=sscanf(inline,"%f",val);
        if ((rtn!=1) || (*val<min) || (*val>max))
        {

            okay=FALSE;
            printf("Invalid input <%s>\n",inline);

        }

        else okay=TRUE;

    } while (!okay);

}
```

Test run 12.2 shows a sample run.

---

🖳 **Test run 12.2**

```
    Program to determine the current flow in a
    diode given an applied voltage. The program
    assumes a temperature of 27 degrees C

Enter reverse saturation current >>   -1
Invalid saturation current please re-enter
Enter reverse saturation current >> 1e-12
Enter end voltage                 >> -43
Invalid end voltage please re-enter
Enter end voltage                 >> 0.8
Enter number of voltage steps      >> 120
Invalid number of steps, max is 100
Enter number of voltage steps      >> 20
    VOLTAGE    CURRENT(uA)
       0.00          0.00
       0.04          0.00
       0.08          0.00
       0.12          0.00
       0.16          0.00
       0.20          0.00
       0.24          0.00
       0.28          0.02
       0.32          0.09
       0.36          0.41
       0.40          1.92
       0.44          9.01
       0.48         42.29
       0.52        198.57
       0.56        932.46
       0.60       4378.63
       0.64      20561.13
       0.68      96550.87
       0.72     453383.15
       0.76    2128994.46
```

---

## 12.3 Boolean circuit

Refer to section 5.5 for some background on this problem.

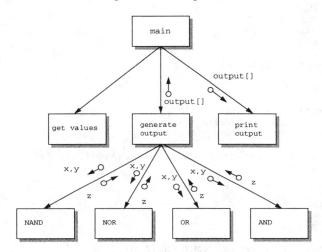

**Figure 12.3:** Structure chart for program 12.3

Program 12.3 determines the truth table for a Boolean circuit.

📄 **Program 12.3**

```
/*****************************************************************/
/* File:        prog12_3.c                               */
/* Title:       Boolean circuit analysis                 */
/* Function:    Program to determine the truth table  for */
/*              the function NAND(OR(NOR(A,B),AND(A,C)),C) */
/* Author(s):           Bill Buchanan                    */
/* Version:             1.00                             */
/* Created:             18-JAN-94                        */
/* Last Modified:       18-JAN-94                        */
/* Recent Modifications:   NONE                          */
/*****************************************************************/
#include <stdio.h>

#define   MAXSTATES   8
#define   TRUE        1
#define   FALSE       0

int    AND(int x,int y);
int    NAND(int x,int y);
int    OR(int x,int y);
int    NOR(int x,int y);
int    NOT(int x);
void   generate_output(int z[]);
void   print_output(int z[]);
void   start_up_screen(void);
```

```
int     main(void)
{
int     output[MAXSTATES];

   start_up_screen();
   generate_output(output);
   print_output(output);
   return(0);
}
void    generate_output(int z[])
{
int     A,B,C,state=0;

   for (A=FALSE;A<=TRUE;A++)
     for (B=FALSE;B<=TRUE;B++)
       for (C=FALSE;C<=TRUE;C++)
       {
          z[state]=NAND(OR(NOR(A,B),AND(A,C)),C);
          state++;
       }
}
void    print_output(int z[])
{
int     A,B,C,state=0;

   puts("Boolean function NOR( AND(A,B),C)");
   puts("   A     B     C     Z");

   for (A=FALSE;A<=TRUE;A++)
     for (B=FALSE;B<=TRUE;B++)
       for (C=FALSE;C<=TRUE;C++)
       {
          printf("%4d %4d %4d %4d\n",A,B,C,z[state]);
          state++;
       }
   puts("");
}

int  AND(int x,int y)
{
   return(x&y);
}

int  NAND(int x,int y)
{
   return( !(x&y) );
}

int  OR(int x,int y)
{
   return( x|y );
}

int  NOR(int x,int y)
{
   return ( !(x|y) );
       /* possible also with bit-masking ie return((~(x|y))&1);*/
}
```

```
int  NOT(int x)
{
  return(!(x));
}

void start_up_screen(void)
{
  puts("");
  puts("\tProgram to determine truth table for the");
  puts("\tboolean function NAND(OR(NOR(A,B),AND(A,C)),C) ");
  puts("");
}
```

Test run 12.3 shows a sample run.

---

🖳 **Test run 12.3**

```
Program to determine truth table for the
boolean function NAND(OR(NOR(A,B),AND(A,C)),C)
```

```
Boolean function NAND(OR(NOR(A,B),AND(A,C)),C)
    A    B    C    Z
    0    0    0    1
    0    0    1    0
    0    1    0    1
    0    1    1    1
    1    0    0    1
    1    0    1    0
    1    1    0    1
    1    1    1    0
```

---

## 12.4 Decimal to binary convertor

Program 12.4 displays the binary equivalent of a signed integer. Refer to section 1.7 for background.

📄 **Program 12.4**
```
/*************************************************************/
/* File:                  prog12_4.c                     */
/* Title:                 Signed Decimal To Binary Program  */
/* Function:    Program to convert from signed decimal   */
/*              to 2's complement binary                 */
/* Author(s):                Bill Buchanan               */
/* Version:                   1.00                       */
/* Created:                   18-JAN-94                  */
/* Last Modified:             18-JAN-94                  */
/* Recent Modifications:    NONE                         */
/*************************************************************/
#include <stdio.h>
#include <math.h>
#define   TRUE    1
#define   FALSE   0
```

```
void    start_up_screen(void);
void    print_binary(int dec);
void    get_int(char msg[],int min,int max,int *val);

int     main(void)
{
int     decimal;

   start_up_screen();

   do
   {
      get_int("Enter a decimal value >> ",-32768,32767,&decimal);
      if (decimal!=0) print_binary(decimal);

   } while (decimal!=0);
   return(0);
}

void    start_up_screen(void)
{
   puts("");
   puts("\tProgram to determine the binary equivalent of");
   puts("\tof a signed decimal value. Note that this program");
   puts("\twill determine the number of bits used to store an");
   puts("\tinteger value. To end program enter a decimal value");
   puts("\tof zero.");
   puts("");
}

void    print_binary(int dec)
{
unsigned bytes,bits,i;

   bytes=sizeof(int);
          /* Determine number of bytes in an integer   */
   bits=8*bytes;
          /* Determine the number of bits          */

   puts("");

   printf("The binary equivalent of %10d is ",dec);
   for (i=pow(2,bits-1);i>0;i>>=1)
      if (dec & i) printf("1"); else printf("0");

   puts("");
}

void    get_int(char msg[],int min,int max,int *val)
{
char    inline[BUFSIZ];
int     rtn,okay;

   do
   {
      printf("%s",msg);
      gets(inline);
      rtn=sscanf(inline,"%d",val);
```

```
    if ((rtn!=1) || (*val<min) || (*val>max))
    {
       okay=FALSE;
       printf("Invalid input <%s>\n",inline);
    }
    else okay=TRUE;
  } while (!okay);
}
```

Test run 12.4 shows a sample run.

---

🖥 **Test run 12.4**
```
Program to determine the binary equivalent of
of a signed decimal value. Note that this program
will determine the number of bits used to store an
integer value. To end program enter a decimal value
of zero.
Enter decimal value >> -1
The binary equivalent of    -1 is 1111111111111111
Enter decimal value >>  43
The binary equivalent of    43 is 0000000000101011
Enter decimal value >> 1024
The binary equivalent of  1024 is 0000010000000000
Enter decimal value >>  -453
The binary equivalent of  -453 is 1111111000111011
Enter decimal value >>  22
The binary equivalent of    22 is 0000000000010110
Enter decimal value >>  10000
The binary equivalent of 10000 is 0010011100010000
```

---

## 12.5 Resistor colour code program

Resistors are normally identified by means of a colour coding system. The colour banding system is given in Table 12.1.

**Table 12.1:** Resistor colour coding

| digit | colour | multiplier | no. of zeros |
|-------|--------|------------|--------------|
|       | silver | 0.01       | -2           |
|       | gold   | 0.1        | -1           |
| 0     | black  | 1          | 0            |
| 1     | brown  | 10         | 1            |
| 2     | red    | 100        | 2            |
| 3     | orange | 1k         | 3            |
| 4     | yellow | 10k        | 4            |
| 5     | green  | 100k       | 5            |
| 6     | blue   | 1M         | 6            |
| 7     | violet | 10M        | 7            |
| 8     | gray   |            |              |
| 9     | white  |            |              |

The first two bands give a digit, the third a multiplier and the fourth the tolerance. Table 12.2 gives a list of the tolerance bands.

**Table 12.2:** Tolerence colour band of a resistor

| Colour | Tolerance |
|--------|-----------|
| red    | 2%        |
| gold   | 5%        |
| silver | 10%       |
| none   | 20%       |

Figure 12.4 shows a 4-band resistor.

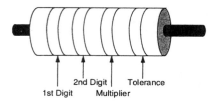

**Figure 12.4:** 4-band resistor colour code

For example,

RED-RED-BROWN-SILVER          220 Ω 10%
GREEN-BLUE-YELLOW-GOLD        560k 5%

📄 **Program 12.5**

```
/*****************************************************************/
/* File:         prog12_5.c                                      */
/* Title:        Resistor Colour Code Program                    */
/* Function:     Program to determine the colour                 */
/*               bands for a 4-band resistor                     */
/* Author(s):                Bill Buchanan                       */
/* Version:                  1.01                                */
/* Created:                  20-JAN-94                           */
/* Last Modified:            22-JAN-94                           */
/* Recent Modifications:     NONE                                */
/*****************************************************************/
#include <stdio.h>

#define   TRUE 1
#define   FALSE  0

typedef struct
{
   int  first_digit,second_digit,no_zeros;
   int  tolerance;
} res_colour_band;
enum cols {SILVER=-2,GOLD,BLACK,BROWN,RED,ORANGE,YELLOW,
                        GREEN,BLUE,VIOLET,GREY,WHITE};
```

```
char
   *colours[12]={"SILVER","GOLD","BLACK","BROWN","RED","ORANGE",
              "YELLOW","GREEN","BLUE","VIOLET","GREY","WHITE"};

void    get_res_codes(res_colour_band *c_bands);
void    show_colours(res_colour_band c_bands);
void    get_int(char msg[],int min,int max,int *val);

int     main(void)
{
res_colour_band resistor;

   get_res_codes(&resistor);
   show_colours(resistor);
   return(0);
}

void    get_res_codes(res_colour_band *c_band)
{
   get_int("Enter 1st colour band >>",
           BLACK,WHITE,&c_band->first_digit);

   get_int("Enter 2nd colour band >>",
           BLACK,WHITE,&c_band->second_digit);

   get_int("Enter number of zeros >>",
           SILVER,VIOLET,&c_band->no_zeros);
   get_int("Enter tolerance >>",0,100,&c_band->tolerance);
}

void    show_colours(res_colour_band c_bands)
{
   printf("Resistor colour bands %s %s %s ",
      colours[c_bands.first_digit+2],
      colours[c_bands.second_digit+2],
      colours[c_bands.no_zeros+2]);

   if (c_bands.tolerance>=20)          printf("NONE");
   else if (c_bands.tolerance>=10)  printf("SILVER");
   else if (c_bands.tolerance>=5)   printf("GOLD");
   else printf("RED\n");
}


void    get_int(char msg[],int min,int max,int *val)
{
char    inline[BUFSIZ];
int     rtn,okay;

   do
   {
     printf("%s",msg);
     gets(inline);
     rtn=sscanf(inline,"%d",val);
     if ((rtn!=1) || (*val<min) || (*val>max))
     {
       okay=FALSE;
       printf("Invalid input <%s>\n",inline);
```

```
        }

        else okay=TRUE;

    } while (!okay);

}
```

Test run 12.5 shows a sample run.

## 12.6 Tutorial

Q12.1    The parallel plate capacitor, shown in Figure 12.5, consists of two parallel plates separated by an air dielectric. Write a program which determines the capacitance of this set-up. The program should prompt for the area of the plates and the separation distance. Test run 12.6 gives a sample run.

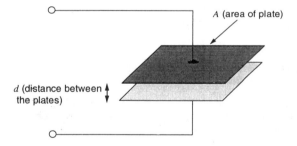

**Figure 12.5:** Parallel plate capacitor

The capacitance of a capacitor with a plates separated by a dielectric of dielectric constant of $\varepsilon_r$ is given by the following.

$$C = \frac{\varepsilon_0 \varepsilon_r A}{d} \quad \text{F}.$$

where $\varepsilon_0 = 8.854 \times 10^{-12}$ F.m$^{-1}$

The area of the plates should be entered in mm$^2$ and the distance between the plates in mm. Capacitance should be displayed in the most appropriate units (mF, μF, nF or pF). For example, if the capacitance is greater than 0.001 F then the units displayed are mF; if it is greater than 0.000 001 then μF, etc. Table 12.3 gives the ranges of the entered values.

**Table 12.3:** Minimum and maximum values

|  | Minimum | Maximum |
|---|---|---|
| $d$ | 0.1 μm | 1 000 mm |
| $A$ | 0.001 mm$^2$ | 10 000 mm$^2$ |
| $\varepsilon_r$ | 1 | 12 |

---

🖥 **Test run 12.6**

```
***********************************************************
*  CAPACITOR Version 1.00                                 *
*  Author: Bill Buchanan                                  *
*  Description:                                           *
*  Program to determine the capacitance of a              *
*  parallel plate capacitor given the distance            *
*  between the plates, the area of the plates             *
*  and the dielectric constant of the material            *
*  separating the plates                                  *
***********************************************************

Enter plate separation (mm) >> 0.1
Enter area of plates (mm2) >>   1000
Enter the dielectric constant of material >> 10
The capacitance is    885.40 pF

Enter plate separation (mm) >> 0.01
Enter area of plates (mm2) >>   10000
Enter the dielectric constant of material >> 10
The capacitance is     88.54 nF
```

---

Q12.2  The gate of a FET is isolated from the substrate by a layer of silicon dioxide (SiO$_2$). The capacitance of the gate-source junction can be approximated and by means of a parallel plate capacitor can be approximated to:

$$C = \frac{\varepsilon_o \varepsilon_r WL}{T_{OX}}$$

where   $W$ - width of gate
   $L$   - length of gate
   $\varepsilon_r$   - dielectic contstant of silicon dioxide (SiO$_2$);
   $T_{OX}$ - thickness of SiO$_2$.

Write a program which displays the gate-source capacitance for the entered values of $W$, $L$, $\varepsilon_r$ and $T_{OX}$. The valid range of the entered values are given in Table 12.4.

**Table 12.4:** Minimum and maximum values

|        | Minimum   | Maximum    |
|--------|-----------|------------|
| $W$    | 0.1 μm    | 100 μm     |
| $L$    | 0.1 μm    | 100 μm     |
| $\varepsilon_r$ | 2 | 3          |
| $T_{OX}$ | 0.1 μm  | 100 μm     |

Q12.3   Figure 12.6 gives an active filter using an op-amp. This circuit has high gain at low frequencies and low gain at high frequencies. It therefore acts as a low-pass filter.

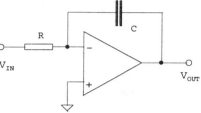

**Figure 12.6:** RC active filter

The magnitude of the gain of this circuit is given by:

$$|Gain| = \frac{1}{2\pi fRC}$$

Write a program in which the user enters a frequency, resistance and capacitance. The program should determine the gain (in dB) for the entered values. Table 12.5 gives the valid ranges of component values.

**Table 12.5:** Minimum and maximum values

|       | Minimum | Maximum  |
|-------|---------|----------|
| $f$   | 1 Hz    | 100 MHz  |
| $R$   | 0 Ω     | 10 MΩ    |
| $C$   | 1 pF    | 1 mF     |

Q12.4   The resistance of a cylindrical conductor is a function of its resistivity, area and length, and is given by the formula:

$$R = \frac{\rho l}{A} \quad \Omega$$

where

ρ  -  resistivity of conductor (Ω.m);
$l$  -  length of the conductor (m);

$A$ - area of conductor (m$^2$).

Write a program which determines the resistance of one of four metals: copper, silver, manganese and aluminimum. Table 12.6 lists the resistivities of these metals. The program should determine the resistance for a selected metal, length and area of conductor, and should display it in the most appropriate units (n$\Omega$, $\mu\Omega$, m$\Omega$, $\Omega$, k$\Omega$, etc.).

**Table 12.6:** Resistor colour coding

| Metal | Resistivity ($\Omega$.m) |
|---|---|
| copper | $17\times10^{-9}$ |
| aluminium | $25.4\times10^{-9}$ |
| silver | $16\times10^{-9}$ |
| manganese | $1400\times10^{-9}$ |

Test run 12.7 shows a sample run. In this case an aluminium conductor is used with a radius of 1 mm and length 1000 m. The resistance is found to be 8.09 $\Omega$.

```
🖥  Test run 12.7
Type of conductor >>
(c)opper
(a)luminium
(s)ilver
(m)anganese
Option >>    a
Enter radius and length of conductor >> 1e-3 1000
Resistance of conductor is 8.09e+00 ohm
```

Q12.5 Write a program to determine the truth table for the following equations:

$$Z = \overline{\overline{A+B}+B\overline{C}}$$

$$Z = \overline{(A+B).(\overline{B}+C)}$$

$$Z = \overline{A+B+C}+B\overline{C}+A$$

$$Z = \overline{A+B+D+(C.D)}+\overline{A}$$
$$Z = \overline{A+B+C}+(\overline{B}.C.D)+A$$

Q12.6 A Butterworth filter circuit produces a flat passband response. The amplitude of this response is given by:

$$\frac{V_{OUT}}{V_{IN}} = \frac{1}{\sqrt{1+\left(f/f_C\right)^{2n}}}$$

where $n$ is the order of the filter and $f_C$ is the cut-off (or -3 dB) frequency. Write a program which displays the response for $n=1, 2, 4, 8, 16$ and $32$. A sample run with a cut-off frequency of 1 kHz is given in test run 12.8. The program in this test run displays 20 frequency steps (excluding 0 Hz) in the range from 0 Hz up to twice the cut-off frequency. Notice that at the cut-off frequency the gain is 0.707 for all filter orders.

🖥 **Test run 12.8**

```
Enter cut-off frequency >>1e3
```

| Frequency | n=1 | n=2 | n=4 | n=8 | n=16 | n=32 |
|---|---|---|---|---|---|---|
| 0.000 | 1.000 | 1.000 | 1.000 | 1.000 | 1.000 | 1.000 |
| 100.000 | 0.995 | 1.00) | 1.000 | 1.000 | 1.000 | 1.000 |
| 200.000 | 0.981 | 0.999 | 1.000 | 1.000 | 1.000 | 1.000 |
| 300.000 | 0.958 | 0.996 | 1.000 | 1.000 | 1.000 | 1.000 |
| 400.000 | 0.928 | 0.987 | 1.000 | 1.000 | 1.000 | 1.000 |
| 500.000 | 0.894 | 0.970 | 0.998 | 1.000 | 1.000 | 1.000 |
| 600.000 | 0.857 | 0.941 | 0.992 | 1.000 | 1.000 | 1.000 |
| 700.000 | 0.819 | 0.898 | 0.972 | 0.998 | 1.000 | 1.000 |
| 800.000 | 0.781 | 0.842 | 0.925 | 0.986 | 1.000 | 1.000 |
| 900.000 | 0.743 | 0.777 | 0.836 | 0.919 | 0.983 | 0.999 |
| 1000.000 | 0.707 | 0.707 | 0.707 | 0.707 | 0.707 | 0.707 |
| 1100.000 | 0.673 | 0.637 | 0.564 | 0.423 | 0.213 | 0.047 |
| 1200.000 | 0.640 | 0.570 | 0.434 | 0.227 | 0.054 | 0.003 |
| 1300.000 | 0.610 | 0.509 | 0.330 | 0.122 | 0.015 | 0.000 |
| 1400.000 | 0.581 | 0.454 | 0.252 | 0.068 | 0.005 | 0.000 |
| 1500.000 | 0.555 | 0.406 | 0.194 | 0.039 | 0.002 | 0.000 |
| 1600.000 | 0.530 | 0.364 | 0.151 | 0.023 | 0.001 | 0.000 |
| 1700.000 | 0.507 | 0.327 | 0.119 | 0.014 | 0.000 | 0.000 |
| 1800.000 | 0.486 | 0.295 | 0.095 | 0.009 | 0.000 | 0.000 |
| 1900.000 | 0.466 | 0.267 | 0.077 | 0.006 | 0.000 | 0.000 |
| 2000.000 | 0.447 | 0.243 | 0.062 | 0.004 | 0.000 | 0.000 |

Q12.7    A π-configuration Butterworth filter is shown in Figure 12.7.

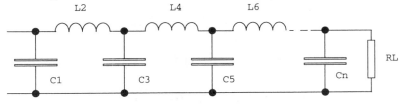

**Figure 12.7:** Butterworth π low-pass filter

The components can be calculated using the normalized values given in Table 12.7 and scaling these for the required load resistance and cut-off frequency.

**Table 12.7:** Normalized component values

| n | C1 | L2 | C3 | L4 | C5 |
|---|------|------|------|------|------|
| 2 | 1.4142 | 1.4142 | | | |
| 3 | 1.0 | 2.0 | 1.0 | | |
| 4 | 0.7654 | 1.8478 | 1.8478 | 0.7654 | |
| 5 | 0.6180 | 1.6180 | 2.0 | 1.6180 | 0.6180 |

These normalized values are then scaled to produce actual values using the formulas:

$$C_n(actual) = \frac{C_n(table)}{2.\pi.f.R_L}$$

$$L_n(actual) = \frac{R_L.L_n(table)}{2.\pi.f}$$

where $n$ is the order of the filter, $R_L$ is the load resistance and $f$ is the cut-off frequency. For example, for a second-order filter the component values will be:

$$C_1 = \frac{1.4142}{2.\pi.f.R_L}$$

$$L_2 = \frac{1.4142.R_L}{2.\pi.f}$$

A sample test run for a fifth-order filter with a cut-off frequency of 1 MHz is shown in test run 12.9.

---

🖳 **Test run 12.9**

```
Butterworth Low Pass Filter Program
************************************
Enter cut-off frequency      >> 1e6
Enter order of filter (2-5)  >> 5
Enter load impedance (ohms)  >> 75

C1=  1.31e-9 F
L2= 19.30e-6 H
C3=  4.24e-9 F
L4= 19.30e-6 H
C5=  1.31e-9 F
```

---

Modify the program so that it displays the component values in the most appropriate unit. A modified sample run is given in test run 12.10.

---

🖳  **Test run 12.10**

```
Butterworth Low Pass Filter Program
*************************************
Enter cut-off frequency     >> 1e6
Enter order of filter (2-5) >> 5
Enter load impedance (ohms) >> 75

C1=  1.31 nF
L2= 19.30 uH
C3=  4.24 nF
L4= 19.30 uH
C5=  1.31 nF
```

---

Q12.8   The low-pass Butterworth filter in Figure 12.7 can be modified to become a high-pass filter by replacing the capacitors with inductors and the inductors with capacitors, and using the following component values:

$$C_n(actual) = \frac{1}{2.\pi.f.R_L L_n(table)}$$

$$L_n(actual) = \frac{R_L}{2.\pi.f.C_n(table)}$$

A sample run is given in test run 12.11.

---

🖳  **Test run 12.11**

```
Butterworth High Pass Filter Program
*************************************
Enter cut-off frequency     >> 6e6
Enter order of filter (2-5) >> 3
Enter load impedance (ohms) >> 50
C1=  5.10 nF
L2=  0.69 uH
C3=  5.10 nF
```

---

Q12.9   Figure 12.8 shows a simple base resistor biased bipolar transistor circuit.

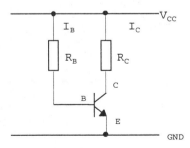

**Figure 12.8:** Simple base resistor biased bipolar circuit

Typically, to produce the maximum output swing the collector voltage is biased at a point halfway between the supply rails, in this case $V_{cc}/2$. Thus, for a specified collector current ($I_c$), the collector resistor ($R_c$) can be determined (see equation 1). The base current is then determined by dividing the collector current by the DC current gain $h_{FE}$ (see equation 2). If the transistor is ON then the base-emitter junction will have a conducting silicon diode voltage across it ($V_{BE}$(ON)). Using an approximation for this voltage (~0.65 V) the base resistance can be determined (equation 3). The circuit equations are:

$$R_C = \frac{V_{cc}/2}{I_C} \quad \Omega \quad (1)$$

$$I_B = \frac{I_C}{h_{FE}} \quad A \quad (2)$$

$$R_B = \frac{V_{cc} - V_{BE}}{I_B} \quad \Omega \quad (3)$$

Write a program which determines $R_B$ for given inputs of $I_c$ and $V_{cc}$. Assume that $V_{BE}$(ON) is 0.65 V and $h_{FE}$ is 100. Entered values for $V_{cc}$ should be limited between 5 and 30 V, and those for $I_c$ between 0.1 and 10 mA. Test run 12.12 gives a sample output.

---

🖥  **Test run 12.12**

```
Enter Vcc (5->15V) >> 15
Enter Ic   (mA)    >> 1
Collector resistance is 15000 ohms
Base resistance is    1435000 ohms
```

---

Q12.10 A self-biasing common-emitter amplifier circuit is given in Figure 12.9. Write a program which determines the values of all resistances given user inputs of collector current, collector voltage and supply voltage. The user should be re-prompted for all out-of-range values. A sample run is given in test run 12.13. Approximations:

$$R_C = \frac{V_{CC} - V_C}{I_C} \quad \Omega$$

$$V_E = \frac{V_{CC}}{10} \quad V$$

$$R_E = \frac{V_E}{I_C} \quad \Omega$$

$$I_B = \frac{I_C}{h_{FE}} \quad A$$

$$V_B = V_{BE} + V_E \quad V$$

$$I_1 = 10.I_B \qquad \text{A}$$

$$R_1 = \frac{V_{CC} - V_B}{I_1} \qquad \Omega$$

$$R_2 = \frac{V_B}{I_1 - I_B} \qquad \Omega$$

where

| | | | |
|---|---|---|---|
| $V_{CC}$ | - | supply voltage | (V) |
| $V_C$ | - | collector voltage | (V) |
| $I_C$ | - | collector current | (A) |
| $V_E$ | - | emitter voltage | (V) |
| $V_B$ | - | base voltage | (V) |

Use approximations of $h_{FE}$=100 and $V_{BE}$(ON)=0.65 V.

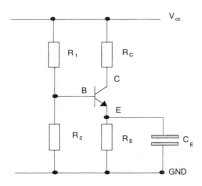

**Figure 12.9:** Common-emitter amplifier

---

💻 **Test run 12.13**
Enter Vcc (V) : 15
Enter Collector Current (mA) :  1
Enter Collector Voltage (V) : 7.5

R1= 128000 ohm R2=24444 ohm R3= 1500 ohm R4=7500 ohm

---

Q12.11  Modify the program in Q12.10 so that the resistances are displayed in the most appropriate units. Test run 12.14 shows a sample run.

---

💻 **Test run 12.14**
Enter Vcc (V) : 15
Enter Collector Current (mA) :  1
Enter Collector Voltage (V) : 7.5
R1= 128.0 Kohm  R2=24.4 Kohm R3= 1.5 Kohm R4=7.5 Kohm

---

Q12.12 Modify the program in Q12.11 so that they determine the nearest preferred value. A list of the normalized preferred values is given in Table 12.8. Test run 12.15 shows a sample run.

**Table 12.8:** Resistor colour coding

| 10 | 16 | 27 | 43 | 68 |
|----|----|----|----|-----|
| 11 | 18 | 30 | 47 | 76 |
| 12 | 20 | 33 | 51 | 82 |
| 13 | 22 | 36 | 56 | 91 |
| 15 | 24 | 39 | 62 | 100 |

🖥 **Test run 12.15**
```
Enter Vcc (V):15
Enter Collector Current (mA):  1
Enter Collector Voltage (V):7.5

R1= 130.0 Kohm  R2=24.0 Kohm R3=1.5 Kohm R4=7.5 Kohm
```

Q12.13 Modify the program in Q12.12 so that the user also enters the AC current gain $h_{fe}$ and the AC input impedance of the transistor $h_{ie}$. The program will determine the AC gain and the AC. input impedance. An *h*-parameter equivalent circuit for a simple base resistor biased circuit is given in Figure 12.10.

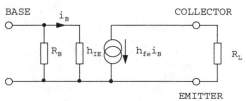

**Figure 12.10:** h-parameter equivalent circuit for base resistor biased circuit

# CHAPTER 13

# Applied Software Engineering

This section analyzes the development of a software project from the initial requirements analysis phase to final testing and installation. It provides a basic introduction to software engineering and notes have been added in italics to explain some of the phases.

## 13.1  Software development

Software development is normally a multi-stage process; the diagram in Figure 13.1 shows the main steps. The first stage normally involves determining whether there is a need for the system (the requirements analysis). If there is a need, the design team produces a design specification. This normally involves the production of a document that defines the functionality of the complete system. These two steps are normally the most difficult in the development process. Typical documents produced at these stages are the requirements analysis and requirements specification documents.

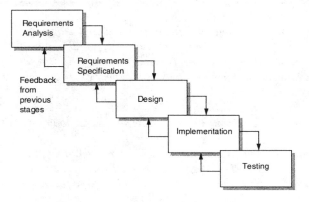

**Figure 13.1:** Software development process

After the production of the requirements specification and when all parties involved find it acceptable, a full design takes place. The document produced at the end of this stage is known as a Function Design Specification (FDS). This design solution must be implementable on the required computer system(s) and should comply exactly with the requirements specification. Next, the design is implemented using an appropriate programming language.

The aim of the testing phase is to verify the implementation to show that it satisfies the original specification. Testing a program can only show the presence of errors; it can never prove their absence. It is normally necessary at this stage to produce a test specification and test data.

The last stage, the installation and maintenance phase, covers two quite distinct activities:

- to correct errors that were missed at an earlier stage but have been detected once the program is in service;
- to add modifications due to additions or changes in the user's requirements.

The development process is iterative, not sequential; any feedback from one stage updates earlier stages.

## 13.2  RLC circuit program

### 13.2.1  Requirements analysis and specification

*The requirements analysis and specification is the first stage of the process and is typically the most difficult part. Any failure in analyzing the requirements can be very costly in future work. At this stage decisions are made as to the nature and bounds of the project and how the problem is to be solved. These decisions  involve:*

- *stating how the problem is to be solved;*
- *stating the requirements that define successful solution of the problem.*

*If after this stage a requirement has been identified then a requirements specification is generated. This defines the technical requirements of the system and should state exactly how the system is intended to operate and all operational constraints.*

## 13.2.2 Requirements analysis

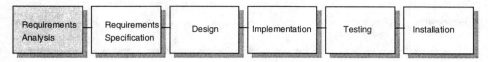

Passive electrical circuits are made up of three basic elements: resistance ($R$), inductance ($L$) and capacitance ($C$). Resistance is normally frequency independent, whereas the reactances of an inductor and a capacitor depend on the applied frequency. The reactance of an inductor with inductance $L$ is given by:

$$X_L = 2 \cdot \pi \cdot f \cdot L$$

and that for a capacitor of capacitance C it is

$$X_C = \frac{1}{2 \cdot \pi \cdot f \cdot C}$$

From these reactances the impedance can be determined; for an inductor and a capacitor these are given as $jX_L$ and $-jX_C$, respectively. Using these equations many simple circuits can be modelled.

The objective of this project is to design and implement a system which will determine the input impedance of a simple RLC circuit arranged either in a series or a parallel configuration. In order for the project to proceed a requirement for this system needs to be identified. This need is thought to exist for two main reasons:

1) Calculations of the impedance using pen, paper and calculator can take some time to complete and can be prone to errors. A well tested computer based package should be less prone to error. After initial testing it should be much faster in determining the required result.
2) Electronic Computer Aided Design (ECAD) packages can be expensive, and may be difficult to use when modelling simple RLC circuits. There may also be problems in obtaining access to these packages.

The user of the package is assumed to have little knowledge of the operation of the program and may be a computer novice. For this reason strong error checking and warnings are required when the user is entering data. A simple text-based menu system will be used to select circuit configurations.

Most likely, the program will be run on a PC-based computer system, although the package should be as portable as possible. The system should also be flexible, allowing for expansion to include other circuit configurations and options.

No major time constraints exist and the system should be designed using structured design techniques.

### 13.2.3  Requirements specification

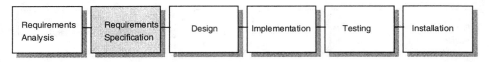

#### *Introduction*

*This section defines the system (both hardware and software) requirements and any constraints or limitations. All functions performed by the system will be specified and all error and warning conditions are documented.*

#### *Circuit types*

The basic package will contain six circuit configurations, these are:

- series RL circuit;
- series RC circuit;
- series LC circuit;
- parallel RL circuit;
- parallel RC circuit;
- parallel LC circuit.

Future work may include other configurations, such as mixed series/ parallel circuits.

#### *Circuit equations*

The impedances of the circuit are:
Series RL circuit:

$$X_L = 2\pi f L \qquad \Omega$$

$$Z = R + jX_L \qquad \Omega$$

$$|Z| = \sqrt{R^2 + X_L^2} \qquad \Omega$$

$$\langle Z \rangle = \tan^{-1}\left(\frac{X_L}{R}\right)$$

Series RC circuit:

$$X_C = \frac{1}{2\pi f C} \qquad \Omega$$

$$Z = R - jX_C \qquad \Omega$$

$$|Z| = \sqrt{R^2 + X_C^2} \qquad \Omega$$

$$\langle Z \rangle = -\tan^{-1}\left(\frac{X_C}{R}\right)$$

Series LC circuit:

$$X_C = \frac{1}{2\pi f C} \qquad \Omega$$

$$X_L = 2\pi f L \qquad \Omega$$

$$Z = j(X_L - X_C) \qquad \Omega$$

$$|Z| = \sqrt{(X_L + X_C)^2} \qquad \Omega$$

$$if \ \ (X_L > X_C) \ \ \langle Z \rangle = \frac{\pi}{2}$$

$$else \ \ \langle Z \rangle = -\frac{\pi}{2}$$

Parallel RC circuit: *TO BE COMPLETED AS A TUTORIAL QUESTION*
Parallel RL circuit: *TO BE COMPLETED AS A TUTORIAL QUESTION*
Parallel LC circuit: *TO BE COMPLETED AS A TUTORIAL QUESTION*

### *Structured analysis*

A flow chart representation of the data within the problem is shown in Figure 13.2. *This is referred to as a data-flow diagram.* The user will initially be prompted for the circuit type, and upon select of a valid circuit type the component values will be prompted for. Next the frequency values will be entered and these and the component values will be used to determine an impedance array for the required sweep of frequencies. Finally, the results will be printed in tabular form using the impedance array values and the frequency data.

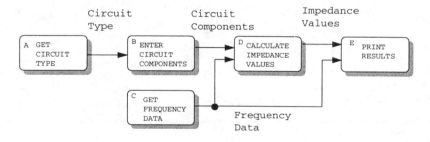

**Figure 13.2:** Highest Level Data-flow Diagram

### *Menu system*

The menu system will be a simple text-based approach. Circuit types are chosen by entering an integer in the range 1-6 for each of the circuit configurations, or 7 to exit the program. All other inputs will give the message INVALID OPTION! and the program will redisplay the main menu. The required menu screen is shown in test run 13.1.

---

⌨ **Test run 13.1**
```
Select one of the following circuits >>
1- SERIES RL    circuit
2- SERIES RC    circuit
3- SERIES LC    circuit
4- PARALLEL RC circuit
5- PARALLEL RL circuit
6- PARALLEL LC circuit
7- EXIT
```

---

### Data input

After the circuit type has been selected the user will be prompted for the required component values. For example, if a series LC circuit is selected then the program will prompt for the values of $L$ and $C$. After valid component values have been entered the user will be prompted for the start and end frequencies, and the number of frequency steps. For example, if the start frequency is entered as 0 Hz, the end frequency as 1000 Hz with 10 frequency steps, then the program will determine the impedance at the frequencies 0, 100, 200, 300, 400, 500, 600, 700, 800, 900 and 1000 Hz. Thus the frequency points will be given by:

$$f_i = f_{start} + i \cdot \frac{(f_{end} - f_{start})}{n} \quad \text{Hz}$$

where

$$f_{start} - \text{start frequency} \quad \text{(Hz)}$$
$$f_{end} - \text{end frequency} \quad \text{(Hz)}$$
$$n - \text{number of frequency points}$$
$$i = 0,1,2,3,..n$$

A sample data entry is shown in test run 13.2.

---

⌨ **Test run 13.2**
```
Enter L and C > 1e-3 1e-6
Enter start and end frequencies > 1000 10000
Enter number of frequency steps > 20
```

---

Values entered into the program will be read from the keyboard as a string and converted into numerical values. These values will be tested for to determine whether they are in the valid range. Out-of-range values will be reported with an error message, the user will be prompted to re-enter the values. Data limits are given in Table 13.1.

**Table 13.1:** Maximum and minimum values for entered values

|           | Minimum | Maximum |
|-----------|---------|---------|
| *frequency* | 0 Hz    | 1 GHz   |
| *R*       | 0 Ω     | 0 Ω     |
| *L*       | 1 nH    | 1 H     |
| *C*       | 1 pF    | 1 F     |

## Data storage

The impedance values will be stored as complex numbers (magnitude and amplitude) in a single array. The size of this array will be defined during compilation and it must be able to change it globally within the program. If the user exceeds the number of points in this array an error message will be displayed and the user will be prompted to re-enter the number of frequency points.

## Error and warning conditions

Several error or warning conditions can occur. These can either make the program act in a unreliable manner or give incorrect results. A program crash can be caused by a divide-by-zero condition and thus it should be avoided by always testing the denominator of a calculation before it is calculated. Entered values for the components should be checked to determine whether they are out-of-range (such as negative). It is thus not necessary to test for the square-root of a negative number.

Checks should also apply to the entered values of the start and end frequencies. Additional tests will be conducted to determine that the end frequency is greater than start frequency. If this if not the case an error message should be displayed and the user will be prompted to re-enter the values.

**Table 13.2:** Error and warning conditions

| No | Condition | Action |
|----|-----------|--------|
| 1 | A divide by zero error has occurred when calculating $X_c$ because either the frequency or capacitance are zero. | A flag is set to identify an infinite value, i.e. reactance will equal `INFINITY_FLAG`, where `INFINITY_FLAG` has a value of $-1$. |
| 2 | Entered values for start and end frequencies are invalid. This can occur if the start frequency is greater than or equal to the end frequency or any of the entered frequencies are negative. | User is prompted to re-enter the start and end frequencies. |
| 3 | The user requests too many frequency points so that the pre-compiled limit for the impedance array is exceeded. | User is prompted to re-enter the number of frequency points. |
| 4 | Values of components are out of range, such as negative, they or exceed a maximum value. | User is prompted to re-enter the component values. |
| 5 | Invalid option from main menu. | Reprint menu and the user is prompted for a new option. |

A value of infinity can occur when the frequency applied to a capacitor in a series circuit is zero, which will cause the impedance of the circuit to be infinite. Values which are infinity will be represented by INFINITY_FLAG. This flag will be set to a −1, which cannot occur in normal calculations of impedance or reactance.. Table 13.2 gives a list of error and warning conditions.

### Printing results

The results will be displayed in tabular form showing the frequency point (0,1,...,*n*), the actual frequency, and the magnitude and the angle of the impedance. A frequency point is displayed as an integer with 6 reserved spaces, and the frequency value and the magnitude of the impedance should be displayed in exponent format with 3 decimal places. The angle of the impedance will be displayed in floating point notation with 2 decimal places. If infinite impedance is detected via the INFINITY_FLAG then "INFINITY" will be displayed in the impedance magnitude. A sample screen is given in test run 13.3.

---

🖳  **Test run 13.3**

```
F_PNT    FREQUENCY      Z_MAGNITUDE      Z_ANGLE
   0     X.YYYe+ZZZ     X.YYYe+ZZZ     XXXXXXX.YY
   1     X.YYYe+ZZZ     X.YYYe+ZZZ     XXXXXXX.YY
   2     X.YYYe+ZZZ     X.YYYe+ZZZ     XXXXXXX.YY
   3     X.YYYe+ZZZ     X.YYYe+ZZZ     XXXXXXX.YY
     ::                  ::     ::
```

---

The outputting of the results should be paused when the bottom of the screen is reached. The user will be prompted to press the ENTER key to continue, which will cause the next screen to be displayed. As a default the screen size will be set to 24 lines. This value can be changed via a single constant value and a re-compilation of the program.

### Project management

The project is small enough for one person to complete the requirements and no time scales exist. Resources required include a computer (likely to be a PC) and the relevant compiler. For system portability the preferred language is ANSI-C.

### Test concepts

Testing of the program will be conducted using standard circuits with typical values. Error conditions will be forced. A test specification is given in section 13.2.8.

### Management of files

A directory named CIRCUIT will be set up. This directory will contain three main sub-directories: SRC, DOCS and BIN. The SRC directory will contain sub-directories which will store current and previous versions of the program. The sub-directory DOCS will be used to store documents such as a user manual, readme file, etc. The BIN directory will contain a working executable program. A sample directory and file structure is shown in Figure 13.3.

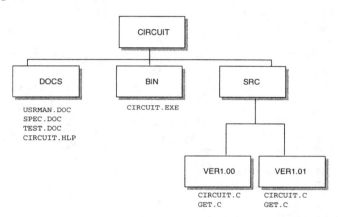

**Figure 13.3:** File organization

### 13.2.4  Design

*After the requirements analysis and specification phase a design process is conducted. The object of this phase is to construct a solution that matches the needs of the analysis and specification phase.*

### Detailed design

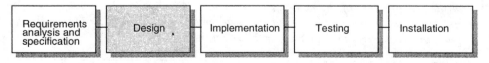

Figure 13.4 shows a first approach at the design. This is a reasonably good design as most of the important data within the program are passed from the main module.

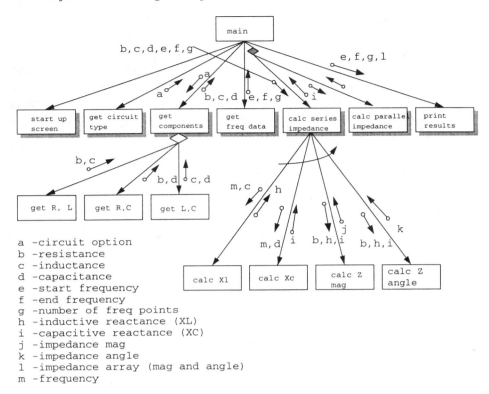

a —circuit option
b —resistance
c —inductance
d —capacitance
e —start frequency
f —end frequency
g —number of freq points
h —inductive reactance (XL)
i —capacitive reactance (XC)
j —impedance mag
k —impedance angle
l —impedance array (mag and angle)
m —frequency

**Figure 13.4:** Design

### 13.2.5 Module specifications

*After the top-level design phase each of the modules within the structure chart can be specified with module specifications. These define the input and output parameters, and the functionality of the modules to be coded. The module specifications used in this section are programming language independent and do not contain data type definitions.* A sample of the module specifications is given next.

| Module | start up screen |
|---|---|
| Function | To display basic information such as version number and the author(s) |
| Input parameters | NONE |
| Output parameters | NONE |
| Return value | NONE |
| Remarks | |

| Module | select circuit |
|---|---|
| Function | To display menu and select circuit configuration |
| Input parameters | NONE |
| Output parameters | option |
| Return value | select circuit returns the circuit option |
| | 1- RL series circuit, 2- RC series circuit, 3- LC series circuit, 4- RL parallel circuit, 5- RC parallel circuit, 6- LC parallel circuit, 7- program exit |
| Remarks | Displays the circuit menu and prompts the user for the circuit type. |

| Module | calc_Xl |
|---|---|
| Function | To determine the reactance of an inductor |
| Input parameters | inductance, frequency |
| Output parameters | NONE |
| Return value | inductive reactance |
| Remarks | The reactance of an inductor is given by $X_L = 2\pi f L$   $\Omega$ |

| Module | calc series imp |
|---|---|
| Function | To determine the impedance of an RLC series circuit |
| Input parameters | resistance, inductance, capacitance, fstart, fend, fsteps |
| Output parameters | impedance magnitude and phase angle array structure |
| Return value | NONE |
| Remarks | A NOVALUE (i.e. -1) flag is passed into the module if the component is not contained in the circuit. For example, in a series RC circuit, the inductance value is sent as NOVALUE. If the magnitude of the impedance is infinite then it will be set to a value of INFINITY_FLAG. |

| Module | get freq values |
|---|---|
| Function | To get the start and end frequencies and the number of frequency steps |
| Input parameters | NONE |
| Output parameters | fstart, fend, fsteps |
| Return value | NONE |
| Remarks | The start frequency is fstart and the end frequency is fend. The number of simulation frequency steps is set by fsteps. |

*Normally the module specifications would be used to code the module and to provide in-program comments. These comments are known as module headers (refer module header for calc_series_imp() in program 13.1).*

### 13.2.6 Implementation

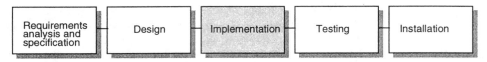

*The program implementation contains three types of comments: a program header comment, module header comments and line comments. The program header comment documents the title of the program, the author(s) of the program (including sources of borrowed code), the current version number, the date last modified and the basic functionaility of the program. In order to save space only one module header has been included. This module header is for* `calc_series_imp()` *and its text is taken from the module specification. In a complete program all modules would have a module header comment. Some in-code comments are also added to explain some operations.*

The coding of the design is shown in Program 13.1.

📄 **Program 13.1**

```
/* Program 13.1 */
/*******************************************************/
/* CIRCUIT.C                                        */
/* Title: Series/ Parallel Impedance Program        */
/* Function: To determine the series and parallel    */
/*    impedances for an RLC circuit. The impedance is */
/*    calculated as a magnitude and angle            */
/* Author(s):           Bill Buchanan               */
/* Version:             1.10                         */
/* Created:             12-JAN-94                    */
/* Last Modified:       1-MAR-94                     */
/* Recent Modifications:  change to get_float() and  */
/*                        get_int() to display ranges */
/*******************************************************/
#include   <stdio.h>
#include   <math.h>

#define    TRUE    1
#define    FALSE   0
typedef    struct {float mag; float angle;} complex;

   /* ANSI C Function protypes */
void    start_up_screen(void);
void    start_up_screen(void);
void    circuit_select(int);
void    get_components(int option,float *r,float *1,float *c);
void    calc_series_imp(float r,float 1,float c,
           float f1,float f2,int fn,complex Z[]);
void    calc_parallel_imp(float r,float 1,float c,
           float f1,float f2,int fn,complex Z[]);
```

```c
void    print_results(float fstart,float fend,int fsteps,complex Z[]);
float   calc_Xl(float f,float l);
float   calc_Xc(float f,float c);
float   calc_mag(float x,float y);
float   calc_angle(float x,float y);
void    get_freq_values(float *f1,float *f2,int *fn);
float   rad_to_deg(float rad);
void    pause_screen(void);
int     select_circuit(void);
void    get_int(char msg[],int min,int max,int *val);
void    get_float(char msg[],float min,float max,float *val);

#define    INFINITY_FLAG        -1
#define    PI                   3.14157
#define    SCREEN_SIZE          23
#define    MAX_IMPED_VALUES     100
#define    NOVALUE              -1

enum       circuits_options { SERIES_RL=1,SERIES_RC,SERIES_LC,
                    PARALLEL_RL,PARALLEL_RC,PARALLEL_LC,EXIT};

int        main(void)
{
int        option,fsteps;
complex    Zin[MAX_IMPED_VALUES];
float      res,cap,ind,fstart,fend;

   start_up_screen();
   do
   {
      option=select_circuit();
      if (option==EXIT) break;
      get_components(option,&res,&ind,&cap);
      get_freq_values(&fstart,&fend,&fsteps);
      if (option<PARALLEL_RL)
        calc_series_imp(res,ind,cap,fstart,fend,fsteps,Zin);
      else
        calc_parallel_imp(res,ind,cap,fstart,fend,fsteps,Zin);

      print_results(fstart,fend,fsteps,Zin);

   } while (option!=EXIT);
        return(0);
}

void    start_up_screen(void)
{
   puts("\t***********************************");
   puts("\t* CIRCUIT.EXE Version 1.10        *");
   printf("\t* Date last modified %s   *\n",__DATE__);
   printf("\t* Program author: BILL BUCHANAN   *\n");
   puts("\t***********************************");
}

int     select_circuit(void)
{
int     opt;
```

```
      puts("Select one of the following circuits >>");
      puts("1- SERIES    RL circuit");
      puts("2- SERIES    RC circuit");
      puts("3- SERIES    LC circuit");
      puts("4- PARALLEL RL circuit");
      puts("5- PARALLEL RC circuit");
      puts("6- PARALLEL LC circuit");
      puts("7- EXIT");
      get_int("Option >> ",1,7,&opt);
      return(opt);
}

void    get_components(int option,float *r,float *1,float *c)
{
   if (option==SERIES_RC || option==PARALLEL_RC)
   {
      get_float("Enter R >>",0,100e6,r);
      get_float("Enter C >>",1e-12,1,c);
      *1=NOVALUE;
   }
   else if (option==SERIES_RL || option==PARALLEL_RL)
   {
      get_float("Enter R >>",0,100e6,r);
      get_float("Enter L >>",1e-9,1,1);
      *c=NOVALUE;
   }

   else if (option==SERIES_LC || option==PARALLEL_LC)
   {
      get_float("Enter L >>",1e-9,1,r);
      get_float("Enter C >>",1e-12,1,c);
      *r=NOVALUE;
   }
}

void    calc_parallel_imp(float r,float 1,float c,float f1,float f2,
                   int fn,complex Z[])
{
   /* Not yet Implemented */
}

/*Module:          calc series imp
 * Function:       To determine the impedance of an RLC series
                   circuit
 * Input           resistance, inductance, capacitance, fstart,
param:             fend, fsteps
 * Output          impedance magnitude and phase angle array
param:             structure
 * Return          NONE
value:
 * Remarks:        A NOVALUE (i.e. -1) flag is passed into the
                   module if the component is not contained in
                   the circuit. For example in a series RC
                   circuit, the inductance value is sent as
                   NOVALUE. If the magnitude of the impedance
                   is infinite then it will be set to a value
                   of INFINITY_FLAG. */
void    calc_series_imp(float r,float 1,float c,float f1,float f2,
```

```
                    int fn,complex Z[])
{
int    i=0;
float  f,Xl=0,Xc=0;

   for (f=f1;f<=f2;f+=(f2-f1)/fn,i++)
   {
      if (l!=NOVALUE) Xl=calc_Xl(f,l);
      if (c!=NOVALUE) Xc=calc_Xc(f,c);
      if (r==NOVALUE) r=0;
      if (Xc==INFINITY_FLAG)
      {
         Z[i].mag=INFINITY_FLAG;
         Z[i].angle=-90; /* if Xc is infinite then angle is -90 deg */
      }
      else
      {
         Z[i].mag=calc_mag(r,Xl-Xc);
         Z[i].angle=calc_angle(r,Xl-Xc);
      }
   }
}

void   print_results(float f1,float f2,int fn,complex Z[])
{
float  f;
int    i=0;
   puts(" F_PNT FREQUENCY   Z_AMPLITUDE   Z_ANGLE");

   for (f=f1;f<=f2;f+=(f2-f1)/fn,i++)
   {
      if (Z[i].mag==INFINITY_FLAG)
         printf("%6d %10.3e   INFINITY  %10.2f\n",i,f,Z[i].angle);
              else
         printf("%6d %10.3e %10.3e %10.2f\n",i,f,Z[i].mag,Z[i].angle);

      if (!((i+1)%SCREEN_SIZE)) pause_screen();
   }
}

float  calc_Xl(float f,float l)
{
   return(2*PI*f*l);
}
float  calc_Xc(float f,float c)
{
   if (f==0 || c==0)  return(INFINITY_FLAG);
   else               return(1/(2*PI*f*c));
}
float  calc_mag(float x,float y)
{
   /* Calculate the magnitude of a complex value x+jy */
   return(sqrt(x*x+y*y));
}

float  calc_angle(float x,float y)
{
   /* Calculate the angle of a complex value x+jy */
```

```
      if (x==0 && y>0) return(90);          /* if only Xl then angle 90 d */
      else if (x==0 && y<0) return(-90);/* if only Xc then angle -90 d*/
      else if ((x==0) && (y==0)) return(0);
      else return(rad_to_deg(atan(y/x)));
}

void    get_freq_values(float *f1,float *f2,int *fn)
{
   /* Get start and end frequency values (f1 and f2)        */
   /* and the number of frequency steps (fn)                */
   get_float("Enter start frequency >>",0,100e6,f1);
   get_float("Enter end frequency >>",*f1,100e6,f2);
   get_int("Enter number of frequency steps >>",
                                    1,MAX_IMPED_VALUES,fn);
}

float   rad_to_deg(float rad)
{
   /* Convert from radians to degrees */
   return(180*rad/PI);
}

void    pause_screen(void)
{
   printf("Press any <ENTER> to continue >>");
   getchar();
}

void    get_float(char msg[],float min,float max,float *val)
{
char    inline[BUFSIZ];
int     rtn,okay;

   do
   {
      printf("%s",msg);
      gets(inline);
      rtn=sscanf(inline,"%f",val);
      if ((rtn!=1) || (*val<min) || (*val>max))
      {
         okay=FALSE;
         printf("Invalid input <%s> Valid values are %g to %g\n",
                                    inline,min,max);
      }
      else okay=TRUE;

   } while (!okay);
}

void    get_int(char msg[],int min,int max,int *val)
{
char inline[BUFSIZ];
int rtn,okay;
   do
   {
      printf("%s",msg);
      gets(inline);
      rtn=sscanf(inline,"%d",val);
```

```
    if ((rtn!=1) || (*val<min) || (*val>max))
    {
       okay=FALSE;
       printf("Invalid input <%s> Valid values are %d to %d\n",
                       inline,min,max);
    }
    else okay=TRUE;
 } while (!okay);
}
```

### 13.2.7  Version control

A version log is kept on the current and previous versions of the program. Each *working* version of the program is stored in a directory so that the previous version can be restored (especially if things go wrong with the current development version). The version number given to the program is in the form X.YZ, where X is an increment when a major change occurs in the program, Y for a relatively large modification and Z for a small change. A version number is only given once the program has been tested and confirmed to be working. All versions of the program should be traceable and known bugs in the program documented. The initial screen of the program should always display the version number as this will help to isolate problems within the program, such as a user running an old version of the program, or that a certain version contains bugs, etc. *A sample version log is shown next. Some systems, such as SCCI on UNIX-based computers, provide automatic version control.*

| Version | Modifications | DATE |
|---------|--------------|------|
| 1.00 | Initial program created | 12-JAN-94 |
| 1.10 | Update to functions get_float() and get_int() so that they display the valid range of entered values | 1-MAR-94 |

### 13.2.8  System testing

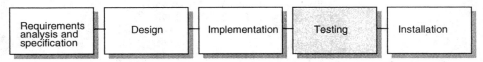

### *Test specification*

The test specification will be written in the form of a checklist; a basic outline is shown in Figure 13.5. The tester's name and the current date are inserted at the top of the document.

Table 13.3 contains known impedance values for a series RL circuit with $R=1$ k$\Omega$ and $L=1$ mH for a sweep of frequencies from 0 to 1 MHz with 20 frequency steps. Table 13.4 shows the known impedance values for a series RC circuit with $R=1$ k$\Omega$ and $C=1$ $\mu$F for a sweep of frequencies from 0 to 1 kHz.

**Table 13.3:** Results of an RL circuit with $R$=1 k$\Omega$ and $L$=1 mH

| Frequency | Zmag | Zangle |
|-----------|----------|--------|
| 0.00e+00 | 1.00e+03 | 0.00 |
| 5.00e+04 | 1.05e+03 | 17.44 |
| 1.00e+05 | 1.18e+03 | 32.14 |
| 1.50e+05 | 1.37e+03 | 43.30 |
| 2.00e+05 | 1.61e+03 | 51.49 |
| 2.50e+05 | 1.86e+03 | 57.52 |
| 3.00e+05 | 2.13e+03 | 62.05 |
| 3.50e+05 | 2.42e+03 | 65.55 |
| 4.00e+05 | 2.70e+03 | 68.30 |
| 4.50e+05 | 3.00e+03 | 70.52 |
| 5.00e+05 | 3.30e+03 | 72.34 |
| 5.50e+05 | 3.60e+03 | 73.86 |
| 6.00e+05 | 3.90e+03 | 75.14 |
| 6.50e+05 | 4.20e+03 | 76.24 |
| 7.00e+05 | 4.51e+03 | 77.19 |
| 7.50e+05 | 4.82e+03 | 78.02 |
| 8.00e+05 | 5.13e+03 | 78.75 |
| 8.50e+05 | 5.43e+03 | 79.40 |
| 9.00e+05 | 5.74e+03 | 79.97 |
| 9.50e+05 | 6.05e+03 | 80.49 |
| 1.00e+06 | 6.36e+03 | 80.96 |

**Table 13.4:** Results of an RC circuit with $R$=1 k$\Omega$ and $C$=1 $\mu$F

| Frequency | Zmag | Zangle |
|-----------|----------|--------|
| 0.00e+00 | INFINITY | -90.00 |
| 5.00e+01 | 3.34e+03 | -72.56 |
| 1.00e+02 | 1.88e+03 | -57.86 |
| 1.50e+02 | 1.46e+03 | -46.70 |
| 2.00e+02 | 1.28e+03 | -38.51 |
| 2.50e+02 | 1.19e+03 | -32.48 |
| 3.00e+02 | 1.13e+03 | -27.95 |
| 3.50e+02 | 1.10e+03 | -24.45 |
| 4.00e+02 | 1.08e+03 | -21.70 |
| 4.50e+02 | 1.06e+03 | -19.48 |
| 5.00e+02 | 1.05e+03 | -17.66 |
| 5.50e+02 | 1.04e+03 | -16.14 |
| 6.00e+02 | 1.03e+03 | -14.86 |
| 6.50e+02 | 1.03e+03 | -13.76 |
| 7.00e+02 | 1.03e+03 | -12.81 |
| 7.50e+02 | 1.02e+03 | -11.98 |
| 8.00e+02 | 1.02e+03 | -11.25 |
| 8.50e+02 | 1.02e+03 | -10.61 |
| 9.00e+02 | 1.02e+03 | -10.03 |
| 9.50e+02 | 1.01e+03 | -9.51 |
| 1.00e+03 | 1.01e+03 | -9.04 |

| Tester:*Bill Buchanan*        Date: *06-DEC-94* | P /F | Notes |
|---|---|---|
| 1. Start program and check that the introduction page and current version number are shown<br>>>Shown correctly | ✓ | *Ver 1.10* |
| 2. Select each of the menu options for the menu and confirm that they select the correct circuit configurations:<br>>>RL series circuit selected OK<br>>>RC series circuit selected OK<br>>>LC series circuit selected OK<br>>>RL parallel circuit selected OK<br>>>RC parallel circuit selected OK<br>>>LC parallel circuit selected OK | <br><br>✓<br>✓<br>✓<br>✗<br>✗<br>✗ | *Parallel circuits are not implemented in this version* |
| 3. Select each of the menu options and enter invalid values for the components; the program should re-prompt for valid values.<br>>>Enter a resistance less than 0; program should re-prompt for another value<br>>>Enter an inductance less than 1e-9; program should re-prompt for another value<br>>>Enter a capacitance greater than 1e-12; program should re-prompt for another value<br>>>Enter a resistance greater than 100e6; program should re-prompt for another value<br>>>Enter an inductance greater than 1; program should re-prompt for another value<br>>>Enter a capacitance greater than 1; program should re-prompt for another value | <br><br>✓<br>✓<br><br>✓<br><br>✓<br>✓<br>✓ | |
| 4. Select RL series circuit and test for invalid frequency ranges.<br>>>Enter a start frequency greater than end frequency; program should re-prompt for a value<br>>>Enter a start frequency equal to end frequency; program should re-prompt for a value<br>>>Enter a start frequency value is less than zero; program should re-prompt for a value<br>>>Enter a start frequency value greater than 100e6; program should re-prompt for a value<br>>>Enter an end frequency value greater than 100e6; program should re-prompt for a value | <br>✓<br><br>✓<br><br>✓<br><br>✓<br><br>✓ | |
| 5. Select RL circuit and enter the following parameters: R=1e3, L=1e-3, fstart=0, fend=1e6, number of frequency steps=20 and compare results against known results.<br>>> Results are the same as known results | <br><br>✓ | |
| 6. Select RC circuit and enter the following parameters: R=1e3, C=1e-6, fstart=0, fend=1e3, number of frequency steps=20 and compare results against known results.<br>>> Check that INFINITY is displayed for impedance at zero frequency<br>>> Results are the same as known results | <br><br>✓<br>✓ | |
| 7. Exit from the program using the exit menu option<br>>> Program exits correctly | ✓ | |
| 8. Observe that the operating system is still in operation<br>>> Operating system environment is operating correctly | ✓ | |

**Figure 13.5:** Simple test specification

## Test results

Test run 13.4 shows a sample run from Version 1.10 of the program.

---

🖥  **Test run 13.4**

```
*************************************
* CIRCUIT.EXE Version 1.10          *
* Date last modified Oct 11 1994    *
* Program author: BILL BUCHANAN     *
*************************************
Select one of the following circuits >>
1- SERIES    RL circuit
2- SERIES    RC circuit
3- SERIES    LC circuit
4- PARALLEL RL circuit
5- PARALLEL RC circuit
6- PARALLEL LC circuit
7- EXIT

Option >> 1

Enter R >>1e3
Enter L >>1e-3
Enter start frequency >>0
Enter end frequency >>1e6
Enter number of frequency steps >>20

F_PNT   FREQUENCY    Z_AMPLITUDE    Z_ANGLE
    0    0.00e+00    1.00e+03         0.00
    1    5.00e+04    1.05e+03        17.44
    2    1.00e+05    1.18e+03        32.14
    3    1.50e+05    1.37e+03        43.30
    4    2.00e+05    1.61e+03        51.49
    5    2.50e+05    1.86e+03        57.52
    6    3.00e+05    2.13e+03        62.05
    7    3.50e+05    2.42e+03        65.55
    8    4.00e+05    2.70e+03        68.30
    9    4.50e+05    3.00e+03        70.52
   10    5.00e+05    3.30e+03        72.34
   11    5.50e+05    3.60e+03        73.86
   12    6.00e+05    3.90e+03        75.14
   13    6.50e+05    4.20e+03        76.24
   14    7.00e+05    4.51e+03        77.19
   15    7.50e+05    4.82e+03        78.02
   16    8.00e+05    5.13e+03        78.75
   17    8.50e+05    5.43e+03        79.40
   18    9.00e+05    5.74e+03        79.97
   19    9.50e+05    6.05e+03        80.49
   20    1.00e+06    6.36e+03        80.96

Select one of the following circuits >>
1- SERIES    RL circuit
2- SERIES    RC circuit
3- SERIES    LC circuit
4- PARALLEL RL circuit
5- PARALLEL RC circuit
```

```
6- PARALLEL LC circuit
7- EXIT

Option >> 2

Enter R >>1e3
Enter C >>1e-6
Enter start frequency >>0
Enter end frequency >>1e3
Enter number of frequency steps >>20

    F_PNT  FREQUENCY    Z_AMPLITUDE    Z_ANGLE
      0    0.00e+00     INFINITY       -90.00
      1    5.00e+01     3.34e+03       -72.56
      2    1.00e+02     1.88e+03       -57.86
      3    1.50e+02     1.46e+03       -46.70
      4    2.00e+02     1.28e+03       -38.51
      5    2.50e+02     1.19e+03       -32.48
      6    3.00e+02     1.13e+03       -27.95
      7    3.50e+02     1.10e+03       -24.45
      8    4.00e+02     1.08e+03       -21.70
      9    4.50e+02     1.06e+03       -19.48
     10    5.00e+02     1.05e+03       -17.66
     11    5.50e+02     1.04e+03       -16.14
     12    6.00e+02     1.03e+03       -14.86
     13    6.50e+02     1.03e+03       -13.76
     14    7.00e+02     1.03e+03       -12.81
     15    7.50e+02     1.02e+03       -11.98
     16    8.00e+02     1.02e+03       -11.25
     17    8.50e+02     1.02e+03       -10.61
     18    9.00e+02     1.02e+03       -10.03
     19    9.50e+02     1.01e+03        -9.51
     20    1.00e+03     1.01e+03        -9.04

Select one of the following circuits >>

1- SERIES    RL circuit
2- SERIES    RC circuit
3- SERIES    LC circuit
4- PARALLEL  RL circuit
5- PARALLEL  RC circuit
6- PARALLEL  LC circuit
7- EXIT

Option >> 7
PROGRAM EXIT, BYE !
```

### 13.2.9 Installation

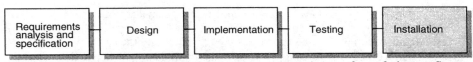

The program will be installed as an executable and can be run free of charge. Source code will not be released. A READ.ME file will also be installed which contains some basic information such as version number, contact names, recent modifications, basic description, how to run the program, etc. A sample READ.ME file is shown next.

```
                           CIRCUIT.EXE
        Author:     Bill Buchanan
        Version:    1.10
        E-mail:
        Description:
        This program determines the impedance of 6 RLC circuits.
           These circuits are:
           - series RL
           - series RC
           - series LC
           - parallel RL
           - parallel RC
           - parallel LC
                  etc
```

## 13.3  Linear feedback shift register

### 13.3.1  Requirements analysis

A linear feedback shift register circuit is used in many applications such as pseudo-random sequence generation and signature analysis of digital circuits. Figure 13.6 shows that a linear feedback shift register (LFSR) is a shift register with the output of some stages fed back to the input through exclusive-OR gates. The output of such a shift register is a pseudo-random binary sequence. By choosing different feedback points (or tappings), the length and composition of the sequence can be changed. The maximum-length sequence that can be generated by an $N$-stage LFSR is $2^N$-1 (the all-zero state is never entered).

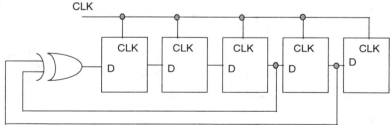

**Figure 13.6:** 4-bit LFSR which generates a maximum-length sequence

Test circuits which use signature analysis feed an input into the exclusive-OR circuit. This results in a output signature that relates to the input data. In order to determine the output pattern for a given input a simulation of the states is required. Figure 13.7 shows an LFSR with an input stream of data.

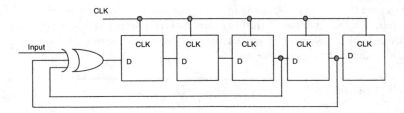

**Figure 13.7:** 4-bit LFSR with input stream

There is thus a requirement for a program which will generate an output signature for a given LFSR tapping arrangement and a given input of binary data.

### 13.3.2 Requirements specification

#### *Introduction*

Refer to requirements analysis for a background on this problem.

#### *System setup*

The program will have two taps for feedback which will be set up at compilation. A program with variable taps will be set up at a future stage (*this is left as a tutorial question*). The program should be structured so that this modification is relatively simple. The fixed tappings will be at positions 2 and 5.

The user will enter the number of stages up to a maximum of 20. Figure 13.6 shows a sample set-up for 6 stages with feedback from the second and fifth stages.

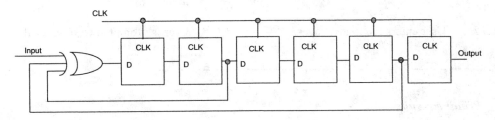

**Figure 13.8:** 6 stage LFSR with feedback taps at stages 2 and 5

#### *Data input*

The user will enter the number of states required and the program will display the states of each of the outputs for each clock cycle. A fixed input sequence of 100101b will be set up *(a variable input sequence is left as a tutorial question)* . The number of stages is determined by the number of shift registers and the number of states is the number of clock cycles (or the number of shifts to be conducted). Test run 13.5 shows a sample run with 8 output states and 5 stages.

---

🖥  **Test run 13.5**

```
Enter number of states required    >>   8
Enter number of stages required    >>   5

State 0 >> XXXXX
State 1 >> XXXXX
State 2 >> XXXXX
State 3 >> XXXXX
State 4 >> XXXXX
State 5 >> XXXXX
State 6 >> XXXXX
State 7 >> XXXXX

INPUT        >> 10010100
OUTPUT       >> XXXXXXXX
```

---

### Error and warning conditions

There are only two main errors that can occur in this program. These are outlined in Table 13.3.

**Table 13.5:** Error and warning conditions

| No | Condition | Warning | Action |
|----|-----------|---------|--------|
| 1 | User enters too many states | `Max states is XX` | User is prompted to re-enter the number of states |
| 2 | User enters too many stages | `Max stages is XX` | User is prompted to re-enter the number of stages |

### Printing results

Test run 13.5 shows a sample run. The outputs from each of the stages should be displayed and the serial input and output sequences will be displayed after the final state output.

### 13.3.3  Design

A basic design for the specification is given in Figure 13.9.

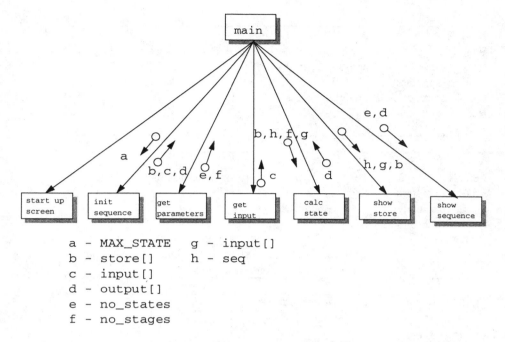

a - MAX_STATE    g - input[]
b - store[]      h - seq
c - input[]
d - output[]
e - no_states
f - no_stages

**Figure 13.9:** Structure chart for LFSR program

The main variables used are described in Table 13.6.

**Table 13.6:** Variables and constants used in the program

| Parameter | Description |
|-----------|-------------|
| MAX_STATE | maximum number of simulated states |
| store[] | processed array containing the output from each stage at a given state |
| input[] | array containing the input sequence (10010000..00) |
| output[] | processed array containing the output sequence from the final shift register |
| seq | sequence state number |

### 13.3.4  Module specifications

A sample of the modules to be used is given next.

| Module | start up screen |
|---|---|
| Function | To display basic information such as version number and the author(s) |
| Input parameters | NONE |
| Output parameters | NONE |
| Return value | NONE |
| Remarks | |

| Module | init seq |
|---|---|
| Function | To initialize three binary arrays to a sequence of 0's. |
| Input parameters | |
| Output parameters | store, input, output |
| Return value | NONE |
| Remarks | store[] contains the output from the shift registers after each state, input[] is the input sequence and output[] is the output sequence. |

| Module | get parameters |
|---|---|
| Function | To get the main circuit parameters |
| Input parameters | |
| Output parameters | no states, no states |
| Return value | NONE |
| Remarks | |

| Module | get input |
|---|---|
| Function | To set up the initial input sequence |
| Input parameters | |
| Output parameters | input |
| Return value | NONE |
| Remarks | The input sequence is fixed at 10010....0. |

### 13.3.5  Coding

A listing of the final coding is given in program 13.2.

📄 **Program 13.2**

```
/***********************************************************/
/* Program LSFR.C                                        */
/* Title: Linear Feedback Shift Register                 */
/* Function: Program to display the stored states        */
/* and output sequence for an N-stage LFSR               */
/* Author(s):              Bill Buchanan                 */
/* Version:                1.00                          */
/* Created:                11-APR-94                     */
/* Recent Modifications:   NONE                          */
```

```
/ * * * * * * * * * * * * * * * * * * * * * * * * * * * * * * * * * * * * * * * * * * * * * * * * * * * * * * * * /
#include  <stdio.h>

#define   MAX_STATES      20
#define   MAX_STAGES      20
#define   FIRST_TAP       2
#define   SECOND_TAP      5
#define   TRUE            1
#define   FALSE           0

void    calc_state(int seq,int stages,int in[],int st[],
            int out[]);
void    init_seq(int values,int st[],int in[],int ou[]);
int     X_OR(int a,int b, int c);
void    get_input(int in[]);
void    show_store(int seq,int stages,int st[]);
void    show_sequence(int vals,int arr[]);
void    start_up_screen(void);
void    get_parameters(int *no_stat,int *no_stag);
void    get_int(char msg[],int min,int max,int *val);

int     main(void)
{
int     input[MAX_STATES],output[MAX_STATES],store[MAX_STATES];
int     seq,no_stages,no_states;

    start_up_screen();

    init_seq(MAX_STATES,store,input,output);

    get_parameters(&no_states,&no_stages);

    get_input(input);

    for (seq=0;seq<no_states;seq++)
    {
       calc_state(seq,no_stages,input,store,output);
       show_store(seq,no_stages,store);
    }
    printf("INPUT   >>");show_sequence(no_states,input);
    printf("OUTPUT  >>");show_sequence(no_states,output);
    return(0);
}

void    init_seq(int values,int st[],int in[], int ou[])
{
int     i;

    for (i=0;i<values;i++)
    {
       st[i]=0;
       in[i]=0;
       ou[i]=0;
    }
}

void    get_parameters(int *no_stat,int *no_stag)
{
```

```
        get_int("Enter number of states required >>",
                                    1,MAX_STATES,no_stat);
        get_int("Enter number of stages required >>",
                                    1,MAX_STAGES,no_stag);
    }


    void    get_input(int in[])
    {
        /* setup fixed data input of 100101 */
        in[0]=1;in[1]=0;
        in[2]=0;in[3]=1;
        in[4]=0;in[5]=1;
    }


    void    calc_state(int seq,int stages,int in[],int st[],int out[])
    {
    int    i;

        st[0]=X_OR(in[seq],st[FIRST_TAP],st[SECOND_TAP]);

        for (i=stages;i>0;i--)
        {
            st[i]=st[i-1];
        }
        out[seq]=st[stages];

    }

    void    show_store(int seq,int stages,int st[])
    {
    int    i;
        printf("State %2d >> ",seq);

        for (i=1;i<=stages;i++)
            printf("%d",st[i]);
        printf("\n");
    }

    void    show_sequence(int vals,int arr[])
    {
    int    i;
        for (i=0;i<vals;i++)
            printf("%d",arr[i]);
        printf("\n");
    }

    int  X_OR(int a,int b, int c)
    {
        return((a^b^c));
    }

    void    start_up_screen(void)
    {
        puts("");
        puts("\t***********************************");
        puts("\t* LFSR.EXE     Version 1.00        *");
```

```
      printf("\t* Date last modified %s    *\n",__DATE__);
      printf("\t* Program author: Bill Buchanan   *\n");
      puts("\t**********************************");
}

void   get_int(char msg[],int min,int max,int *val)
{
char   inline[BUFSIZ];
int    rtn,okay;

   do
   {
      printf("%s",msg);
      gets(inline);
      rtn=sscanf(inline,"%f",val);
      if ((rtn!=1) || (*val<min) || (*val>max))
      {
         okay=FALSE;
         printf("Invalid input <%s>. Valid values are %d to %d\n",
                 inline,min,max);
      }
      else okay=TRUE;

   } while (!okay);
}
```

## 13.3.6  System testing

### *Test specification*

| Tester:*Bill Buchanan*  Date: *06-DEC-94* | P/F | Notes |
|---|---|---|
| 1. Start program and check that the introduction page and current version number are shown <br> >>Shown correctly | ✓ | *Ver 1.00* |
| 2. Program should prompt for the required number of stages <br> >> Enter an invalid value of -1. Check that the program displays an error message and re-prompts for a valid value <br> >> Enter an invalid value of 20. Check that the program displays an error message and re-prompts for a valid value. <br> >> Enter a valid value of 15. Check that the program displays accepts this value | ✓ <br> ✓ <br> ✓ | *Max   stages is 20* |
| 3. Program should prompt for the required number of states <br> >> Enter an invalid value of -1. Check that the program displays an error message and re-prompts for a valid value <br> >> Enter an invalid value of 21. Check that the program displays an error message and re-prompts for a valid value. <br> >> Enter a valid value of 5. Check that the program displays accepts this value | ✓ <br> ✓ <br> ✓ | *Max   states is 20* |
| 4. Check the results produced in test run against known results | ✓ | *Results are shown in test run 13.6* |

### Test Results

A sample test run of the program is used to document test results. This is given in test run 13.6.

---

🖳  **Test run 13.6**

```
************************************
* LFSR.EXE     Version 1.00        *
* Date last modified Apr 14 1994    *
* Program author: Bill Buchanan     *
************************************


Enter number of states required >> -1
ERROR: Max states is 20
Enter number of states required >> 21
ERROR: Max states is 20
Enter number of states required >> 15
Enter number of stages required >> -1
ERROR: Max stages is 20
Enter number of stages required >> 21
ERROR: Max stages is 20
Enter number of stages required >> 5

State  0 >> 10000
State  1 >> 11000
State  2 >> 11100
State  3 >> 01110
State  4 >> 10111
State  5 >> 01011
State  6 >> 00101
State  7 >> 10010
State  8 >> 01001
State  9 >> 00100
State 10 >> 00010
State 11 >> 00001
State 12 >> 10000
State 13 >> 01000
State 14 >> 10100

INPUT  >>110101000000000
OUTPUT >>000011101001000
```

---

### 13.3.7  Installation

The program will be installed as an executable and can be run free of charge. Source code will be freely available and a READ.ME file will also be distributed. This will contain some basic information such as version number, contact names, recent modifications, basic description, etc. A sample READ.ME file is shown next.

```
                               LFSR.EXE
        Author:      Bill Buchanan
        Version:     1.00
        E-mail:
        Description:
```

A linear feedback shift register circuit is used in many
applications such as pseudo-random sequence generation and
signature analysis of digital circuits. It is basically a
shift register with the output of some stages fed back to
the input through exclusive-OR gates. The output of such a
shift register is a pseudo-random binary sequence. By
choosing different feedback points, the length and
composition of the sequence can be changed. The maximum-
length sequence that can be generated by an N-stage LFSR is
$2^N-1$ (the all-zero state is never entered).
        Test circuits which use signature analysis feed an input
into the exclusive-OR circuit. This results in a output
signature that relates to the input data. In order to
determine the output pattern for a given input a simulation
of the states is required.
        The program will prompt for the number of states the
circuit is to be simulated for and also for the number of
stages. Ver 1.00 has a limit of 20 for these parameters. The
output of each stage for every state is also displayed.

## 13.4 Tutorial

Q13.1   Modify the code in program 13.1 so that parallel circuits are included. Also
        modify the design to show this upgrade. Remember to change the version
        number of the program. A sample version log file is shown next.

| Version | Modifications | DATE |
|---------|---------------|------|
| 1.00 | Initial program created | 12-JAN-94 |
| 1.10 | Update to functions get_float() and get_int() so that they display the valid range of entered values | 1-MAR-94 |
| 1.20 | Update program to include parallel impedance functions, etc. | XX-YYY-ZZ |

Q13.2   Modify the code in program 13.2 so that the user can enter a variable input
        sequence.

Q13.3   When testing digital circuits the single-stuck-at (s-s-a) model is typically used
        to define a fault. In this model, a fault-free circuit is defined as one in which all
        logic gates work properly and all interconnections assume either logic 1 or
        logic 0 voltages. A faulty circuit is one which has only one gate or one
        interconnection malfunctioning. It is further assumed that all faults, whether

arising from flaws or interconnections or within the gates, manifest themselves as if an interconnection were permanently held at either a 1 or a 0 level. Figure 13.10 shows the faults that can occur for a TTL gate and how they appear as stuck-at conditions.

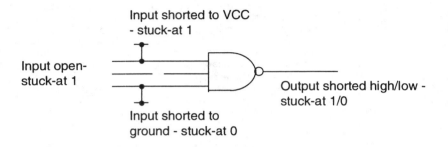

**Figure 13.10:** TTL stuck-at faults

Design and develop a program which will analyze the circuit given in Figure 13.11. A full software engineering process should be conducted i.e. requirements analysis, requirements specification, etc. The program should prompt for the location of the stuck-at fault (i.e. either inputs A, B, C or intermediate connections Z1 and Z2. It should then print the truth table for the circuit with this stuck-at fault giving the correct states for Z1, Z2 and Z. The user should be prompted for the location of the stuck-fault and its state (i.e. 0 or 1). A sample run is given in test run 13.7.

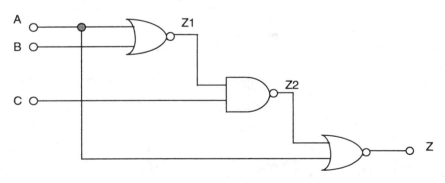

**Figure 13.11:** Boolean circuit

💻  **Test run 13.7**
```
* * * * * * * * * * * * * * * * * * * * * * * * * * * * * * * * * * * *
*  SSA.EXE      Version 1.00                  *
*  Date last modified Apr 14 1994             *
*  Program author: Bill Buchanan             *
* * * * * * * * * * * * * * * * * * * * * * * * * * * * * * * * * * * *
Enter location of fault:
1- A input
2- B input
3- C input
4- Z1 partial output
5- Z2 partial output
6- Exit program
Enter option (1-6) >>> 2
Enter type of fault (0 - stuck at zero or 1 -stuck at one)
>> 0

        Boolean function NOR(NAND( NOR(A,B),C),A)
        A    B    C    Z1    Z2    Z
        0    0    0    1     1     0
        0    0    1    1     0     1
        0    1    0    1     1     0
        0    1    1    1     0     1
        1    0    0    0     1     0
        1    0    1    0     1     0
        1    1    0    0     1     0
        1    1    1    0     1     0
```

Q13.4   The response of an electrical network can be found using ABCD parameters. This allows a circuit to be broken down into cascaded 2-port network segments, each of which is represented by its equivalent ABCD matrix. The resultant ABCD parameters are simply the multiplation of each of the matrixes. For example, for a two stage network the overall ABCD parameters will be:

$$\begin{bmatrix} A & B \\ C & D \end{bmatrix} = \begin{bmatrix} A_1 & B_1 \\ C_1 & D_1 \end{bmatrix} \begin{bmatrix} A_2 & B_2 \\ C_2 & D_2 \end{bmatrix}$$

The input and output voltages are given by:

$$\begin{bmatrix} V_1 \\ I_1 \end{bmatrix} = \begin{bmatrix} A & B \\ C & D \end{bmatrix} \begin{bmatrix} V_2 \\ I_2 \end{bmatrix}$$

A series resistance $R$ has the following ABCD parameters:

$$\begin{bmatrix} 1 & R \\ 0 & 1 \end{bmatrix}$$

and a parallel resistance $R$ has the following ABCD parameters:

$$\begin{bmatrix} 1 & 0 \\ Y_R & 1 \end{bmatrix}$$

For example, for the circuit given in Figure 13.12 the resultant ABCD matrix will be:

$$\begin{bmatrix} A & B \\ C & D \end{bmatrix} = \begin{bmatrix} 1 & 10 \\ 0 & 1 \end{bmatrix} \begin{bmatrix} 1 & 0 \\ \frac{1}{2} & 1 \end{bmatrix} \begin{bmatrix} 1 & 20 \\ 0 & 1 \end{bmatrix}$$

$$= \begin{bmatrix} 1 & 10 \\ 0 & 1 \end{bmatrix} \begin{bmatrix} 1 & 20 \\ \frac{1}{2} & 11 \end{bmatrix}$$

$$= \begin{bmatrix} 6 & 130 \\ \frac{1}{2} & 11 \end{bmatrix}$$

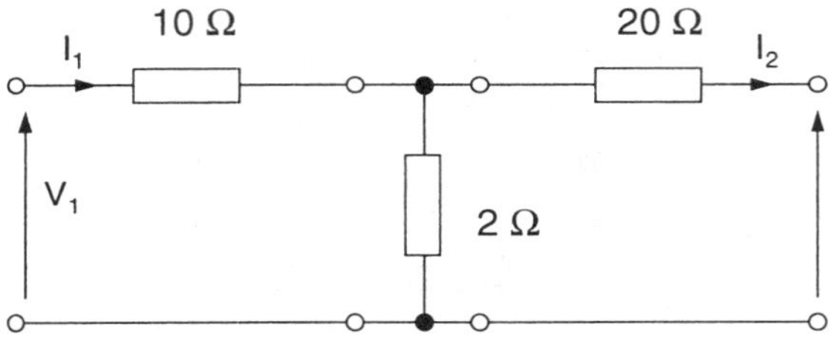

**Figure 13.12:** Example resistor network

The input resistance of a ABCD network can be found to be:

$$R_{IN} = \frac{AR_L + B}{CR_L + D}$$

Write a program which determines the ABCD parameters for a T-network (series resistance/ parallel resistance/ series resistance) or for a Π-network (parallel resistance/ series resistance/ parallel resistance). It should also determine the input impedance of the circuit for an entered load resistance. As a check on the results, *AD–BC* should always equal 1.

Q13.5    Repeat some of the questions in Chapter 12 and conduct a full software engineering process upon them.

# CHAPTER 14

# Introduction to PC graphics using Turbo/ Borland C

Displays can normally be used either in a text or a graphics mode. A PC text display typically displays characters in an array of 80 columns by 25 rows, whereas in graphics mode the screen is made up of individual pixels, such as 640 pixels in the x-direction and 480 in the y-direction. Many currently available software packages display information in graphical form. If the basic interface is displayed in graphical form it is known as a graphical user interface (or GUI). Popular GUIs include Microsoft Windows and X-Windows. Typically, graphics are used in applications which require high-resolution images. These include schematic diagrams, circuit simulation graphs, animation, etc.

Graphics are not an intrinsic part of most programming languages. They are normally found in a graphics library. These contain functions that can range from the generation of simple line drawings to 3D bit-mapped graphics manipulation. Many different libraries can be purchased but this chapter discusses Turbo/Borland C graphics. Note that ANSI-C does not include graphics functions so that the code produced will only work on DOS-based PC using Turbo/ Borland C.

To use the graphics routines the header file *graphics.h* should be included at the top of the file, as shown below. This helps the compiler check for incorrect usage of the functions. It also includes definitions that relate to colours, line styles, fill styles, etc.

```
#include <graphics.h>
```

The Turbo/Borland C libraries implement a complete library of more than 50 graphics routines. The main operations are as follows:

- simple graphics operations, such as `putpixel`, `line` and `rectangle`;
- high-level calls, such as `setviewport`, `circle`, `bar3d`, and `drawpoly`;
- several fill and line styles;
- bit-oriented routines, like `getimage` and `putimage`;
- several fonts that may be magnified, justified and oriented.

The basic graphics screen is made up of pixels, which are accessed using an *x-y* coordinate system. The *x*-direction is horizontally across the screen and the *y*-direction is vertically down the screen. The top left-hand corner is the (0,0) *x-y* point and the bottom of the screen is the (MaxX, MaxY) point. A diagram of this is shown in Figure 14.1.

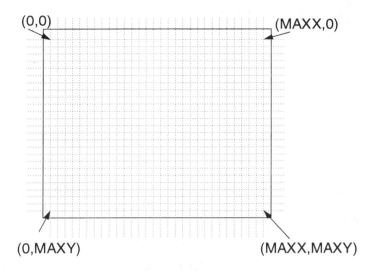

**Figure 14.1:** Screen resolution

A graphics display is interfaced to the PC system using a video driver card. The resolution and the number of displayable colours depends on the type of graphics driver and display used. A program can automatically detect the graphics driver and load the required file that contains information on how the program interfaces to the driver. This file is called a driver file. Table 14.1 shows typical graphics drivers and their associated driver files.

**Table 14.1:** Typical graphics drivers

| Graphics Driver | Resolution | Colours | Driver File |
|---|---|---|---|
| CGA | 320×200 (CGAC0) | 4 (Light Green, L.Red, Yellow) | CGA.BGI |
| | 320×200 (CGAC1) | 4 (L.Cyan, L.Magenta, White) | |
| | 320×200 (CGAC2) | 4 (Green, Red, Brown) | |
| | 320×200 (CGAC3) | 4 (Cyan, Magenta, L.Grey) | |
| | 640×200 (CGAHI) | 2 | |
| EGA | 640×200 (EGALO) | 16 (BLACK..WHITE) | EGAVGA.BGI |
| | 640×350 (EGAHI) | 16 | |
| VGA | 640×200 (VGALO) | 16 | EGAVGA.BGI |
| | 640×350 (VGAMED) | 16 | |
| | 640×480 (VGAHI) | 16 | |
| SVGA | 800×600 | 256 | SVGA256.BGI |
| | 1024×768 | 16 | SVGA16.BGI |

A program makes use of the graphics driver file when the program is run. This allows a single program to be used with several different types of graphics displays. The driver files are identified with a *BGI* filename extension. It is advisable to copy the standard graphics drivers onto a disk or into the current working directory. A listing of these BGI files is shown next. Typically, these files will be found in the \TC or \BORLANDC\BGI directory.

```
C:\TC> dir *.bgi
 Volume in drive C is MS-DOS_5
 Volume Serial Number is 3B33-13D3
 Directory of C:\TC
PC3270   BGI      6029 02/05/89     5:50
IBM8514  BGI      6665 02/05/89     5:50
HERC     BGI      6125 02/05/89     5:50
EGAVGA   BGI      5363 02/05/89     5:50
CGA      BGI      6253 20/04/90     9:23
ATT      BGI      6269 20/04/90     9:23
         6 file(s)        36704 bytes
                      12668928 bytes free
```

Other drivers are available such as *SVGA.BGI* (16 colour SVGA) and *SVGA256.BGI* (256 colour SVGA).

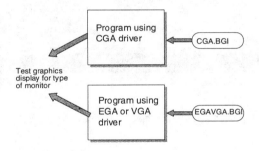

**Figure 14.2:** BGI files required for CGA/EGA and VGA graphics drivers

EGA and VGA monitors can display at least 16 colours. Within a program these are accessed either as a numerical value or by a symbolic name, as given in Table 14.2.

**Table 14.2:** Displayable colours

| Numeric value | symbolic name | Numeric value | symbolic name |
|---|---|---|---|
| 0 | BLACK | 8 | DARKGRAY |
| 1 | BLUE | 9 | LIGHTBLUE |
| 2 | GREEN | 10 | LIGHTGREEN |
| 3 | CYAN | 11 | LIGHTCYAN |
| 4 | RED | 12 | LIGHTRED |
| 5 | MAGENTA | 13 | LIGHTMAGENTA |
| 6 | BROWN | 14 | YELLOW |
| 7 | LIGHTGRAY | 15 | WHITE |

The `setcolor()` function sets the current drawing colour. For example, to set the drawing colour to white the `setcolor(WHITE);` or `setcolor(15);` statement is used. The former is preferable as it is self-documenting.

Table 14.3 outlines the basic graphics functions. An on-line help facility is available by placing the cursor on the function name then pressing the CNTRL and function key F1 (CNTRL-F1) at the same time, or by pressing F1 for more general help. A sample help screen on `initgraph()` is given in Figure 14.3.

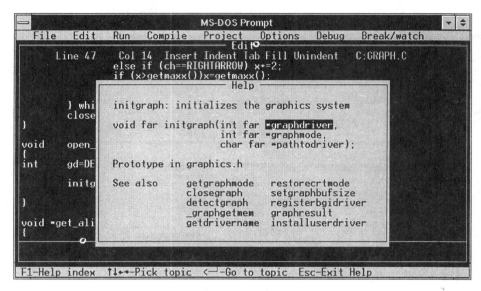

**Figure 14.3:** On-line help screen for `initgraph()`

**Table 14.3:** Sample Borland graphics routines

| Graphic routine | Function | Description |
| --- | --- | --- |
| arc | draws a circular arc | `arc(x,y,stangle,endangle,radius)` arc with centre point x,y at a start angle `stangle`, and end angle `endangle` and the radius is `radius` |
| bar | draws a 2D bar | `bar(left,top,right,bottom)` draws a solid rectangular bar from (left,right) to (right,bottom) using current drawing colour |
| circle | draws a circle of a given radius and centre | `circle(x,y,radius)` |
| cleardevice | clears the graphic screen | `cleardevice()` erases the entire graphics screen |

| | | |
|---|---|---|
| **closegraph** | shuts down the graphics screen | `closegraph()` returns the screen to text mode |
| **drawpoly** | draws the outline of a polygon | `drawpoly(numpoints,polypoints)` draws a polygon with numpoints using array `polypoints`. This array has consecutive *x,y* points. The number of values in the array will be twice the number of points to be displayed. For example, to display the polygon at the points (5,10), (50,100), (40,30) then an array needs to be filled with the values 5, 10, 50, 100, 40, 30. |
| **floodfill** | flood fills a bounded region | `floodfill(x,y,border)` fills an enclosed area where x,y is the seed point with the enclosed area to be filled. The floodfill will continue outwards until the border colour is reached |
| **getimage** | get an image from the screen | `getimage(x1,y1,x2,y2,ptr)` |
| **getmaxx** | get maximum *x*-co-ordinate of the screen | `x=getmaxx()` |
| **getmaxy** | get maximum *y*-co-ordinate of the screen | `y=getmaxy()` |
| **grapherrormsg** | display error message generated by `graphresult()` | `grapherrormsg(err)` |
| **graphresult** | determines if the graphics screen has been initialized correctly | `err=graphresult()` Return codes include: grOk, grNoInitGraph, grNotDetected, grFileNotFound, grInvalidDriver, grFontNotFound, grInvalidMode, grError, grIOerror, grInvalidFont |
| **imagesize** | determines the size of a graphics object | `imagesize(ptr)` |
| **initgraph** | initialises graphics. It can determine the graphics driver and graphics mode to use by checking the hardware | `initgraph(*gdriver,*gmode,pathtodriver)` gmode returns the graphics driver, if gmode is sent as DETECT then the graphics mode will be set to the highest possible resolution. Settings for gmode are DETECT, CGA, EGA, EGA64 and VGA. Typical settings for gdriver are given in Table 14.1. For example, VGALO(640x200, 16 colour), VGAMED (640x350, 16 colour), VGAHI (640x480, 16 colour) |
| **line** | draws a line with the current drawing colour | `line(x1,y1,x2,y2)` |

| **outtextxy** | display a string of text to the graphics screen | `outtextxy(x,y,str)`<br>displays the text `str` and coordinate x,y |
|---|---|---|
| **putimage** | put an image from memory onto the screen | `putimage(x,y,ptr,mask)` |
| **putpixel** | puts a single pixel to the screen | `putpixel(x,y,col)`<br>puts a pixel at (x,y) of colour `col`. |
| **rectangle** | draws a rectangle of the current drawing colour | similar to `bar()` but no fill |
| **setbkcolor** | sets the current background colour | `setbkcolour(colour)` |
| **setcolor** | set the current drawing colour | `setcolor(colour)`<br>available colours on EGA/VGA are from BLACK to WHITE. |

## 14.1  Basic graphics routines

There are two main display modes: text and graphics. The `initgraph()` function changes the mode from text to graphics and the `closegraph()` function changes it back into text mode.

### 14.1.1  Closing graphics

The `closegraph()` function shuts down the graphics system. The standard format is given next:

```
void    closegraph(void);
```

### 14.1.2  Initializing graphics

This function initializes the graphics system and puts the hardware into graphics mode. The standard format for the `initgraph()` routine is given next:

```
void    initgraph(int *graphdriver,int *graphmode,char *pathtodriver);
```

PCs can have different graphics drivers, for example:

- CGA (Colour Graphics Adapter);
- EGA (Enhanced Graphics Adapter);
- VGA (Video Graphics Adapter);
- SVGA (Super Video Graphics Adapter);
- IBM 8514;
- PC 3270.

It is possible for this function to automatically detect the graphics driver by setting the graphdriver parameter to DETECT. This has the advantage of setting the display to the maximum possible graphics range. The pathtodriver string informs the program as to where it will find the graphics driver file. This file is loaded when the program is run. If the string is a null (or empty) string " " then the program will assumes that it will be found in the current working directory. Otherwise, if the driver file is to be found in the directory \TC on the C: drive then the string will contain "C:\\TC" (a double slash indicates a sub-directory).

Program 14.1 displays a diagonal line from the top corner to the bottom corner of the screen. The graphics driver is initialized using initgraph(). After initialization the graphresult() routine is used to determine if there were any errors in initializing the driver. A return of grOk indicates that there have been no problems and the graphics screen can now be used. If it does not return grOk then grapherrormsg() is used to display the error. Typical errors are "BGI File not found", "Graphics not initialised", "Invalid Font", etc.

The getmaxx() and getmaxy() functions return the maximum screen size in the *x*- and *y*-directions, respectively. For a typical VGA display the maximum number of pixels in the *x*-direction will be 640 and in the *y*-direction 480.

**Program 14.1**

```
#include <stdio.h>
#include <graphics.h>

int     main(void)
{
int     gdriver=DETECT,gmode,errorcode;

   initgraph(&gdriver,&gmode,"");
                  /*   if driver file is not in the current working   */
                  /*   directory then replace correct path name with  */
                  /*   for example    "C:\\TC" or "C:\\BORLANDC\\BGI"  */
   errorcode=graphresult();

   if (errorcode == grOk)
   {
      setcolor(WHITE);
      line(0,0,getmaxx(),getmaxy());
      closegraph();
   }
   else printf("Graphics error: %s\n",grapherrormsg(errorcode));
   return(0);
}
```

### 14.1.3 Drawing a pixel

The putpixel() function plots at pixel at a given position and colour. The standard format is given next:

```
void putpixel(int x,int y, int colour);
```

Program 14.2 displays pixels of a random colour at a random location. The function random(X) returns a random value from 0 to X-1. This random value is based upon the system timer. The initial value of the timer is set by calling randomize() at the start of the program.

The graphics display is initialized in open_graphics(). This function either returns GRAPHICS_ERROR on an error or NO_ERROR. The return value is then tested in main() and a decision is made as whether to quit the program. If there is no error the program will continue to display pixels until the user presses on the keyboard. The function kbhit() is used for this purpose. It returns a TRUE value when a key is pressed, thus the loop do {..} while (!kbhit()) will continue until the user presses a key.

### Program 14.2

```c
#include <stdio.h>
#include <graphics.h>
#include <time.h>      /* required for randomize()    */
#include <stdlib.h>    /* required for random()       */
#include <conio.h>     /* required for kbhit()        */

enum   errors {NO_ERROR=0,GRAPHICS_ERROR};
int    open_graphics(void);

int    main(void)
{
int    x,y;

   if (open_graphics()==GRAPHICS_ERROR)  return(GRAPHICS_ERROR);

   randomize();  /* initialise random generator */

   do
   {
      x=random(getmaxx());
      y=random(getmaxy());
      putpixel(x,y,random(15));
   } while (!kbhit()); /* do until a key is pressed */

   closegraph();
   return(NO_ERROR);
}

int    open_graphics(void)
{
int    gdriver=DETECT,gmode,errorcode;

   initgraph(&gdriver,&gmode,"");
   errorcode=graphresult();

   if (errorcode != grOk)
   {
      printf("Graphics error: %s\n",grapherrormsg(errorcode));
      return(GRAPHICS_ERROR);
   }
   return(NO_ERROR);
}
```

### 14.1.4 Drawing a line

The line() function draws a line of the current drawing colour from (*x1*, *y1*) to (*x2*, *y2*). The standard format for line() is:

```
void line(int x1,int y1,int x2,int y2);
```

Program 14.3 draws many random lines of random colours.

**Program 14.3**
```
#include <stdio.h>
#include <graphics.h>
#include <time.h>        /* required for randomize() */
#include <stdlib.h>      /* required for random()    */
#include <conio.h>       /* required for kbhit()     */

enum    errors {NO_ERROR=0,GRAPHICS_ERROR};

int     open_graphics(void);

int     main(void)
{
int     maxX,maxY;

   randomize();   /* initialise random generator */

   if (open_graphics()==GRAPHICS_ERROR)  return(GRAPHICS_ERROR);

   maxX=getmaxx();
   maxY=getmaxy();

   do
   {
      setcolor(random(15));
      line(random(maxY),random(maxY),random(maxX),random(maxY));
   } while (!kbhit());

   closegraph();
   return(NO_ERROR);
}

int     open_graphics(void)
{
   see program 14.2
}
```

### 14.1.5 Drawing a rectangle

The rectangle() function draws a rectangle using the current drawing colour. The standard format for the rectangle() routine is given next:

```
void rectangle(int x1,int y1,int x2,int y2);
```

Program 14.4 displays a single resistor on the screen. The draw_resistor(x,y) function draws this resistor at a point starting at (*x,y*). One problem in displaying graphics is that graphics displays can vary in the number of displayable pixels. If absolute coordinates are used then the object will appear relatively small on a high-resolution display or relatively large on a low-resolution display. For this reason the resistor is scaled with respect to the maximum *x*- and *y*- coordinates, this makes its coordinates relative to the screen size. The scaling of the resistor is given in Figure 14.4.

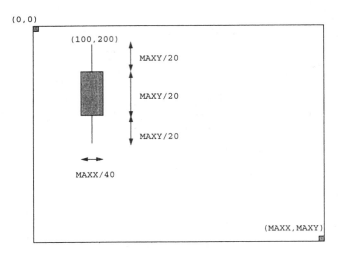

**Figure 14.4:** Layout of resistor graphic

📄 **Program 14.4**

```
#include  <stdio.h>
#include  <graphics.h>

enum    errors {NO_ERROR=0,GRAPHICS_ERROR};

int     open_graphics(void);
void    draw_resistor(int x,int y);

int     main(void)
{
   if (open_graphics()==GRAPHICS_ERROR)  return(GRAPHICS_ERROR);

   draw_resistor(100,200);

   getchar();
   closegraph();
   return(NO_ERROR);
}

int     open_graphics(void)
{
   see program 14.2
}

void    draw_resistor(int x,int y)
{
int     maxx,maxy;
```

```
struct
{
    int length, width, connectline;
}   res;

  maxx=getmaxx();
  maxy=getmaxy();

  res.length=maxy/20;
  res.width=maxx/40;
  res.connectline=maxy/20;

  line(x,y,x,y+res.length);
  rectangle(x-res.width/2,y+res.connectline,
        x+res.width/2,y+res.connectline+res.length);
  line(x,y+res.connectline+res.length,
        x,y+res.length+2*res.connectline);
}
```

### 14.1.6 Displaying text

The outtextxy() function sends a string to the output device. Numerical values cannot be displayed to the screen directly and must be converted into a string before they are displayed. The standard format for the outtextxy() routine is given next:

```
void outtextxy(int x,int y,char *textstring);
```

Program 14.5 uses outtextxy() to display a resistor value string within the draw_resistor() function.

📄 **Program 14.5**
```
#include  <stdio.h>
#include  <graphics.h>

enum    errors {NO_ERROR=0,GRAPHICS_ERROR};

int     open_graphics(void);
void    draw_resistor(int x,int y, char str[]);

int     main(void)
{
  if (open_graphics()==GRAPHICS_ERROR)
    return(GRAPHICS_ERROR);

  draw_resistor(100,200,"100 K");
  draw_resistor(200,200,"200 K");

  getchar();
  closegraph();
  return(NO_ERROR);
}

int     open_graphics(void)
{
    see program 14.2
}
```

```
void    draw_resistor(int x,int y, char str[])
{
int     maxx,maxy;
struct
{
  int length, width, connectline;
} res;

  maxx=getmaxx();
  maxy=getmaxy();

  res.length=maxy/20;
  res.width=maxx/40;
  res.connectline=maxy/20;

  line(x,y,x,y+res.length);
  rectangle(x-res.width/2,y+res.connectline,
          x+res.width/2,y+res.connectline+res.length);
  line(x,y+res.connectline+res.length,
          x,y+res.length+2*res.connectline);

  outtextxy(x+res.width,y+res.length/2+res.connectline,str);
}
```

### 14.1.7  Drawing a circle

The circle() function draws a circle at a centre (*x,y*) of a given radius. The standard format for the circle() routine is given next:

```
void circle(int x,int y,int radius);
```

Program 14.6 uses circle() to display a voltage source.

**Program 14.6**

```
#include <stdio.h>
#include <graphics.h>

enum    errors {NO_ERROR=0,GRAPHICS_ERROR};

int     open_graphics(void);
void    draw_resistor(int x,int y, char str[]);
void    draw_voltage_source(int x,int y, char str[]);

int     main(void)
{
  if (open_graphics()==GRAPHICS_ERROR)
    return(GRAPHICS_ERROR);

  draw_resistor(200,200,"100 K");
  draw_resistor(300,200,"200 K");
  draw_voltage_source(100,200,"5 V");

  getchar();
  closegraph();
  return(NO_ERROR);
}
```

```
int     open_graphics(void)
{
   see program 14.2
}

void    draw_resistor(int x,int y, char str[])
{
   see program 14.5
}

void    draw_voltage_source(int x,int y, char str[])
{
int     maxy;
struct
{
   int radius, connectline;
} volt;

   maxy=getmaxy();

   volt.radius=maxy/40;
   volt.connectline=maxy/20;

   line(x,y,x,y+volt.connectline);

   circle(x,y+volt.connectline+volt.radius,volt.radius);

   line(x,y+volt.connectline+2*volt.radius,
      x,y+2*volt.radius+2*volt.connectline);

   outtextxy(x+volt.connectline+volt.radius,
      y+volt.radius+volt.connectline,str);
}
```

### 14.1.8  Bit-mapped graphics

Program 14.7 will display a face which can be moved around the screen using the arrowkeys. Figure 14.5 shows a sample screen.

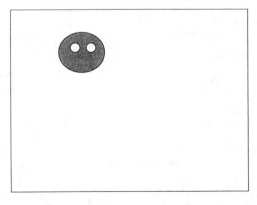

**Figure 14.5:** Face to be displayed

The getch () function is used to get a single keystroke from the keyboard. If the return value is a 0 then the keystroke is an extended character, such as a function key (F1..F12), page up, page down, arrowkeys, etc. The extended character can be determined by calling getch () again. Sample return values are given in Table 14.4.

**Table 14.4:** Sample returns for extended characters

| Return value | Key |
| --- | --- |
| Up arrow | 72 |
| Down arrow | 80 |
| Left arrow | 75 |
| Right arrow | 77 |
| Escape key | 27 |

The following code determines whether a function key has been pressed.

```
ch=getch(); if (ch==0) ch=getch();
```

For example, if the Escape key is pressed then ch will store the value 27.

The getimage(x1,y1,x2,y2) function capture, the image from the coordinates (x1,y1) to (x2,y2) into memory and putimage(x,y, BITMASK) is used to display the image and to clear it from the screen. The quickest way to get rid of a graphics object is to exclusive-OR all the bits in the object bit map with itself. The putimage(x,y,BITMASK) function allows a bit mask to be applied to the image. An exclusive-OR function is defined with XOR_PUT. For example, if the bits on a section of the screen are 11001010, then when this is exclusive-OR'ed with itself the result will be 00000000.

📄 **Program 14.7**
```
/*****************************************************/
/* FACE.C                                         */
/* Title: Shape moving program                    */
/* Function: Program to display a shape which     */
/* can be moved using the arrow-keys              */
/* Author(s): Bill Buchanan                       */
/* Version: 1.00                                  */
/* Created: 07-MAR-94                             */
/* Last modified:                                 */
/* Recent Modifications: NONE                     */
/*****************************************************/

#include  <conio.h>
#include  <graphics.h>
#include  <alloc.h>
#include  <stdio.h>
#include  <process.h> /* required for exit()  */

#define    UPARROW       72
#define    DOWNARROW     80
#define    LEFTARROW     75
#define    RIGHTARROW    77
#define    ESC           27
```

```
#define   INCREMENT      4

enum    errors {NO_ERROR=0,GRAPHICS_ERROR,GRAPHICS_MEM_ERROR};

int     open_graphics(void);
void    *get_shape(void);

int     main(void)
{
void    *shape;
int     x,y,ch;

   if (open_graphics()==GRAPHICS_ERROR)      return(GRAPHICS_ERROR);

   shape=get_shape();

   if (shape==NULL)
   {
     puts("Cannot allocate enough graphics memory");
     return(GRAPHICS_MEM_ERROR);
   }
   x=getmaxx()/2; y=getmaxy()/2;                 /* start co-ordinates */

   do
   {
     putimage(x, y, shape, XOR_PUT);        /*   draw image        */
     ch=getch(); if (ch==0) ch=getch();     /*   get extended key */
     putimage(x, y, shape, XOR_PUT);        /*   erase image       */

     if      (ch==UPARROW)      y-=INCREMENT;
     else if (ch==DOWNARROW)    y+=INCREMENT;
     else if (ch==LEFTARROW)    x-=INCREMENT;
     else if (ch==RIGHTARROW)   x+=INCREMENT;

        /* test if shape is off the screen */
     if (x>0.9*getmaxx())x=0.9*getmaxx();
     if (x<0)  x=0;
     if (y>0.9*getmaxy())y=0.9*getmaxy();
     if (y<0)  y=0;

   } while (ch!=ESC);
   closegraph();

   return(NO_ERROR);
}

int     open_graphics(void)
{
   see program 14.2
}

void    *get_shape(void)
{
int     startx,starty ;
void    *al;
int     ulx, uly, lrx, lry, size, buffsize;

    /* Draw shape */
   setfillstyle( SOLID_FILL,WHITE );

   startx=getmaxx()/2; starty=getmaxy()/2;
```

```
size=getmaxx()/20;

/* draw face outline   */
circle(startx,starty,size);
floodfill(startx,starty,WHITE);

/* draw eyes           */
setcolor(RED);
circle(startx+size/3,starty,size/3);
floodfill(startx+size/3,starty,WHITE);

circle(startx-size/3,starty,size/3);
floodfill(startx+size/3,starty,WHITE);

/* get size of face */
ulx = startx-size;
uly = starty-size;
lrx = startx+size;
lry = starty+size;

buffsize = imagesize(ulx, uly, lrx, lry);

al = malloc( buffsize );
getimage(ulx, uly, lrx, lry, al);
putimage(ulx, uly, al, XOR_PUT);

return(al);
}
```

## 14.2  Tutorial

Q14.1    Draw a cross which touches each corner of the screen.

Q14.2    Draw a triangle with its base on the bottom of the screen and an apex which reaches the centre of the top of the screen.

Q14.3    Write a program which draws circles of radius 1, 2, 4, 8, 16, 32, 64... units. Each of the circles should be drawn one at a time with a delay of 1 second between updates. The function `delay(milliseconds)` delays the program for a number of milliseconds; for example, `delay(1000)` will delay for 1 second.

Q14.4    Write a program which will cover the screen with random blue pixels.

Q14.5    Write a program which will move a red rectangle across the screen from left to right. Use the `delay()` function to animate it. The rectangle should physically move. A possible method could be:

> 1. display the rectangle in red at *x,y* coordinates;
> 2. delay for a small time period;
> 3. display the rectangle in black (this will erase the red rectangle);
> 4. increment the *x*- coordinate and go back to 1.

Q14.6 Write a program in which the user enters the values of the resistor colour bands and the program will display the resistor with the correct colour bands.

Q14.7 Write a program which will display the schematic given in Figure 14.6.

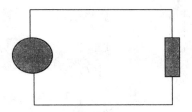

**Figure 14.6:** Schematic

Q14.8 Modify the program in Q14.7 so that the user enters a DC voltage and a resistance and the program will display the voltage, resultant current and resistance on the graphics display. For example, if the user enters a voltage of 10 V and a resistance of 10 Ω then the schematic shown in Figure 14.7 will be displayed.

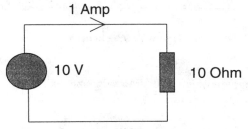

**Figure 14.7:** Schematic

Q14.9 Write a program which will display the schematic given in Figure 14.8.

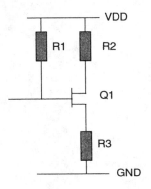

**Figure 14.8:** Schematic

Q14.10  Write a program which will display the schematic given in Figure 14.9.

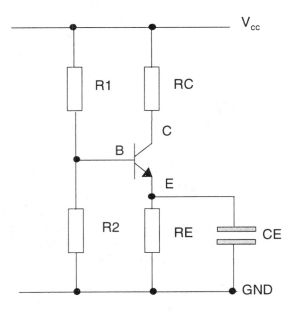

**Figure 14.9:** Schematic

Q14.11  Write a program which will draw a graph axis for $x$ and $y$ with a given maximum $x$ and $y$. For example,

```
void drawaxis(int maxx,int maxy);
```

Q14.12  Change the program in Q14.10 so that it will draw text to the graph (e.g. with maximum $x$ and $y$ values).

# Appendix

## A1 Structure charts

A structure chart is one method used in the design of structured software. Its approach is similar to schematic diagrams used in electronic design where graphical objects represent electronic devices. The structure chart represents each of the functions (or modules) by rectangular boxes, and the relationship between them is represented by connecting arrows. Data flow is also represented by connecting arrows with a circle at their end. If data goes into a module the arrow points into the module, else if it is being returned then the arrow points away from it. Repetition is denoted by a curved arrow and a decision by a diamond. The standard notation for structure charts is given in Figure A1.1.

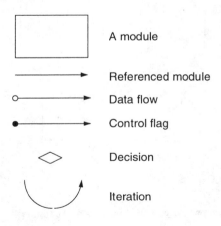

**Figure A1.1:** Structure chart notation

Figure A1.2 shows how the flow of data is represented. The main module represents the controlling module (i.e. `main()`). The diagram shows that `main` initially calls module `mod1` and passes the parameter `val1` to it. This module then returns `val2` back to `main`. This value is then passed into `mod2` which in turn passes back `val3` to `main`.

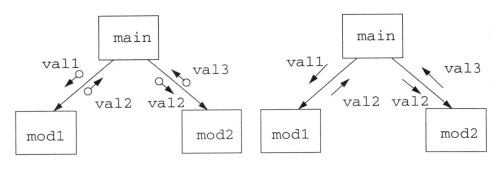

Standard notation          Other possible notation

**Figure A1.2:** Data flow representation

Figure A1.3 shows an example of a decision and iteration. The parameter which controls the decision or iteration may also be shown on the chart.

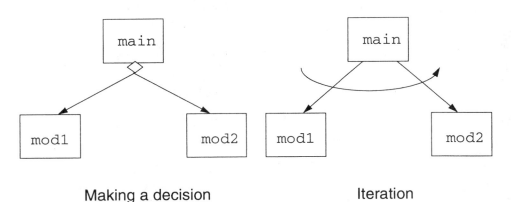

Making a decision                    Iteration

**Figure A1.3:** Decisions and iteration

## A2  Header files and associated functions

The following sections document the range of functions available in ANSI-C.

## A2.1  Classification routines

**Table A2.1:** Classification functions

| Conversion functions | Header file | Description |
|---|---|---|
| `int  isalnum(int ch);` | ctype.h | Function: To determine if character `ch` is a digit ('0'-'9') or a letter ('a'-'z' or 'A'-'Z').<br>Return: A non-zero value if the character is a digit or letter. |
| `int  isalpha(int ch);` | ctype.h | Function: To determine if character `ch` is a letter ('a'-'z', 'A'-'Z').<br>Return: A non-zero value if the character is a letter. |
| `int  iscntrl(int ch);` | ctype.h | Function: To determine if character `ch` is a control character, i.e. ASCII 0-31 or 127 (DEL).<br>Return: A non-zero value if the character is a control character. |
| `int  isdigit(int ch);` | ctype.h | Function: To determine if character `ch` is a digit ('0'-'9').<br>Return: A non-zero value if the character is a digit. |
| `int  isgraph(int ch);` | ctype.h | Function: To determine if character `ch` is a printing character (the space character is excluded).<br>Return: A non-zero value if the character is printable (excluding the space character). |
| `int  islower(int ch);` | ctype.h | Function: To determine if character `ch` is a lowercase letter ('a'- 'z' ).<br>Return: A non-zero value if the character is a lowercase letter. |
| `int  ispunct(int ch);` | ctype.h | Function: To determine if character `ch` is a punctuation character.<br>Return: A non-zero value if the character is a punctuation character. |

| | | | |
|---|---|---|---|
| `int  isprint(int ch);` | | ctype.h | Function: To determine if character `ch` is a printing character.<br>Return: A non-zero value if the character is printable (including the space character). |
| `int  isspace(int ch);` | | ctype.h | Function: To determine if character `ch` is either a space, horizontal tab, carriage return, new line, vertical tab or form-feed.<br>Return: A non-zero value if the character is either a space, horizontal tab, carriage return, new line, vertical tab or form-feed. |
| `int  isupper(int ch);` | | ctype.h | Function: To determine if character `ch` is an uppercase letter ('A'- 'Z' ).<br>Return: A non-zero value if the character is an uppercase letter. |
| `int  isxdigit(int ch);` | | ctype.h | Function: To determine if character `ch` is a hexadecimal digit i.e. '0'-'9','a'-'f', 'A'-'F'.<br>Return: A non-zero value if the character is a hexadecimal digit. |

A sample program is given in program A2.1.

**Program A2.1**

```
#include <stdio.h>
#include <ctype.h>
int  main(void)
{
int  ch;

   do
   {
      printf("\nEnter a character >>");
      fflush(stdin);
      ch=getchar();
      puts("This character has the following attributes");

      if (isalnum(ch)) puts("Alphanumeric");
      if (isalpha(ch)) puts("Alphabetic");
      if (iscntrl(ch)) puts("Control character");
      if (isdigit(ch)) puts("Numeric");
      if (islower(ch)) puts("Lowercase");
      if (isupper(ch)) puts("Uppercase");
      if (ispunct(ch)) puts("Punctuation");
      if (isprint(ch)) puts("Printable character");
      if (isspace(ch)) puts("Space character");
      if (isxdigit(ch)) puts("A hex digit");
   } while (ch!=' ');
}
```

Test run A2.1 shows a sample run.

---

🖥 **Test run A2.1**

```
Enter a character >>  A
This character has the following attributes
Alphanumeric
Alphabetic
Uppercase
Printable character
A hex digit

Enter a character >>  ^V
This character has the following attributes
Control character

Enter a character >>  0
This character has the following attributes
Alphanumeric
Numeric
Printable character
A hex digit
```

---

## A2.2 Conversion routines

**Table A2.2:** Conversion functions

| Conversion functions | Header file | Description |
|---|---|---|
| `double atof(char *str);` | stdlib.h | Function: Converts a string `str` into a floating-point number. Return: Converted floating-point value. If value cannot be converted the return value is 0. |
| `int atoi(char *str);` | stdlib.h | Function: Converts a string `str` into an integer. Return: Converted integer value. If value cannot be converted the return value is 0. |
| `long atol(char *str);` | stdlib.h | Function: Converts a string `str` into a long integer. Return: Converted integer value. If value cannot be converted the return value is 0. |
| `char *itoa(int val, char *str, int radix);` | stdlib.h | Function: Converts `val` into a string `str`. The number base used is defined by `radix`. Return: A pointer to `str`. |

| | | |
|---|---|---|
| `char`<br>`*ltoa(long val, char *str,`<br>`        int radix);` | stdlib.h | Function: Converts `val` into a string `str`. The number base used is defined by `radix`.<br>Return: A pointer to `str`. |
| `int _tolower(int ch);` | ctype.h | Function: Converts character `ch` to lowercase.<br>Return: Converted value lowercase character. Note, `ch` must be in uppercase when called. |
| `int tolower(int ch);` | ctype.h | Function: Converts character `ch` to lowercase.<br>Return: Converted value lowercase character. Return value will be `ch` unless `ch` is in uppercase. |
| `int _toupper(int ch);` | ctype.h | Function: Converts character `ch` to uppercase.<br>Return: Converted value lowercase character. Note, `ch` must be in lowercase when called. |
| `int toupper(int ch);` | ctype.h | Function: Converts character `ch` to uppercase.<br>Return: Converted value lowercase character. Return value will be `ch` unless `ch` is in lowercase. |

## A2.3 Input/ Output routines

**Table A2.3:** Input/ output functions

| Conversion functions | Header file | Description |
|---|---|---|
| `void clearerr(FILE *fptr);` | stdio.h | Function: Resets file error or end-of-file indicator on a file.<br>Return: None. |
| `int fclose(FILE *fptr);` | stdio.h | Function: Closes a file currently pointed to by file pointer `fptr`.<br>Return: A 0 on success, otherwise, EOF if any errors are encountered. |

| | | |
|---|---|---|
| `int feof(FILE *fptr);` | stdio.h | Function: Detects the end-of-file. Return: A non-zero if at the end of a file, otherwise a 0. |
| `int ferror(FILE *fptr);` | stdio.h | Function: Detects if there has been an error when reading from or writing to a file. Return: A non-zero if an error has occurred, otherwise, a 0 if no error. |
| `int fflush(FILE *fptr);` | stdio.h | Function: Flushes a currently open file. Return: A 0 on success, otherwise, EOF if any errors are encountered. |
| `int fgetc(FILE *fptr);` | stdio.h | Function: Gets a character from a file. Return: The character is read. On an error it returns EOF. |
| `char *fgets(char *str, int n, FILE *fptr);` | stdio.h | Function: To read a string from the file pointed to by fptr into string str with n characters or until a new-line character is read (whichever is first). Return: On success, the return value points to string str, otherwise a NULL on an error or end-of-file. |
| `FILE *fopen(char *fname, char *mode);` | stdio.h | Function: Opens a file named fname with attributes given by mode. Attributes include "r" for read-only access, "w" for read/write access to an existing file, "w+" to create a new file for read/write access, "a" for append, "a+" for append and create file is it does not exist and "b" for binary files. Return: If successful a file pointer, otherwise a NULL is returned. |
| `int fprintf(FILE *fptr, char *fmt,arg1...);` | stdio.h | Function: Writes formatted data to a file. Return: The number of bytes outputted. On an error the return is EOF. |
| `int fputc(int ch, FILE *fptr);` | stdio.h | Function: Writes a character ch to a file. Return: The character written, otherwise on an error it returns EOF. |

```
int
fread(void *buff, size_t size,
      size_t n, FILE *fptr);
```
stdio.h

Function: Reads binary data from a file. It reads n items of data, each of length `size` bytes into the block specified by `buff`.

Return: The number of items read. In the event of an error the return will be less than the specified number (n).

```
int   fscanf(FILE *fptr,
      char *format,   &arg1...);
```
stdio.h

Function: Scans and formats input from a file in a format specified by `format`.

Return: The number of fields successfully scanned. In the event of a reading from an end-of-file the return is EOF.

```
int   fseek(FILE *fptr,
      long offset, int whence);
```
stdio.h

Function: The file pointer `fptr` is positioned at an offset specified by `offset` beyond the location specified by `whence`. This location can be either to SEEK_SET (the start of the file), SEEK_CUR (the current file position) or SEEK_END (the end-of-file).

Return: A 0 on success; otherwise, a non-zero value if any errors are encountered.

```
int   fwrite(void *buff,
      size_t size, size_t n,
      FILE *fptr);
```
stdio.h

Function: Writes binary data to a file. It writes n items of data, each of length `size` bytes from the block specified by `buff`.

Return: The number of items written. On the event of an error the return will be less than the specified number (n).

```
int   getc(FILE *fptr);
```
stdio.h

Function: Gets a character ch from a file.

Return: The character read, or in the event of an error it returns EOF.

```
int   getchar(void);
```
stdio.h

Function: Gets a character from the standard input (normally the keyboard).

Return: The character read, or on an error it returns EOF.

| | | |
|---|---|---|
| `char *gets(char *str);` | stdio.h | Function: Gets a string `str` from the standard input (normally the keyboard). String input is terminated by a carriage return (and not with spaces or tabs, as with `scanf()`). Return: On success, the return value points to string `str`, otherwise a NULL on an error. |
| `int printf(char *fmt, arg1....);` | stdio.h | Function: Writes formatted data to the standard output (normally the display). Return: The number of bytes output. On an error the return is EOF. |
| `int putc(int ch, FILE *fptr);` | stdio.h | Function: Puts a character `ch` to a file. Return: The character written, else in the event of an error it returns EOF. |
| `int putchar(int ch);` | stdio.h | Function: Puts a character `ch` to the standard output (normally the display). Return: The character written, else on an error it returns EOF. |
| `int puts(char *str);` | stdio.h | Function: Puts a string `str` to the standard output (normally the display). The string is appended with a new-line character. Return: The character written, else on an error it returns EOF. |
| `void rewind(FILE *fptr);` | stdio.h | Function: Repositions a file pointer to the start of a file. Any file errors will be automatically cleared. Return: None |
| `int scanf(char *format, &arg1...);` | stdio.h | Function: Scans and formats input from the standard input (normally the keyboard) in a format specified by `format`. Return: The number of fields successfully scanned. In the event of a reading from an end-of-file the return is EOF. |

## A2.4 String manipulation routines

### Table A2.4: String functions

| Conversion functions | Header file | Description |
|---|---|---|
| `int strcmp(char *str1,char *str2);` | string.h | Function: Compares two strings `str1` and `str2`. Return: A 0 (zero) is returned if the strings are identical, a negative value if `str1` is less than `str2`, or a positive value if `str1` is greater than `str2`. |
| `int strlen(char *str);` | string.h | Function: Determines the number of characters in `str`. Return: Number of characters in `str`. |
| `char *strcat(char *str1, char *str2);` | string.h | Function: Appends `str2` onto `str1`. The resultant string `str1` will contain `str1` and `str2`. Return: A pointer to the resultant string. |
| `char *strlwr(char *str1);` | string.h | Function: Converts uppercase letters in a string to lowercase Return: A pointer to the resultant string |
| `char *strupr(char *str1);` | string.h | Function: Converts lowercase letters in a string to uppercase. Return: A pointer to the resultant string. |
| `char *strcpy(char *str1, char *str2);` | string.h | Function: Copies `str2` into `str1`. Return: A pointer to the resultant string. |
| `int sprintf(char *str,char *format_str, arg1,....);` | stdio.h | Function: Similar to `printf()` but output goes into string `str`. Return: Number of characters output. |

| int<br>  sscanf(char *str,char *format_str,<br>        arg1,...); | stdio.h | Function: Similar to scanf() but input is from string str.<br>Return: Number of fields successfully scanned. |

## A2.5 Math routines

**Table A2.5:** Math functions

| Conversion functions | Header file | Description |
|---|---|---|
| int abs(int val); | math.h, stdlib.h | Function: To determine the absolute value of val.<br>Return: Absolute value. |
| double acos(double val); | math.h | Function: To determine the inverse cosine of val.<br>Return: Inverse cosine in radians. If the range of val is invalid then errno is set to EDOM (domain error). |
| double asin(double val); | math.h | Function: To determine the inverse sine of val.<br>Return: Inverse sine in radians. If the range of val is invalid then errno is set to EDOM (domain error). |
| double atan(double val); | math.h | Function: To determine the inverse tangent of val.<br>Return: Inverse tangent in radians. |
| double atan2(double val1,<br>        double val2); | math.h | Function: To determine the inverse tangent of val1/val2.<br>Return: Inverse tangent in radians. If val1 and val2 are 0 then errno is set to EDOM (domain error). |
| double ceil(double val); | math.h | Function: Rounds val up to the nearest whole number.<br>Return: The nearest integer value converted to a double. |

| | | |
|---|---|---|
| `double cos(double val);` | math.h | Function: To determine the cosine of `val`.<br>Return: Cosine value. |
| `double cosh(double val);` | math.h | Function: To determine the hyperbolic cosine of `val`.<br>Return: The hyperbolic cosine. If an overflow occurs the return value is `HUGE_VAL` and `errno` is set to `ERANGE` (out of range). |
| `double exp(double val);` | math.h | Function: To determine the exponential e to the power of `val`.<br>Return: The exponentional power. If an overflow occurs the return value is `HUGE_VAL` and `errno` is set to `ERANGE` (out of range). |
| `double fabs(double val);` | math.h | Function: To determine the absolute value of `val`.<br>Return: Absolute value returned as a `double`. |
| `double floor(double val);` | math.h | Function: Rounds `val` down to the nearest whole number.<br>Return: The nearest integer value converted to a `double`. |
| `double fmod(double val1,`<br>`            double val2);` | math.h | Function: Determines the remainder of a divsion of `val1` by `val2` and rounds to the nearest whole number.<br>Return: The nearest integer value converted to a `double`. |
| `double log(double val);` | math.h | Function: Determines the natural logarithm of `val`.<br>Return: The natural logarithm. If the value passed into the function is less than or equal to 0 then `errno` is set to `EDOM` and the value passed back is `HUGE_VAL`. |

| | | |
|---|---|---|
| `double   log10(double val);` | math.h | Function: Determines the base-10 logarithm of `val`.<br>Return: The base-10 logarithm. If the value passed into the function is less than or equal to 0 then `errno` is set with EDOM and the value passed back is HUGE_VAL. |
| `double   pow(double val1,`<br>`          double val2);` | math.h | Function: Determines `val1` to the power of `val2`.<br>Return: The raised power. If an overflow occurs or the power is incalculable then the return value is HUGE_VAL and `errno` is set to ERANGE (out of range) or EDOM (domain error). If both arguments passed are 0 then the return is 1. |
| `int   rand(void);` | math.h | Function: Generates a pseudo-random number from 0 to `val-1`.<br>Return: The generated random number. |
| `double   sin(double val);` | math.h | Function: To determine sine of `val`.<br>Return: Sine value. |
| `double   sinh(double val);` | math.h | Function: To determine hyperbolic sine of `val`.<br>Return: The hyperbolic sine. If an overflow occurs the return value is HUGE_VAL and `errno` is set to ERANGE (out of range). |
| `double   sqrt(double val);` | math.h | Function: Determines the square root of `val`.<br>Return: The square root. If the value passed into the function is less than 0 then `errno` is set with EDOM and the value returned is 0. |
| `void   srand(unsigned int`<br>`          seed);` | stdlib.h | Function: Initializes the random-generator with `seed`.<br>Return: None. |

```
double   tan(double val);
```
math.h

Function: To determine the tangent of val.
Return: The hyperbolic tangent. If an overflow occurs the return value is HUGE_VAL and errno is set to ERANGE (out of range).

```
double   tanh(double val);
```
math.h

Function: To determine the hyperbolic tangent of val.
Return: The hyperbolic tangent.

## A2.6  Time and date routines

**Table A2.6:** Time functions

| Conversion functions | Header file | Description |
|---|---|---|
| `char *asctime(struct tm *ttt);` | time.h | Function: Converts date and time to string. The time passed as a pointer to a tm structure.<br>Return: A pointer to the date string. |
| `char *ctime(time_t *ttt);` | time.h | Function: Converts date and time to string. The time passed as a pointer to by ttt.<br>Return: A pointer to the date string. |
| `double difftime(time_t time2, time_t time1);` | time.h | Function: To determine the number of seconds between time2 and time1.<br>Return: Difference in time returned as a double. |
| `struct tm *gmtime(time_t *ttt);` | time.h | Function: Converts time into Greenwich Mean Time. The time is passed as a pointer to ttt and the result is put into a tm structure.<br>Return: A pointer to the tm structure. |
| `int localtime(time_t *ttt);` | time.h | Function: Converts time into local time. The time is passed as a pointer to ttt and the result is put into a tm structure.<br>Return: A pointer to the tm structure. |

| | | |
|---|---|---|
| `time_t time(time *ttt);` | time.h | Function: To determine the time of day. The time is passed as a pointer to `ttt` and the result gives the number of seconds that have passed since 00:00:00 GMT January 1970. This value is returned through the pointer `ttt`. Return: The number of seconds that have passed since January 1970. |

## A2.7 Other standard routines

**Table A2.7:** Other standard functions

| Conversion functions | Header file | Description |
|---|---|---|
| `void exit(int status);` | stdlib.h | Function: To terminate the program. The value passed `status` indicates the termination status. Typically, a 0 indicates a normal exit and any other value indicates an error. Return: None. |
| `void free(void *block);` | stdlib.h | Function: To free an area of memory allocated to `block`. Return: None. |
| `void *malloc(size_t size);` | stdlib.h | Function: To allocate an area of memory with `size` bytes. Return: If there is enough memory a pointer to an area of memory is returned, otherwise a `NULL` is returned. |
| `int system(char *cmd);` | stdlib.h | Function: Issues a system command given by `cmd`. Return: A 0 on success, otherwise a −1. |

# A3 Things that can go wrong

The following sections document typical compiler errors and warnings, and also run-time errors.

### A3.1 Typical compiler errors

A compiler error must be fixed; otherwise the compiler will not produce object code.

### A3.1.1   Statement missing ; in function XXXX

This is one of the most common compiler errors. It is caused by a statement line not being terminated by a semicolon (;). Typically, the compiler will highlight the next statement after the statement in error. In program A3.1 a semicolon is missing from the statement c=a+b.

📄 **Program A3.1**
```
#include <stdio.h>

int main(void)
{
int     a,b,c;

        a=2; b=5;
        c=a+b
        printf("Answer is %d\n",c);

        return(0);

}
```

In this case, the compiler error was highlighted by the following:

```
Statement missing ;  in function main
```

### A3.1.2   Unexpected end of file in comment started on line X

Unterminated comments can cause considerable problems in a program. They tend to lead to errors that give few clues to their cause. In program 3.2 a comment is started near the top of the program. In this case there is no closing comment so the compiler is able to inform the programmer that it reached the end of the file before a close comment could be found.

📄 **Program A3.2**
```
#include <stdio.h>
/* Program X.Y

void    main(void)
{
int     a,b;

        a=4; b=8;

        return(0);
}
```

In this case, the compiler error was highlighted by the following:

```
Unexpected end of file in comment started on line 2
```

In program A3.3 a comment is started near the top of the program and this is not terminated until the second comment line. This causes a large part of the program to be 'commented-out'. The effects of this compiler error may differ in different situations.

📄 **Program A3.3**

```
#include <stdio.h>
/* Program X.Y


void    main(void)
{
int     a,b;
        /*      This is a comment       */
        a=4; b=8;

        return(0);
}
```

In this case, the compiler error was highlighted by the vague statement:

```
Declaration needs type or storage class
```

### A3.1.3 Extra parameter in call to XXXX in function XXXX

Header files contain function prototypes which allow the compiler to check the parameters passed into a function. In program A3.4 the `puts()` function two parameters are passed from `main()`. This is incorrect syntax as it should only have one parameter passed to it. The compiler will highlight this as an error.

📄 **Program A3.4**

```
#include <stdio.h>

int main(void)
{
        puts("Hello",23);
        return(0);
}
```

In this case, the compiler error was highlighted by the following:

```
Extra parameter in call to puts in function main
```

### A3.1.4 Type mismatch in redeclaration of 'XXXX'

The function prototype defines the syntax of a function. This should be inserted near the top of program it is used in. If it is not prototyped then the compiler assumes that the return type is an `int`. If the compiler then encounters a function that has not been prototyped the parameters passed or returned may differ from the assumed default. This will be highlighted as an error. In program A3.5 the function `myfunction()` is not prototyped and is then defined as returning a `void`.

▤ **Program A3.5**
```
#include <stdio.h>

int main(void)
{
        myfunction();
        return(0);
}

void      myfunction(void)
{

}
```

In this case, the compiler error was highlighted by the following:

```
Type mismatch in redeclaration of 'myfunction'
```

### A3.1.5  Too few parameters in call to 'XXXX' in function XXXX

This is similar to A3.1.3 where the compiler highlights a problem in the parameters passed to a function. In program A3.6 the prototype for myfunction() defines a single value to be passed, but when it is used in main() no parameters are passed.

▤ **Program A3.6**
```
#include <stdio.h>

float     myfunction(int);

int     main(void)
{
      myfunction();
      return(0);
}

void  myfunction(void)
{

}
```

In this case, the compiler error was highlighted by the following:

```
Too few parameters in call to 'myfunction' in function main
```

### A3.1.6  Not an allowed type in function XXXX

The data type of the return value is checked against the data type of the variable to which it is being assigned. If they differ in type the compiler may highlight it. In program A3.7 the return data type from myfunction() is defined as void (i.e. nothing is returned), but the program assigns this return to the variable a.

📄 **Program A3.7**
```
#include <stdio.h>
void      myfunction(void);

int       main(void)
{
int       a;

          a=myfunction();
          return(0);
}

void      myfunction(void)
{
}
```

In this case, the compiler error was highlighted by the following:

```
Not an allowed type in function main
```

## A3.2  Typical compiler warnings

### A3.2.1  Possible use of 'X' before definition in function XXXX

A common programming error is to use a variable before it can be assigned a value. For example, in program A3.8 the variables a and b are used but never assigned values. Note that it cannot be assumed that the initial state of any numerical variable is 0 or that any string is empty.

📄 **Program A3.8**
```
#include <stdio.h>

int main(void)
{
int       a,b,c;

          c=a+b;
          printf("Answer is %d\n",c);

          return(0);
}
```

In this case, the compiler warning was highlighted by the following:

```
Possible use of 'a' before definition in function main
Possible use of 'b' before definition in function main
```

### A3.2.2  'X' is assigned a value that is never used in function XXXX

A common warning is when a variable is assigned a value that is never used. In program A3.9 the variable c takes on the value of a+b but the result is never used.

📄 **Program A3.9**

```
#include <stdio.h>

int     main(void)
{
int     a,b,c;

        a=2; b=5;

        c=a+b;

        printf("Answer is %d\n",a);

        return(0);
}
```

In this case, the compiler warning was highlighted by the following:

```
'c' is assigned a value which is never used in function main
```

### A3.2.3  'X' declared but never used in function XXXX

Another common warning is given when a variable is declared but never used. In program A3.10 the variable c is declared but never used. This type of warning tends to highlight a mistake in the code (e.g. incorrect placement of comments, program typos, etc).

📄 **Program A3.10**

```
#include <stdio.h>

int  main(void)
{
int  a,b,c;

     a=2; b=5;

     printf("Values are %d %d\n",a,b);

     return(0);

}
```

In this case, the compiler warning was highlighted by the following:

```
'c' declared but never used in function main
```

### A3.2.4  Void functions may not return a value in function XXXX

If a function that has been defined as returning a void returns a value using return() a warning will be highlighted (on some compilers this may generate an error). In program A3.11 the main() function has been defined as returning a void, but a return() is used.

📄 **Program A3.11**
```
#include <stdio.h>

void      main(void)
{
int       a,b;

          a=2; b=5;

          printf("Values are %d %d\n",a,b);

          return(0);
}
```

In this case, the compiler warning was highlighted by the following:

```
Void functions may not return a value in function main
```

### A3.2.5  Call to function 'XXXX' with no prototype in function 'XXXX'

This can be caused by calling a standard function when the associated header file is not inserted at the top of the program. For example, in program A3.12 the function puts() is used, but stdio.h is not included.

📄 **Program A3.12**
```
int main(void)
{
        puts("Hello");
        return(0);
}
```

In this case, the compiler warning was highlighted by the following:

```
Call to function 'puts' with no prototype in function main
```

This warning can also be generated because a user-defined function is not prototyped, as shown in program A3.13.

📄 **Program A3.13**
```
#include <stdio.h>

int main(void)
{
        myfunction();
        return(0);

}

myfunction()
{
        return(0);
}
```

In this case, the compiler warning was highlighted by the following:

```
Call to function 'myfunction' with no prototype in function main
```

### A3.2.6  *Function should return a value in function XXXX*

If a function is declared as returning a value and there is no `return()` within it then the compiler will highlight this. In program A3.14 the `main()` function has been declared as returning an `int` but there is no `return()` statement.

📄 **Program A3.14**
```
#include <stdio.h>

int    main(void)
{
     puts("Hello");
}
```

In this case, the compiler warning was highlighted by the following:

```
Function should return a value in function main
```

### A3.2.7  *Possible incorrect assignment in function XXXX*

A typical error in a program is to confuse the assignment operator (=) with the logical equals (==). Note that the compiler may be able to detect an incorrect assignment. For example, in program A3.15 the assignment operator has been used in the `if()` statement.

📄 **Program A3.15**
```
#include <stdio.h>

int    main(void)
{
float    x;

     x=5;

     if (x=6) printf("x is six");

     return(0);
}
```

In this case, the compiler warning was highlighted by the following:

```
Possible incorrect assignment in function main
```

## A3.3  Typical run-time errors

### A3.3.1  Division by zero

A program may 'crash' if there is a divide-by-zero error. All divisions should be tested to determine if the denominator is 0. If it is, then a flag must be set and/or a warning generated. Other mathematical operations can also cause overflows but are generally coped with by the associated functions and return flags.

### A3.3.2  Decisions are incorrect

Many errors may be caused by an incorrectly defined decision statement. A common error is to use the AND and OR bitwise operators (& and |) instead of the AND and OR logical operators (&& and ||). Program A3.16 shows a possible incorrect usage.

📄 **Program A3.16**
```c
#include <stdio.h>

int     main(void)
{
float   x,y;

        x=5; y=6;

        if ( (x==1) | (y==5) ) printf("XXXX");
        return(0);
}
```

### A3.3.3  Loop does not iterate

A typical programming error is to terminate the for() loop statement with a semi-colon.

📄 **Program A3.17**
```c
#include <stdio.h>

int     main(void)
{
float   x;

        for (x=0;x<10;x++);
        {
                printf("Value is %f ",x);
                printf("Square is %f\n",x*x);
        }
        return(0);
}
```

A sample run is shown below.

💻 **Test run A3.1**
```
Value is 10.000000 Square is 100.000000
```

### A3.3.4 Loss of resolution

The resolution of a numerical calculation depends on the number of bits used to represent the values. The more bits used to store the value the higher the accuracy will be. Program A3.18 determines the square of values in powers of 10 starting at 1. These values are 1, 10, 100, 1000, up to 1 000 000 000. Variables val1 and val2 have been declared as a float and a double, respectively. A double data type has a greater resolution than a float.

📄 **Program A3.18**
```c
#include <stdio.h>

int      main(void)
{
float    i;
float    val1;
double   val2;

   for (i=1;i<1e9;i*=10)
   {
      val1=i*i;
      val2=i*i;
      printf("%.2f %.2f %.2f\n",i,val1,val2);
   }
   return(0);
}
```

Test A3.2 run shows an example of a run from a compiler which uses 2 bytes for a float and 4 bytes for a double. It can be seen that as the calculated value becomes larger the float variable calculation gives significant errors.

In a calculation always check the resolution of all data types and assign the result to a variable with the required resolution. If in doubt use a long instead of an int and a double instead of a float.

🖥 **Test run A3.2: Run using Borland C compiler on a PC-based system**
```
1.00 1.00 1.00
10.00 100.00 100.00
100.00 10000.00 10000.00
1000.00 1000000.00 1000000.00
10000.00 100000000.00 100000000.00
100000.00 10000000000.00 10000000000.00
1000000.00 999999995904.00 1000000000000.00
10000000.00 100000000376832.00 100000000000000.00
100000000.00 10000000272564224.00 10000000000000000.00
```

### A3.3.5 Overflow errors

A typical error is where a numerical calculation overflows the range of the data type being used. For example, the range of a 2 byte signed integer is between −32,768 and 32,767. If a calculation results in a value outside this range then the resultant value will be incorrect. Program A3.19 contains two signed integer variables i and j, and a long integer k. The calculation i*i determines the square of 1230. When it is executed a signed integer calculation will be conducted. An overflow results, as the answer is 1,512,900. When the i variable is recast as a long the result is correct, as shown in test run A3.3.

In a calculation always check the ranges of all data types and assign the result to a variable has the required range. If in doubt use a long instead of an int and a double instead of a float.

**Program A3.19**

```
#include <stdio.h>

int     main(void)
{
int     i,j;
long    k;

  i=1230;

  j=i*i;
  k=(long)i*(long)i;

  printf("%d %d %ld\n",i,j,k);

  return(0);
}
```

**Test run A3.3: Run using Borland C compiler on a PC-based system**
1230 5572 1512900

# Index

A copy of all the programs in the text is available by sending a stamped addressed envelope and a 3.5 or 5 inch floppy disk to the following address:

W.J. Buchanan,
Senior Lecturer,
Department of Electrical, Electronic and Computer Engineering,
Napier University,
219 Colinton Road,
Edinburgh EH14 1DJ,
UK.

Helpful tips, requests for advice and comments can be sent via the e-mail address:

w.buchanan@csu.napier.ac.uk (International)
w.buchanan@uk.ac.napier.csu (UK)

Lecturers and tutors can also request a free disk with solutions to all tutorial programs contained in the text.